I0394441

EXPRESSIVE SKETCHBOOKS

This book is dedicated to my wonderful husband, Mark Barker, who has always encouraged me to color outside of the lines.

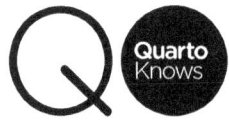

Inspiring | Educating | Creating | Entertaining

Brimming with creative inspiration, how-to projects, and useful information to enrich your everyday life, Quarto Knows is a favorite destination for those pursuing their interests and passions. Visit our site and dig deeper with our books into your area of interest: Quarto Creates, Quarto Cooks, Quarto Homes, Quarto Lives, Quarto Drives, Quarto Explores, Quarto Gifts, or Quarto Kids.

© 2020 Quarto Publishing Group USA Inc.
Text and Artwork © 2020 Helen Wells

First Published in 2020 by Quarry Books, an imprint of The Quarto Group, 100 Cummings Center, Suite 265-D, Beverly, MA 01915, USA.
T (978) 282-9590 F (978) 283-2742 QuartoKnows.com

All rights reserved. No part of this book may be reproduced in any form without written permission of the copyright owners. All images in this book have been reproduced with the knowledge and prior consent of the artists concerned, and no responsibility is accepted by producer, publisher, or printer for any infringement of copyright or otherwise, arising from the contents of this publication. Every effort has been made to ensure that credits accurately comply with information supplied. We apologize for any inaccuracies that may have occurred and will resolve inaccurate or missing information in a subsequent reprinting of the book.

Quarry Books titles are also available at discount for retail, wholesale, promotional, and bulk purchase. For details, contact the Special Sales Manager by email at specialsales@quarto.com or by mail at The Quarto Group, Attn: Special Sales Manager, 100 Cummings Center, Suite 265-D, Beverly, MA 01915, USA.

ISBN: 978-1-63159-835-7

Digital edition published in 2020
eISBN: 978-1-63159-836-4

Library of Congress Cataloging-in-Publication Data

Names: Wells, Helen (Artist), author.
Title: Expressive sketchbooks : developing creative skills, courage, and
  confidence / Helen Wells.
Description: Beverly : Quarry Books, 2020. | Includes index.
Identifiers: LCCN 2019050184 (print) | LCCN 2019050185 (ebook) | ISBN
  9781631598357 | ISBN 9110002367122 (ebook)
Subjects: LCSH: Drawing—Technique. | Notebooks.
Classification: LCC NC730 .W458 2020 (print) | LCC NC730 (ebook) | DDC
  741.2—dc23
LC record available at https://lccn.loc.gov/2019050184
LC ebook record available at https://lccn.loc.gov/2019050185

Design: Laura McFadden
Page Layout: Megan Jones Design
Photography of Artist: Georgina Piper
Photography of Art and Materials: Helen Wells

EXPRESSIVE SKETCHBOOKS

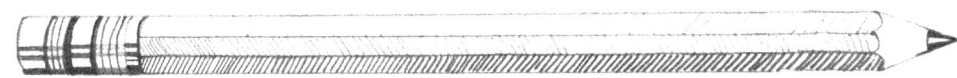

Developing Creative Skills, Courage, and Confidence

HELEN WELLS

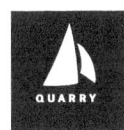

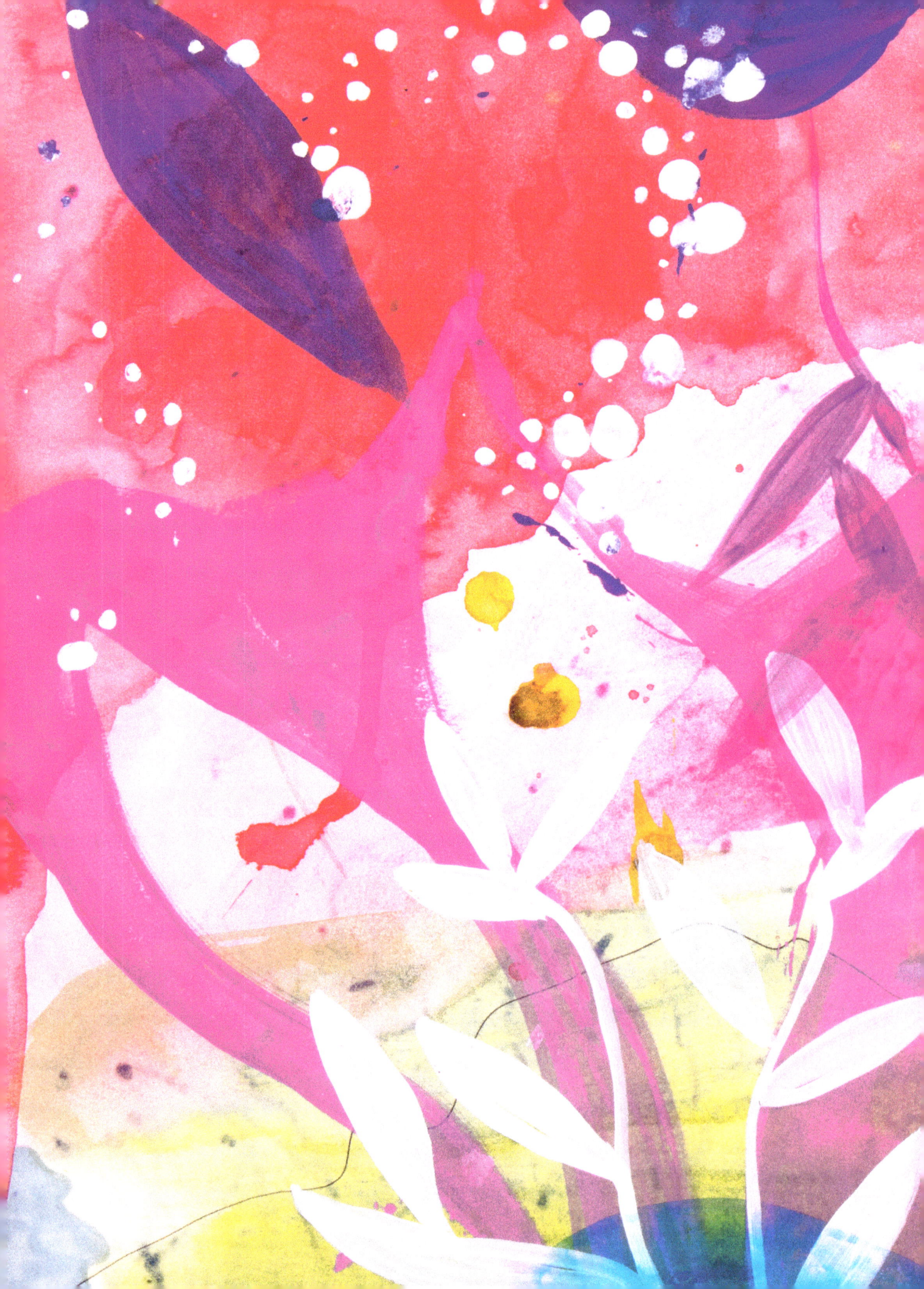

CONTENTS

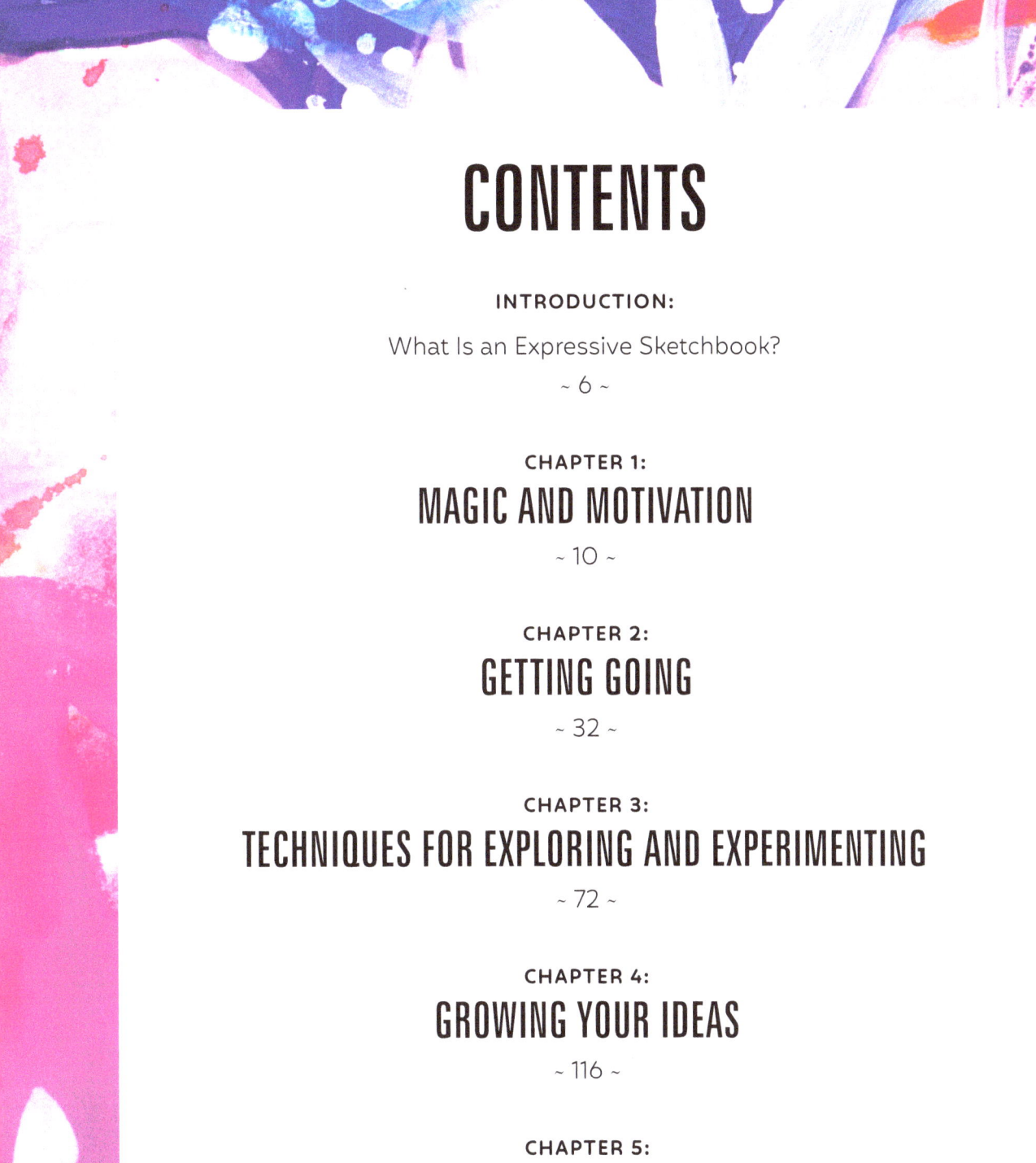

WHAT IS AN EXPRESSIVE SKETCHBOOK?

Nurture Your Creativity

An expressive sketchbook is a playground for your imagination—a place to nurture your creativity and develop your own artistic style. In this book, I provide lots of guideposts to light your way and help you develop a sketchbook that feels uniquely yours.

This book is about exploring your call to create and coaxing those ideas out onto the page. It is about helping you make art that only you can create.

Know that your sketchbook will not be filled with flawless drawings or perfect outcomes. But the sometimes messy and joyful experiments will pave the way to discovering and refining your own visual style and artistic voice. Keep in mind that sketchbooks are where you develop an artistic practice, not where you turn up fully formed. They are part of the artistic journey; they are not the final destination.

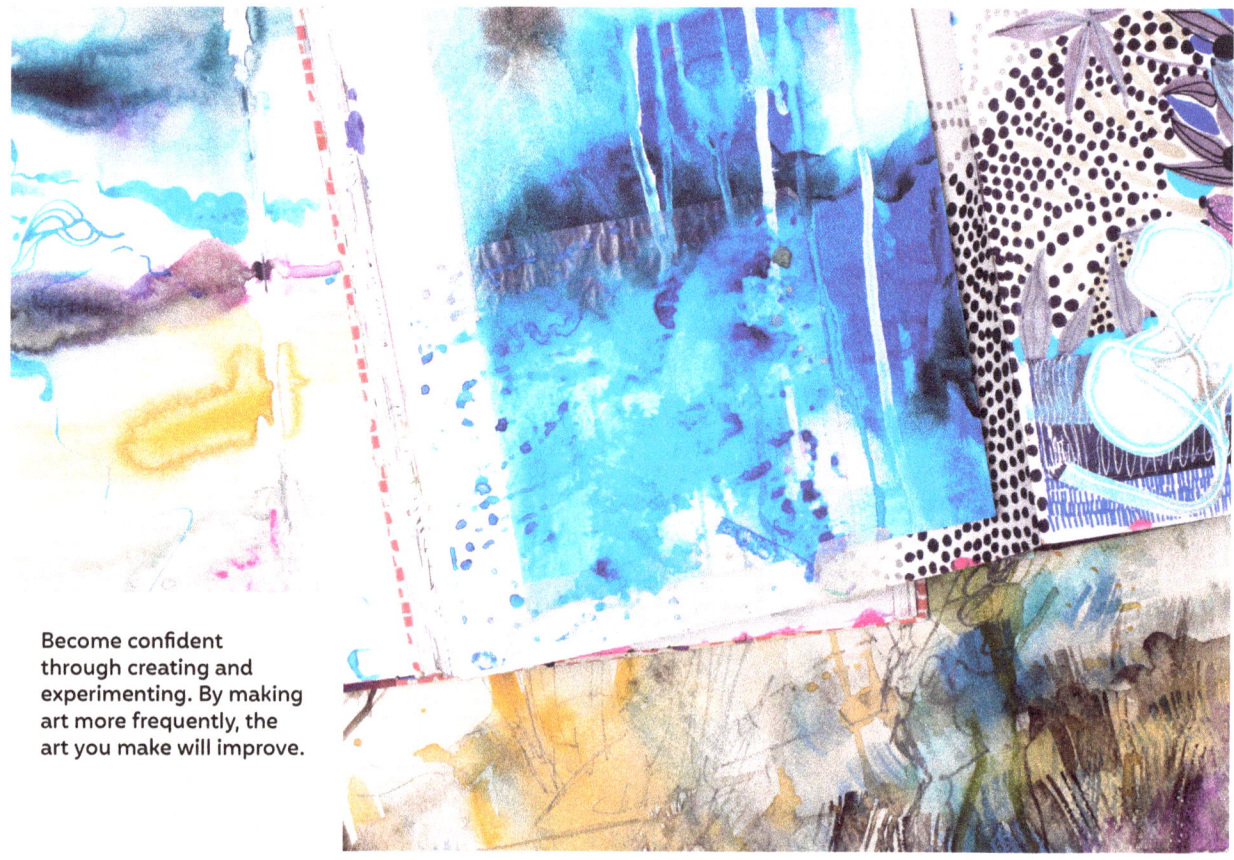

Become confident through creating and experimenting. By making art more frequently, the art you make will improve.

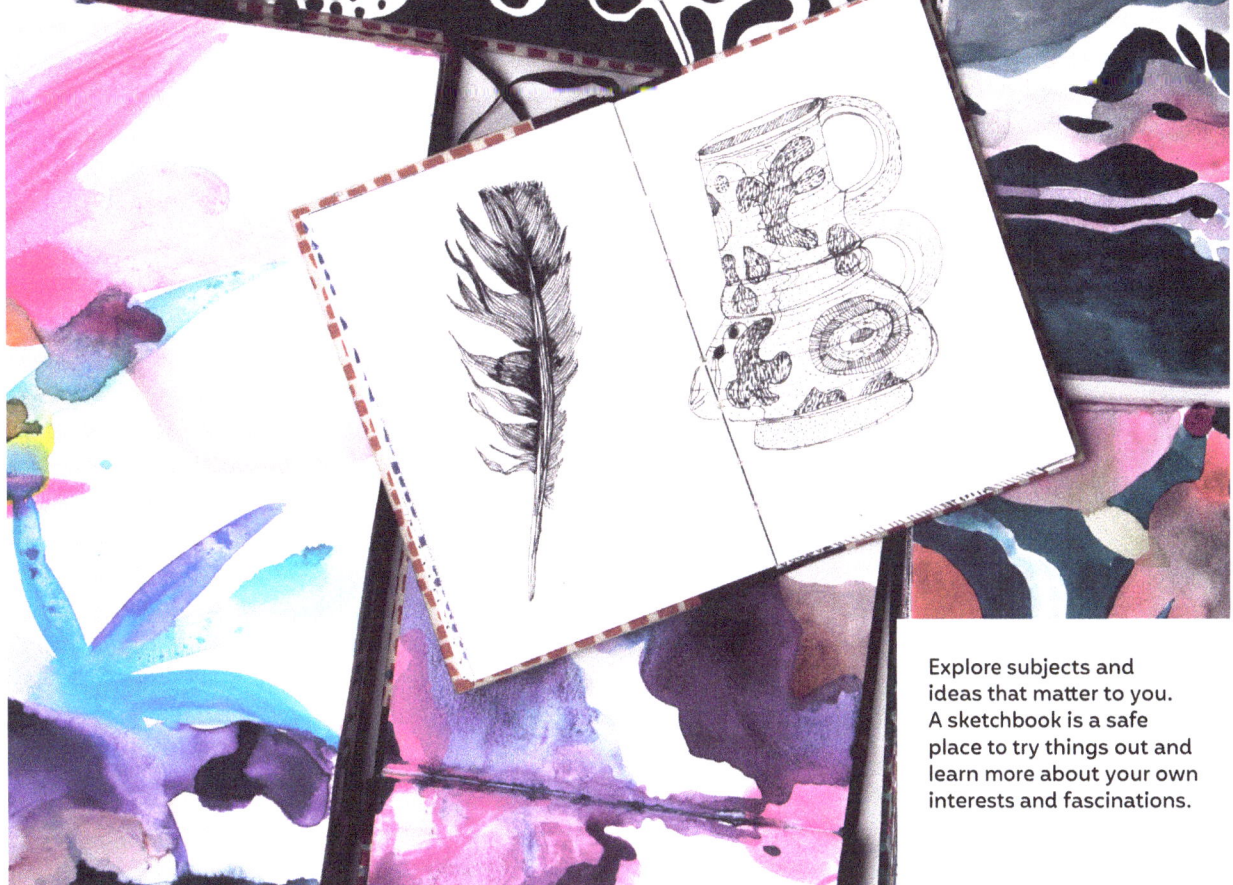

Explore subjects and ideas that matter to you. A sketchbook is a safe place to try things out and learn more about your own interests and fascinations.

Incorporate Art into Your Life

A great sketchbook is not about perfect outcomes. It's about learning and growing through doing. The sketchbook is a safe place to become more confident and courageous about your own creativity. It's also where you can develop an approach to art and a process that lights you up, filling you with energy and enthusiasm. Think of your sketchbook as a place to have a creative conversation with yourself.

Become more inspired by creating more art. Don't wait to feel ready to begin; by beginning and taking action, we become ready.

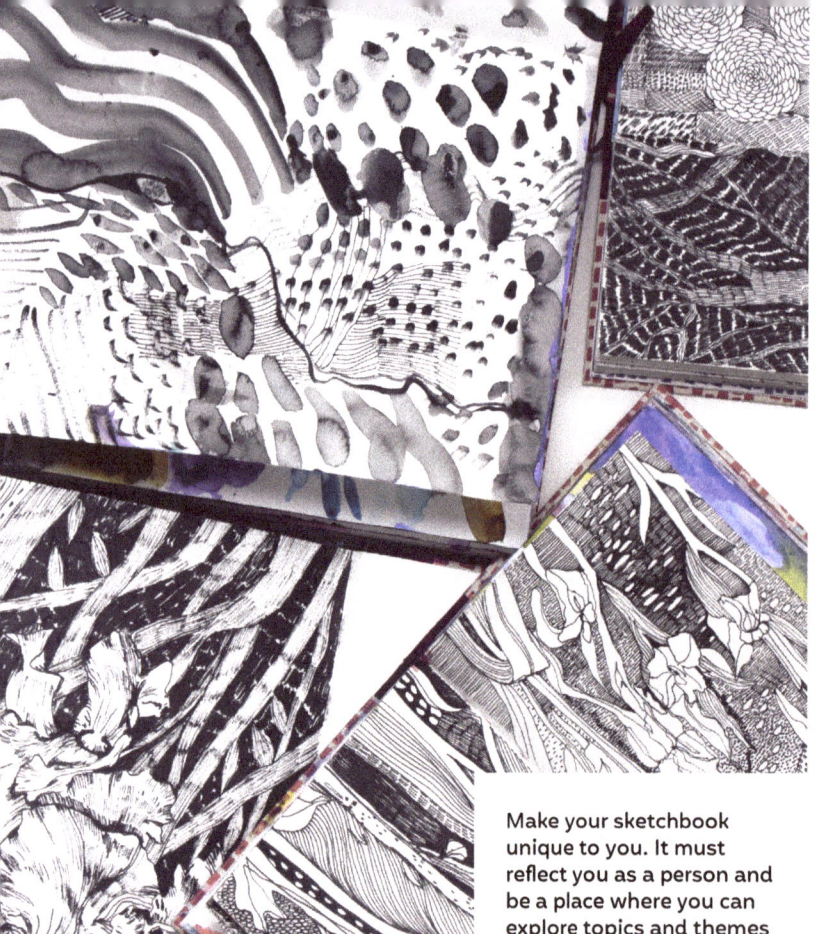

Experimentation and Discovery

There are no rules when it comes to sketch-books, apart from experimentation and discovery. We become creative by creating. Your sketchbook may contain very few actual sketches. For some people, a sketchbook may be all about sketching from life, while for others it is about exploring color and com-position or recording thoughts, memories, or ideas. My hope is that this book gives you a little creative rocket fuel to allow you to take off in your own artistic direction.

Make your sketchbook unique to you. It must reflect you as a person and be a place where you can explore topics and themes that resonate with you.

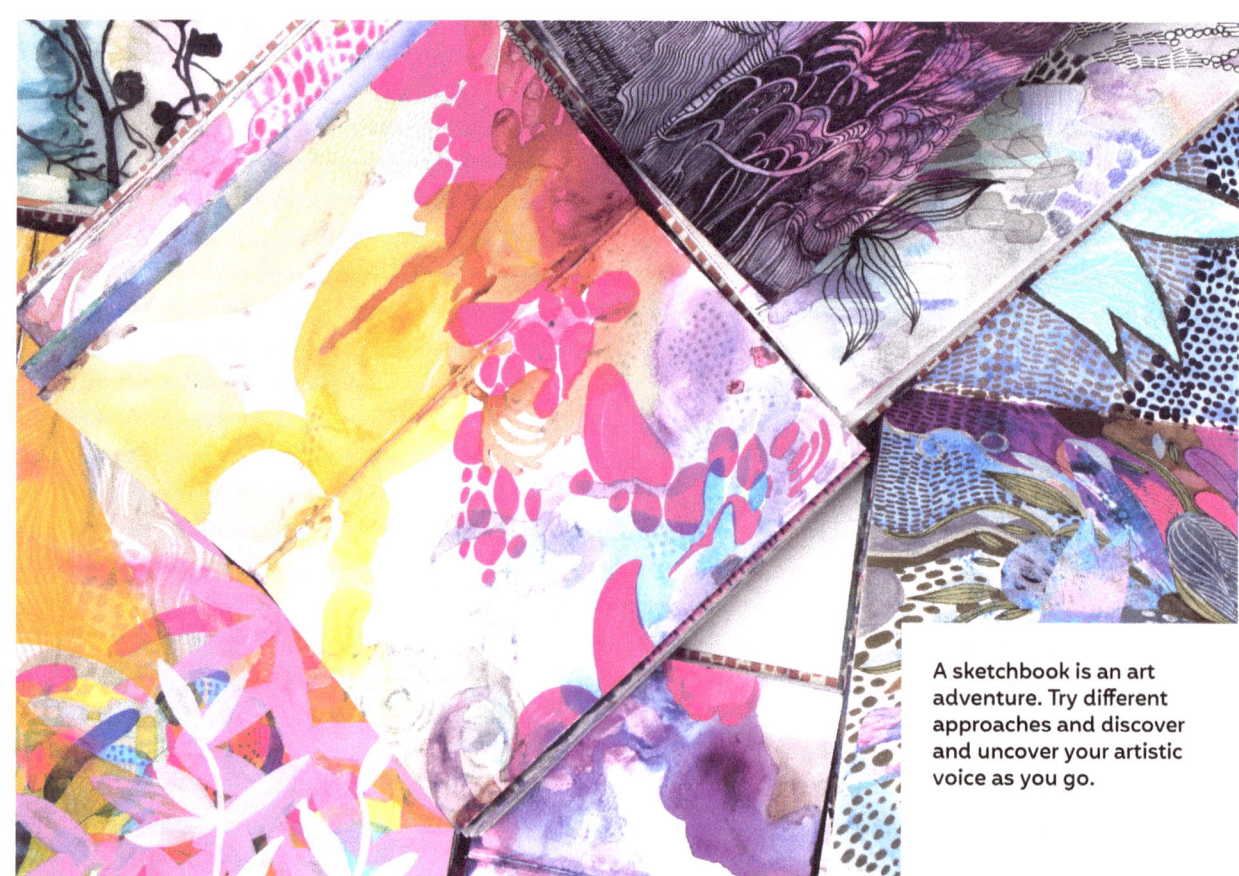

A sketchbook is an art adventure. Try different approaches and discover and uncover your artistic voice as you go.

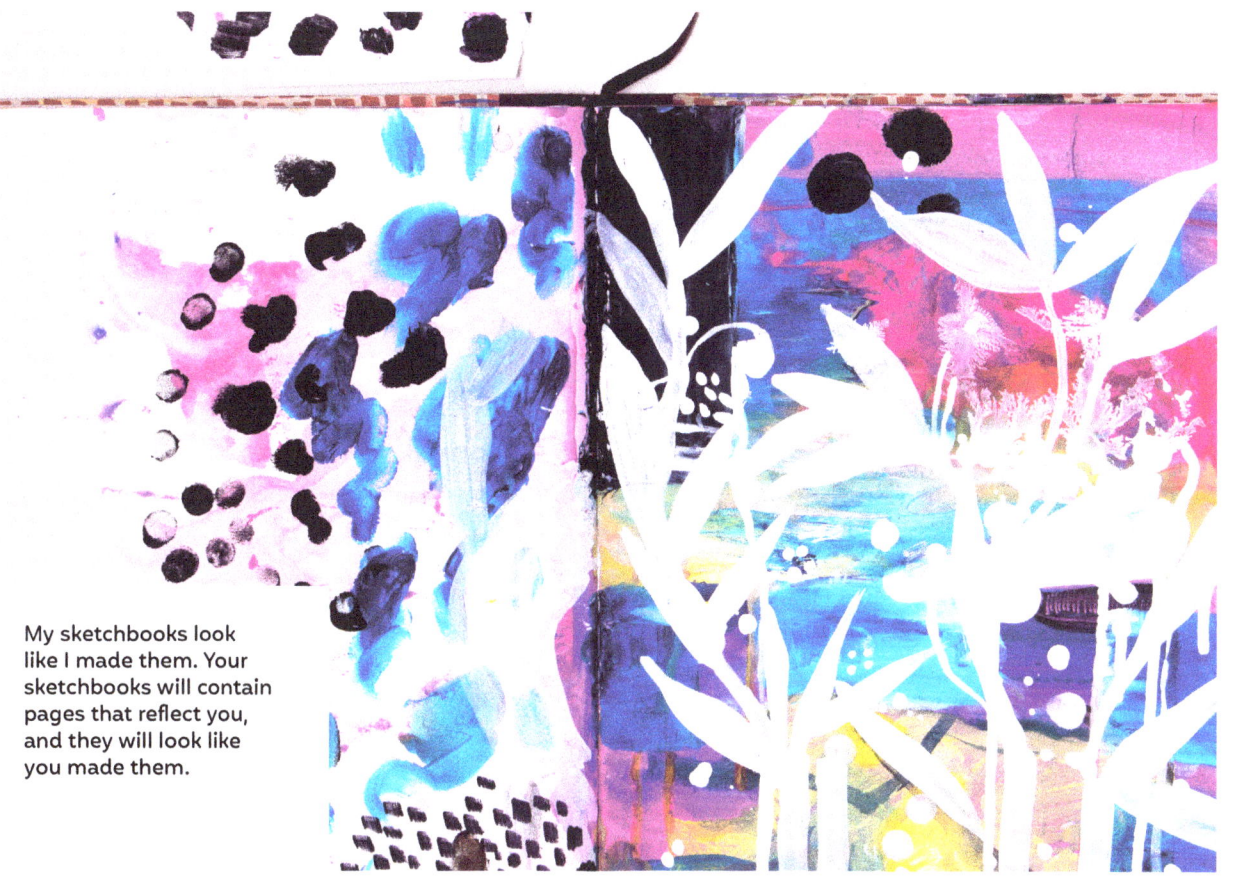

My sketchbooks look like I made them. Your sketchbooks will contain pages that reflect you, and they will look like you made them.

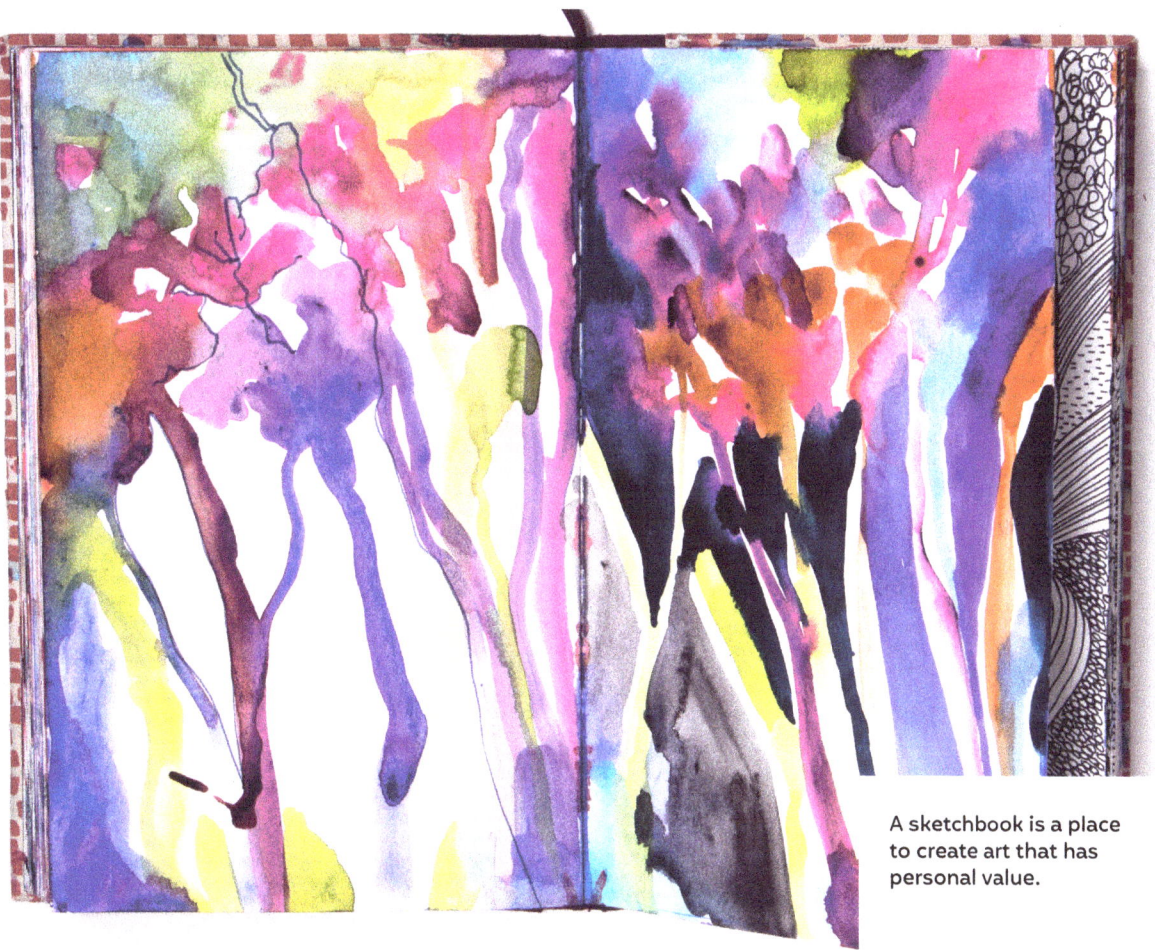

A sketchbook is a place to create art that has personal value.

MAGIC AND MOTIVATION

Why develop your own sketchbook practice? Keeping a sketchbook will help you cultivate your own self-expression and creativity. This chapter is designed to help you unpack any obstacles and barriers that may be blocking your creativity. It will also help you understand your reason for starting a sketchbook and what you'd like your sketchbook to be. Look for tips on ways in which you can reflect upon and document your artistic interests and inspirations.

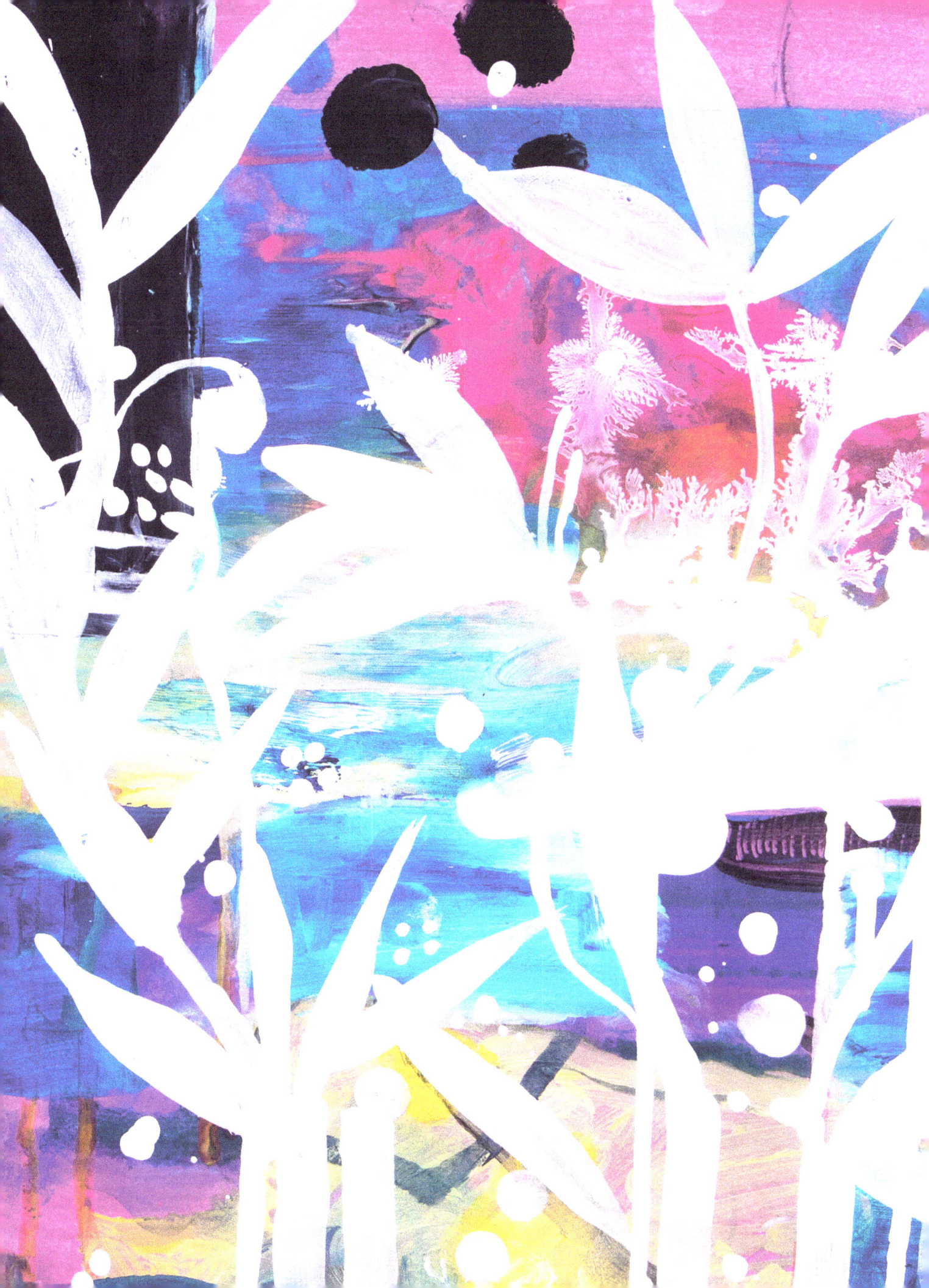

REASONS TO START A SKETCHBOOK

You may not realize it now, but using a sketch-book can be life enhancing. The more you sketch, the more creative alchemy you are inviting into your life. Here are a few reasons to begin your very own sketchbook (or to continue in those moments when you feel stuck).

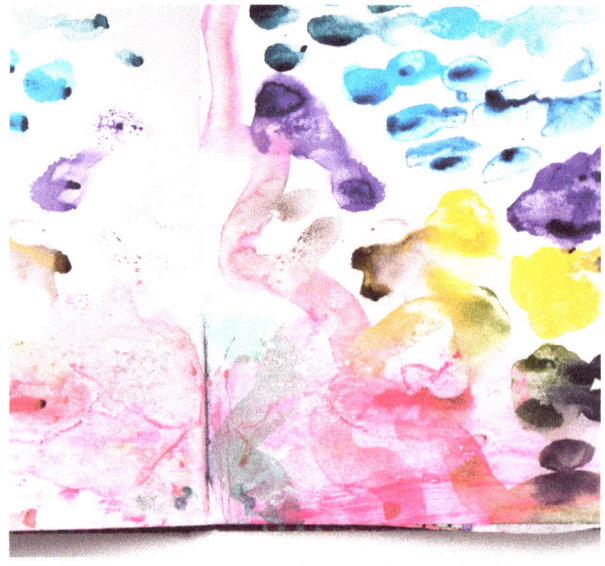

Play in a sketchbook to develop artistic skills. A sketchbook is a place to learn and grow—it will not be full of flawless masterpieces. Some pages will look like a mess, but that doesn't matter.

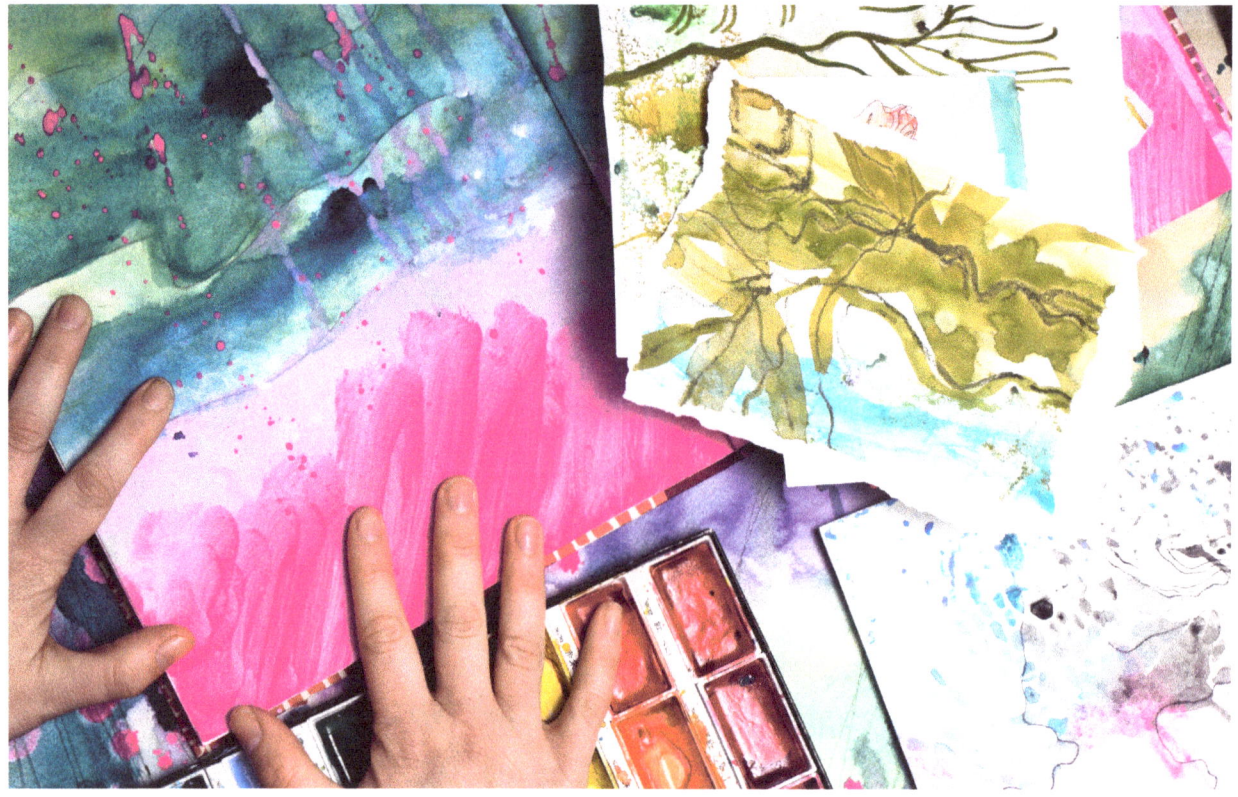

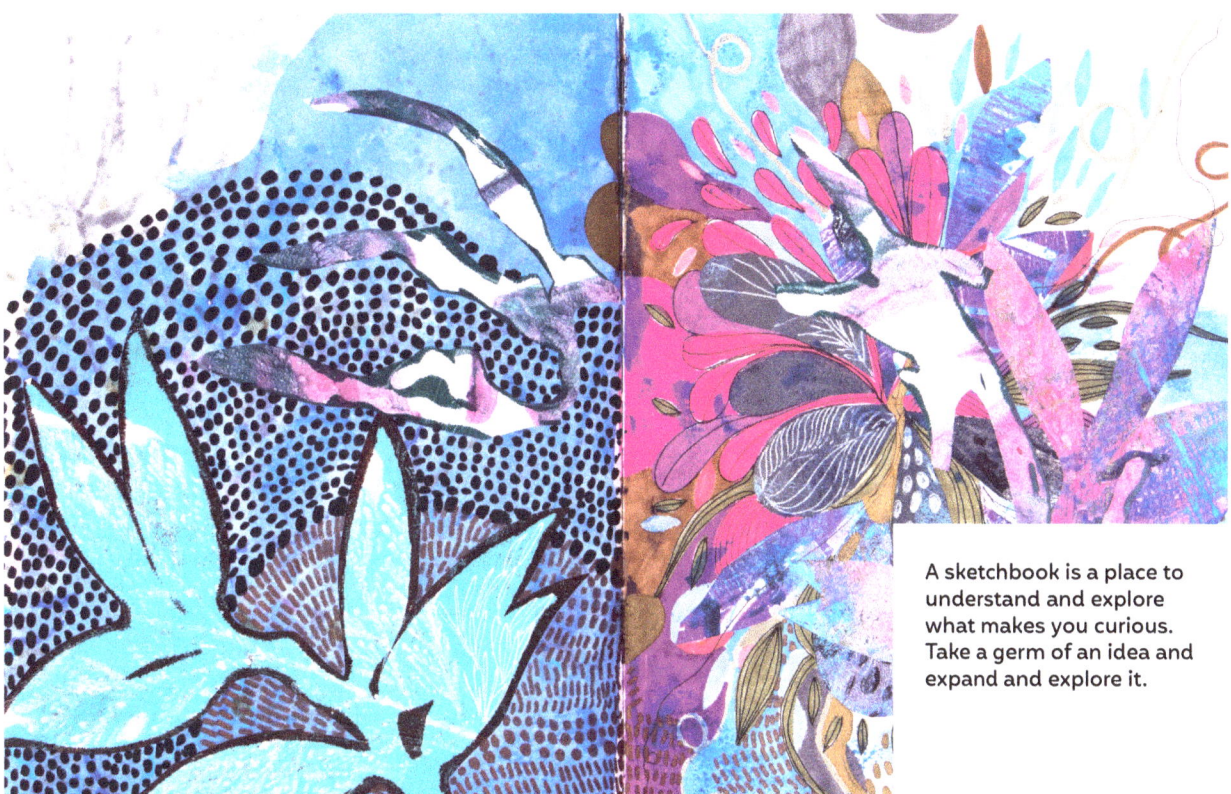

A sketchbook is a place to understand and explore what makes you curious. Take a germ of an idea and expand and explore it.

Explore Ideas

Your sketchbook is a great place for you to understand, develop, and explore your artistic interests or preoccupations. Unpack what makes you curious about art and life and sketch those thoughts out on the pages. In developing a sketchbook, you take ideas from your head or your heart and bring them to life on paper.

Log Your Creative Journey

Use a sketchbook to record your creative awakening. Think of your sketchbook as a friend and companion on your artistic journey.

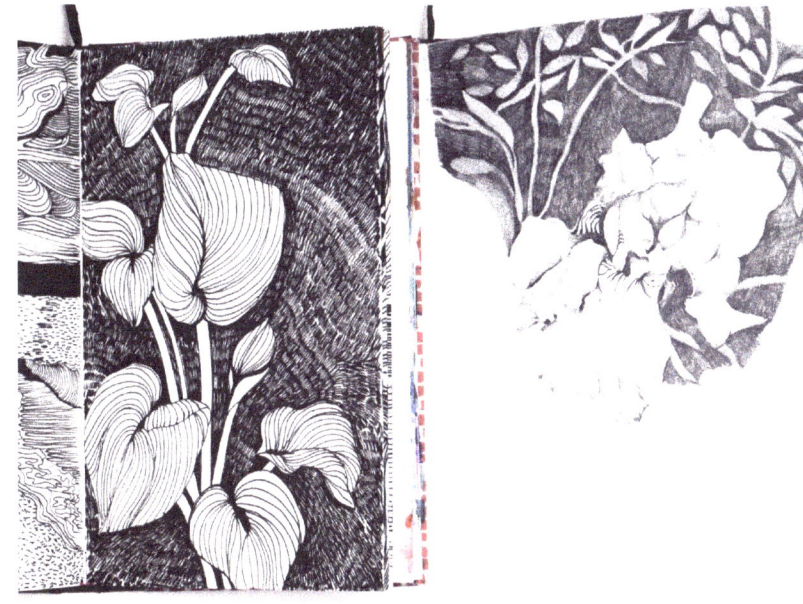

A sketchbook offers an opportunity to spot patterns and recurring themes. These two sketchbook pages were created years apart. Notice the use of white floral silhouettes against a patterned background. By flicking through old sketchbooks, you can spot recurring themes and find connections.

Intimate/Safe Place

Your sketchbook is for you. It can be a private and personal playground. You don't have to share it with anyone. You don't need to display its contents or put them on a wall. If you want to, you can close the cover and keep what is inside private, like your own conversation with yourself.

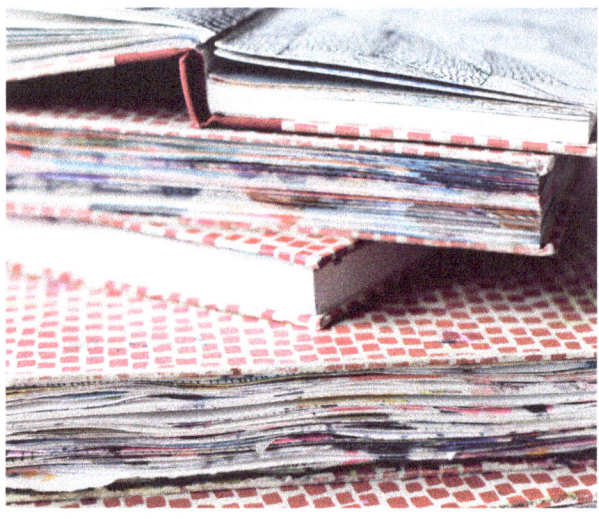

The contents of a sketchbook do not need to be shared publicly. Create art just for yourself, just for the joy of being creative. Sketchbook pages are for discovery, not display.

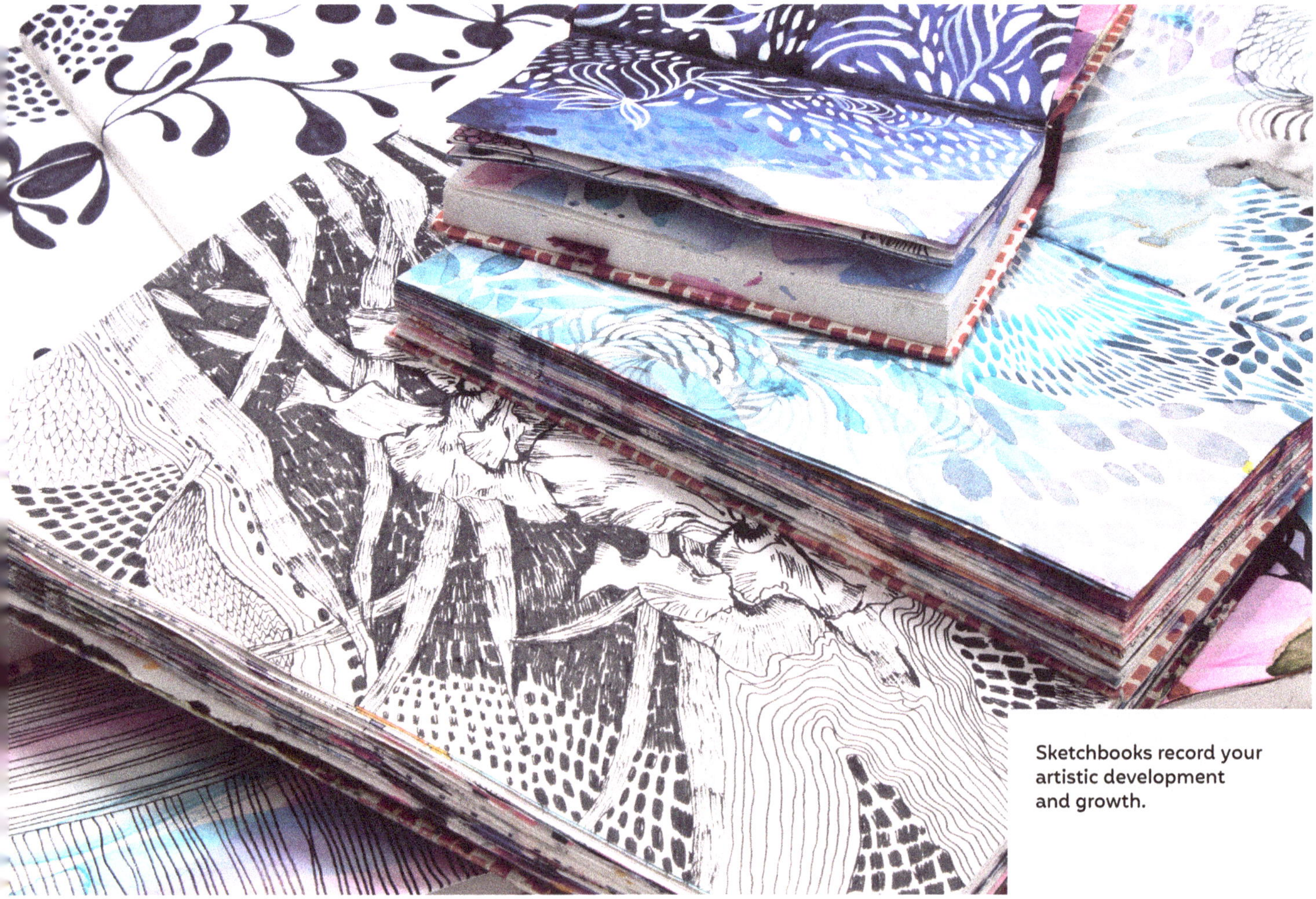

Sketchbooks record your artistic development and growth.

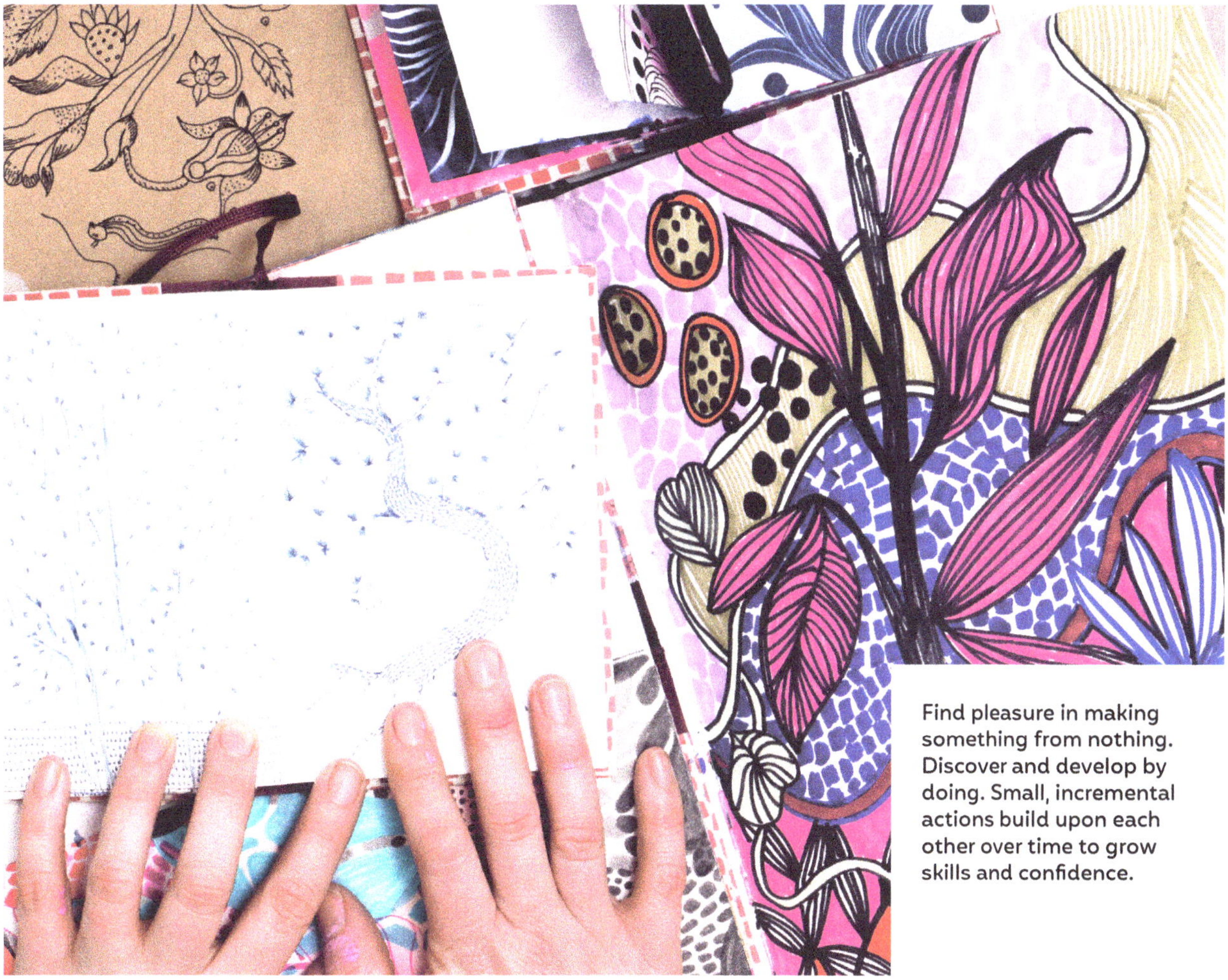

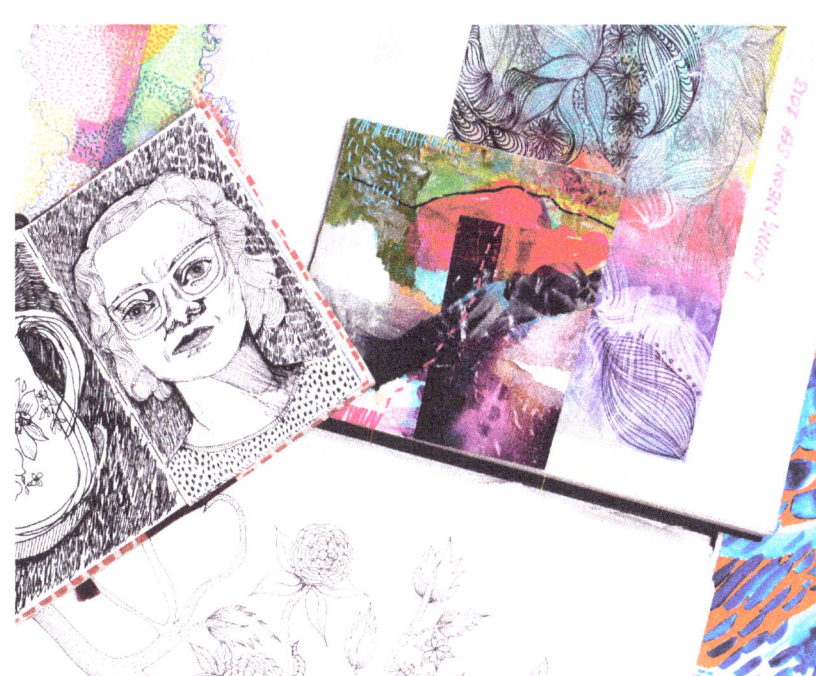

Find pleasure in making something from nothing. Discover and develop by doing. Small, incremental actions build upon each other over time to grow skills and confidence.

Develop Your Skills

We learn to create by creating. We get better by doing. Your sketchbook is a place to create and do, develop and progress.

Look Back in Months or Years to Come

Your sketchbook captures a season of your life. It can be very rewarding to keep all your sketchbooks and look back on where you were or what interested you at a certain time of your life. Social media has made it so easy for us to compare ourselves, our lives, our creative output, and our artwork with others. We often tend to compare our very worst efforts with someone else's best efforts. Instead we should compare our work against our work and ask ourselves: Am I learning? Am I developing? Am I expressing myself? Am I feeling fulfilled by my output? Am I pushing myself?

Look back at old sketchbooks and discover past interests or fascinations. A sketchbook allows you to track ideas and progress over time.

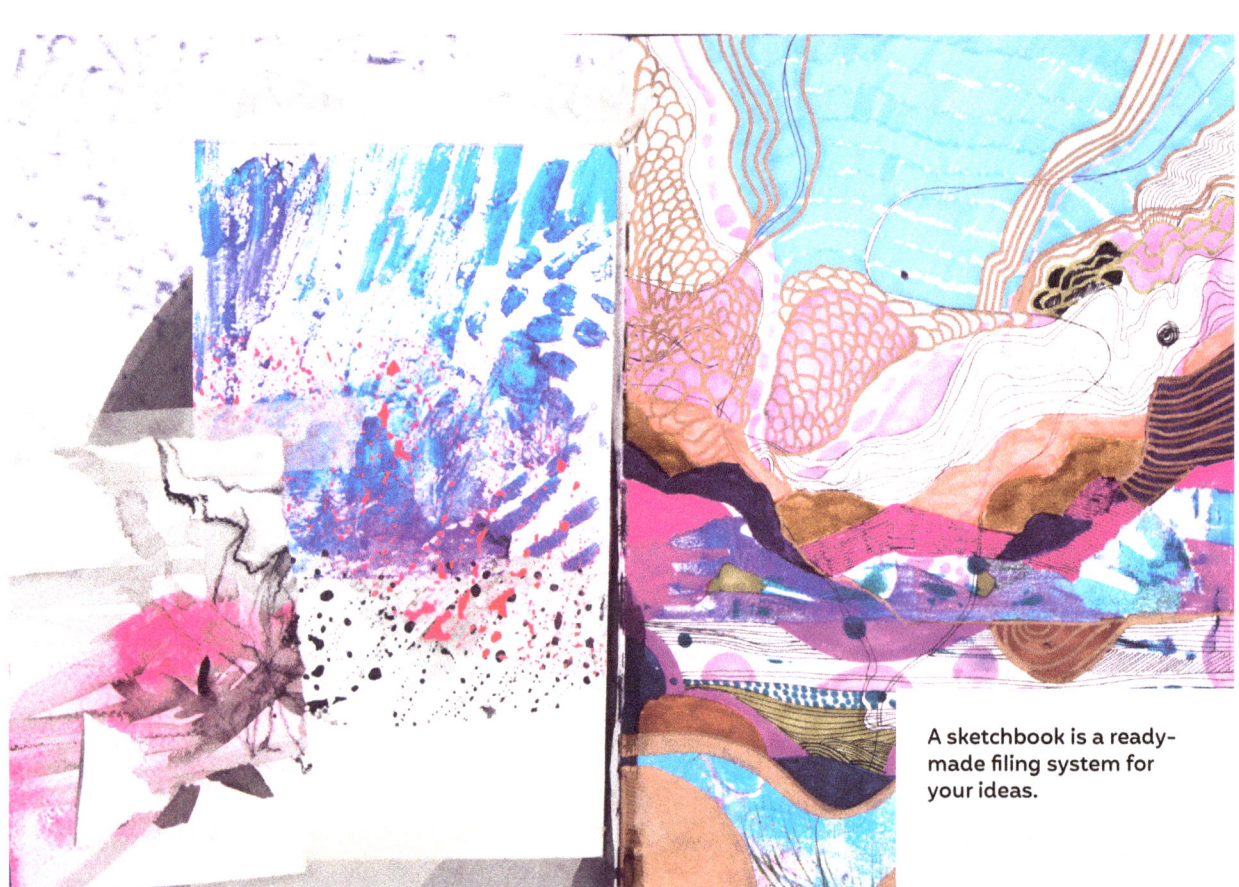

A sketchbook is a ready-made filing system for your ideas.

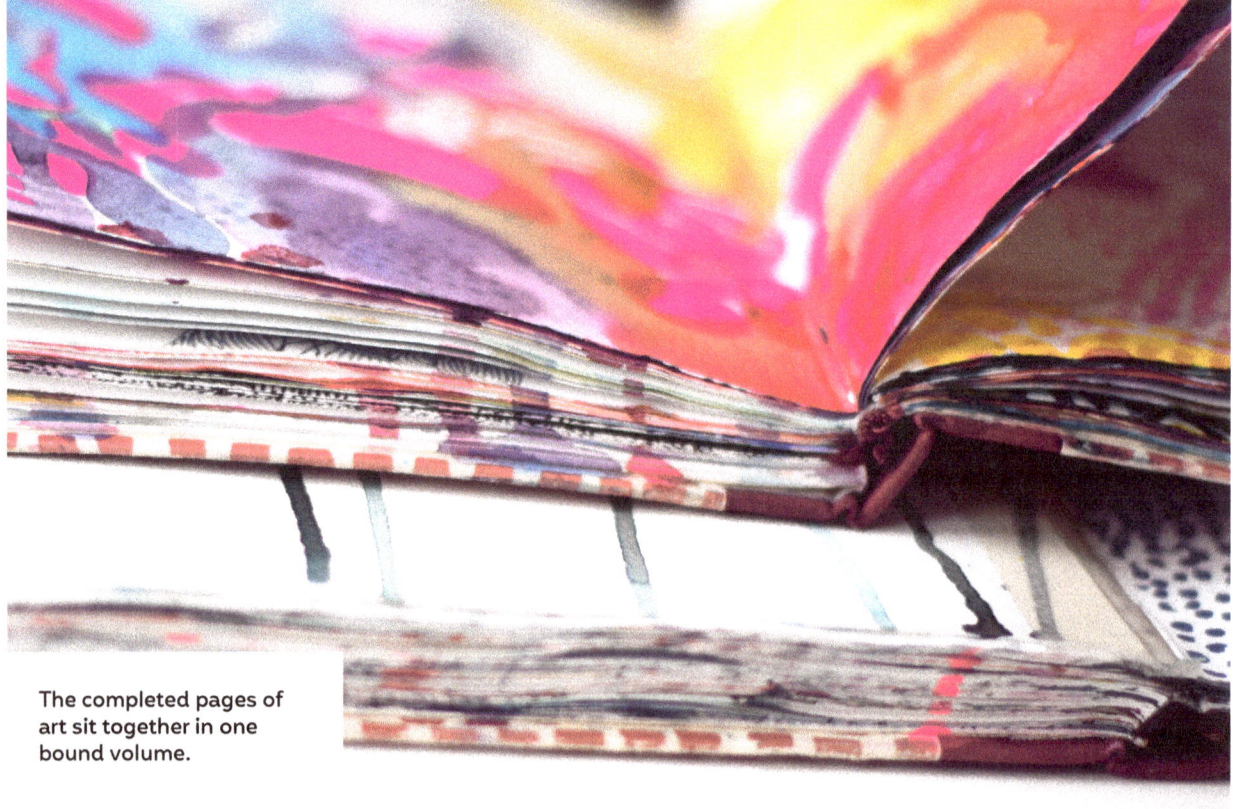

The completed pages of art sit together in one bound volume.

All in One Place

Your sketchbook is a brilliant filing cabinet of ideas, all kept safe and sound in one place.

A Beautiful Object

Your sketchbook can develop into a beautiful object. You may really appreciate the way the completed pages of your sketchbook remain together in one bound volume.

Rewarding

Making art for yourself can be nourishing and rewarding. Experimenting in your sketchbook can lift your spirits and bring joy to your life. There is something extremely satisfying about turning a blank page into something filled with meaning or learning, color or line.

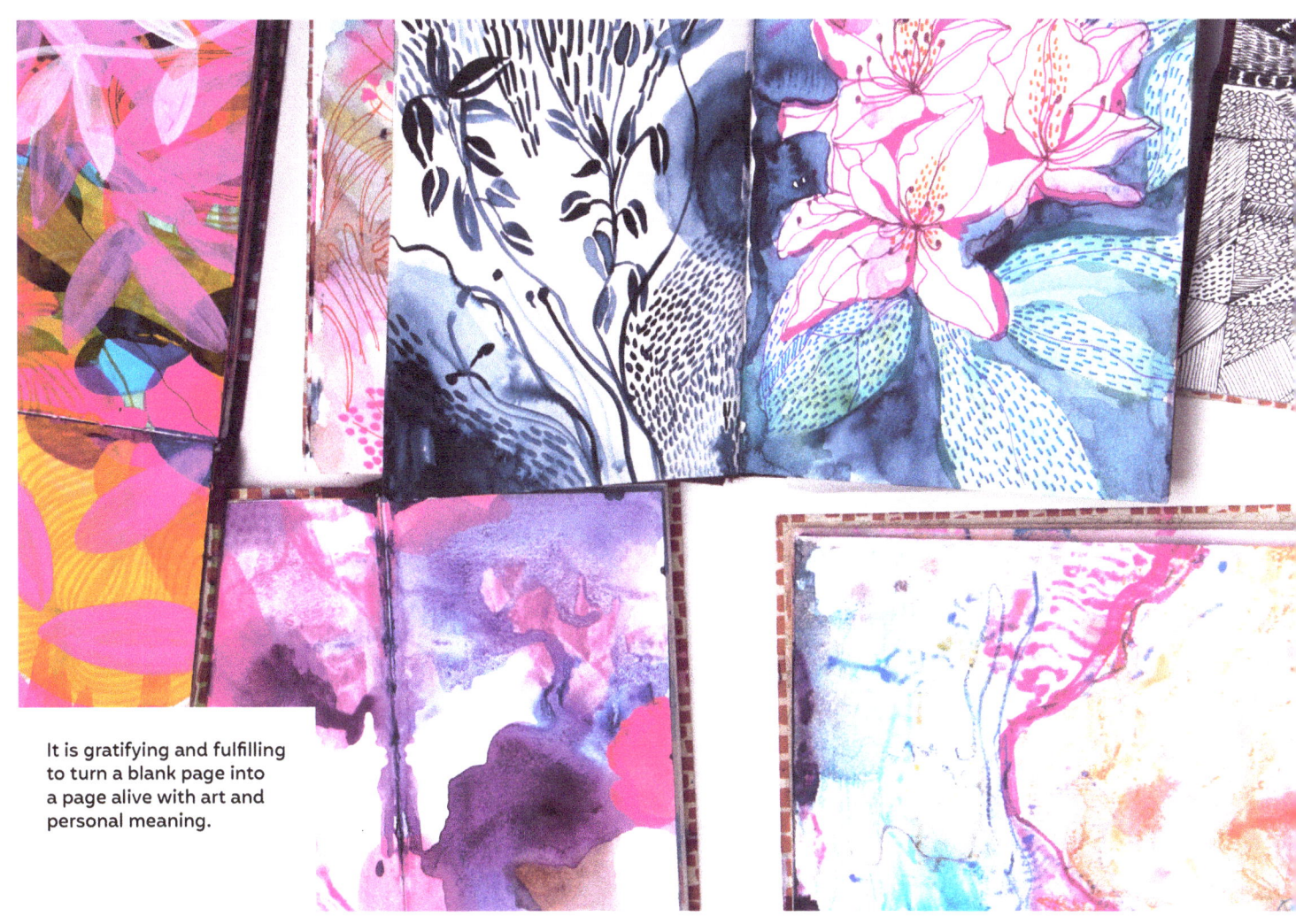

It is gratifying and fulfilling to turn a blank page into a page alive with art and personal meaning.

Process, Not Outcome

Your sketchbook is a place to enjoy and learn from the process of creating. A sketchbook is not about completed art works. It is a place to explore process, expand on small fragments, and develop your own artistic language and lexicon. I often learn the most from my failed attempts, my worst pages—the pages I don't like. Think about your sketchbook as a place where you gain insight and wisdom from the "doing" and that this insight isn't necessarily based on whether you like the result. Sometimes the magic happens in your brain and not on the page. The value can come from what you have learned in the process of creating, not from what you created.

Creating Meaning

Using sketchbooks can help you connect with yourself. It can prompt you to be more conscious about the things in life that energize and enliven you. Using a sketchbook is an exercise in discovery; it invites you to think about what lights you up, what makes you curious, what fascinates you, and what makes you feel expansive. Your sketchbooks will become a place where you define what matters to you, where you unearth messages to yourself, from yourself.

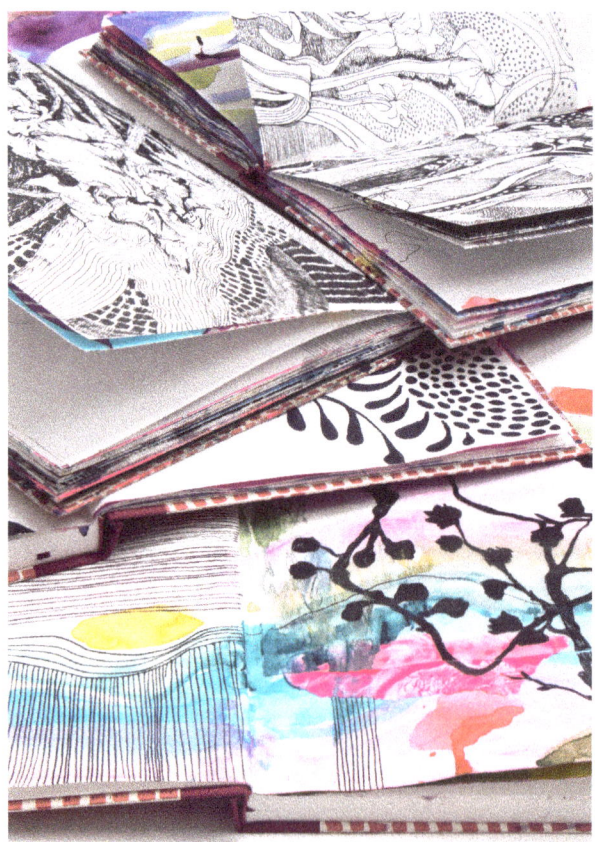

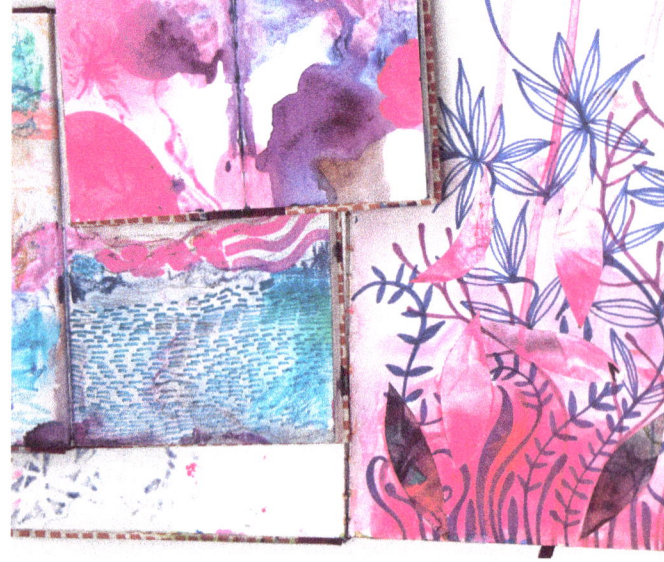

What you learn through creating can be more significant than what you create. The larger sketchbook features felt-tip pen floral patterns pasted over with collaged leaf shapes. It has been finished with a splash of hot pink paint that I allowed to drip down the page. The medium-size sketchbook features felt-tip pen, scribbles of pastels, a splash of watercolor, and blue felt-tip pen marks. In the smaller sketchbook, I was exploring how colors work together.

A sketchbook practice is an exercise in self-discovery. Creating art pages is a way to unearth the things that excite, interest, and expand you.

Interpreting the World

Creating art is a way to interpret the world. When you start to draw, you'll often find that you begin to see things with new eyes. When I draw an object, I learn about it, I appreciate its form, its complexity, its structures, and its patterns.

The act of really looking at something invites you to see it differently. You gain new insight on your subject matter and you might discover something about it that you hadn't noticed before. The act of drawing something, even a mundane object, often reveals a hidden beauty in the subject.

A Springboard

Your sketchbook can be the start of a stimulating conversation with yourself. Its pages can contain the beginnings of ideas that you may want to develop into paintings or larger artworks. It's a place to capture those ideas that otherwise may dissipate or be lost in the ether. It's the start of something that takes you on a path to discovery.

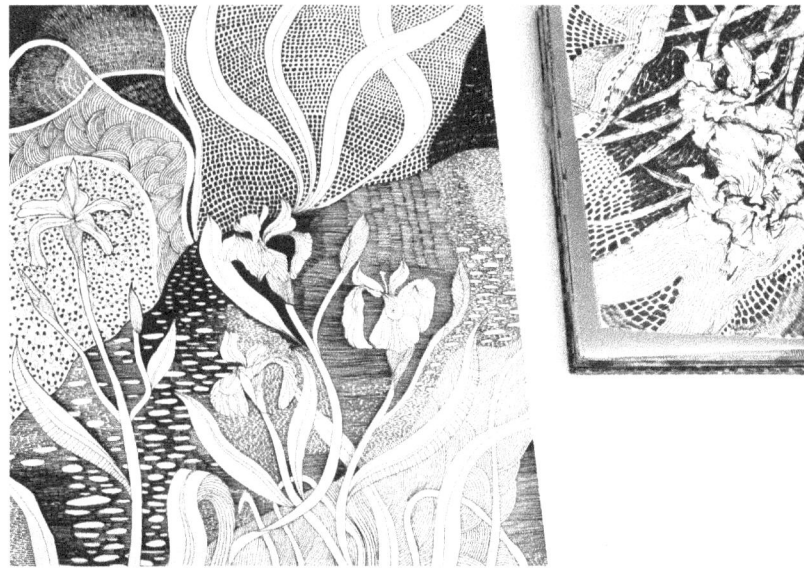

The pages in your sketchbook may contain ideas or fragments of ideas that you may want to expand beyond the pages into larger and more complete artworks.

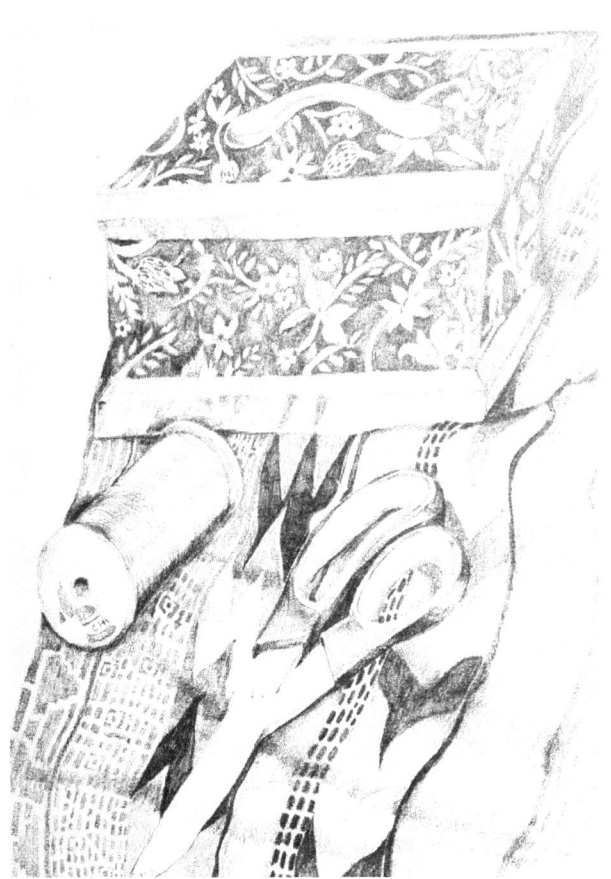

Seek the extraordinary in the ordinary. Drawing can reveal a hidden beauty in an object. By drawing a subject, you'll see it differently and gain a greater understanding of it.

OVERCOMING OBSTACLES

Overcoming obstacles is an integral part of being creative, so let's take a moment to reflect on what these obstacles might be.

Some of us would like to be more creative but we are scared to try and scared to fail. We start and then get lost, or become blocked, or don't know the next step to take. My goal is to help you overcome these obstacles and work through them.

Meet your own creative vulnerabilities with compassion and curiosity.

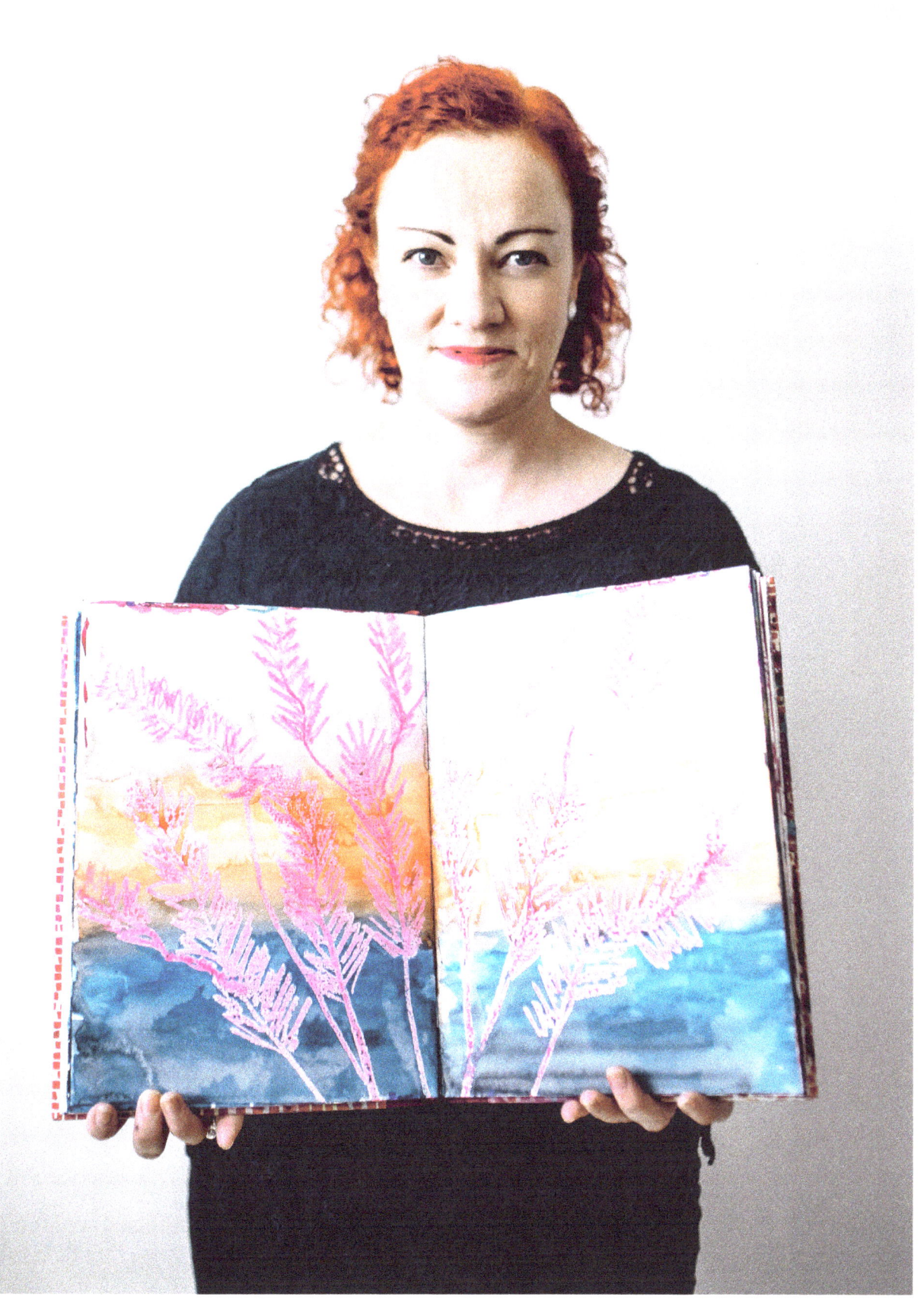

I Can't Draw

There were many years of my life when I stopped drawing and didn't start again. I was so critical of everything I produced. The sad thing is that my mental chatter and self-criticism about not being able to draw well got in the way of me doing something I loved. I listened to my own negative talk and believed it, whether it was true or not.

When we are small children, we draw with an innate sense of joy and curiosity. We draw rainbows and stick people and houses and lollipop trees. When we are young, we draw because it is a way of understanding and exploring the world around us and because it is fun. We need to bring this playful child back to the page and not allow our own criticism to prevent us from enjoying the process.

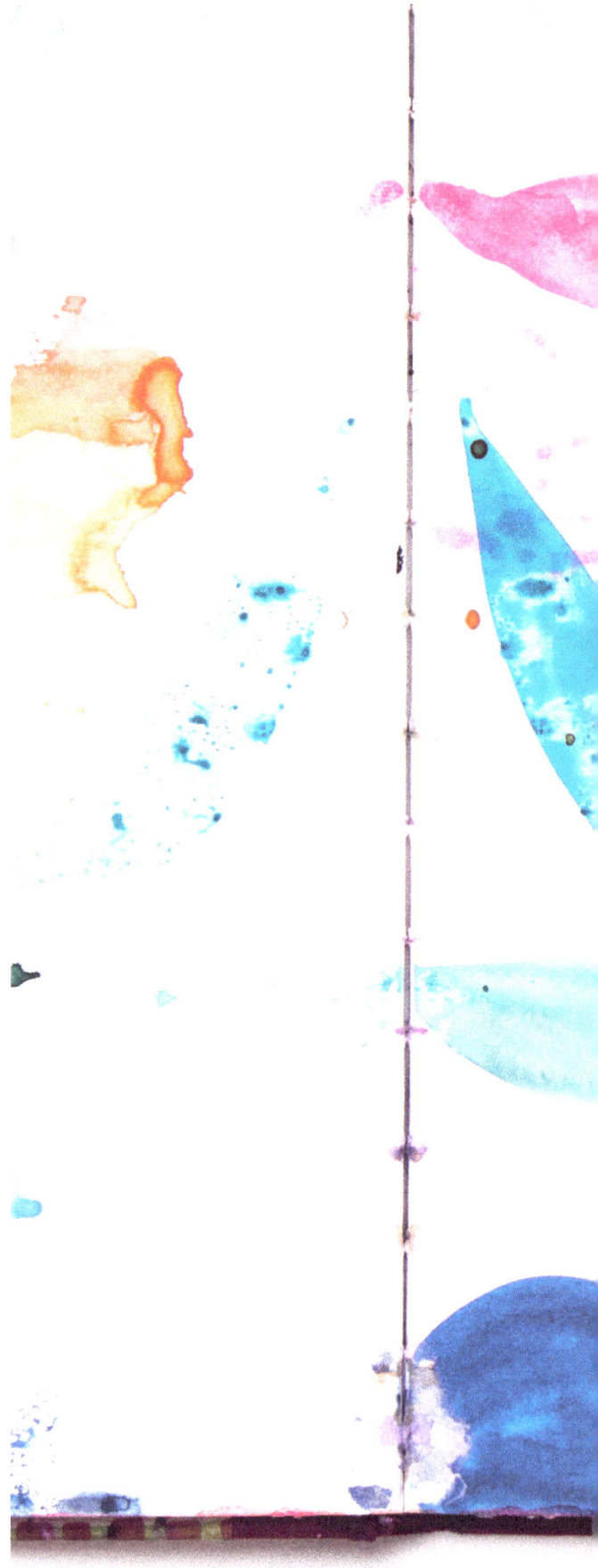

▶ A sketchbook is part of the artistic journey, not the destination. Its contents may be incomplete and experimental. Aim for playful over perfection.

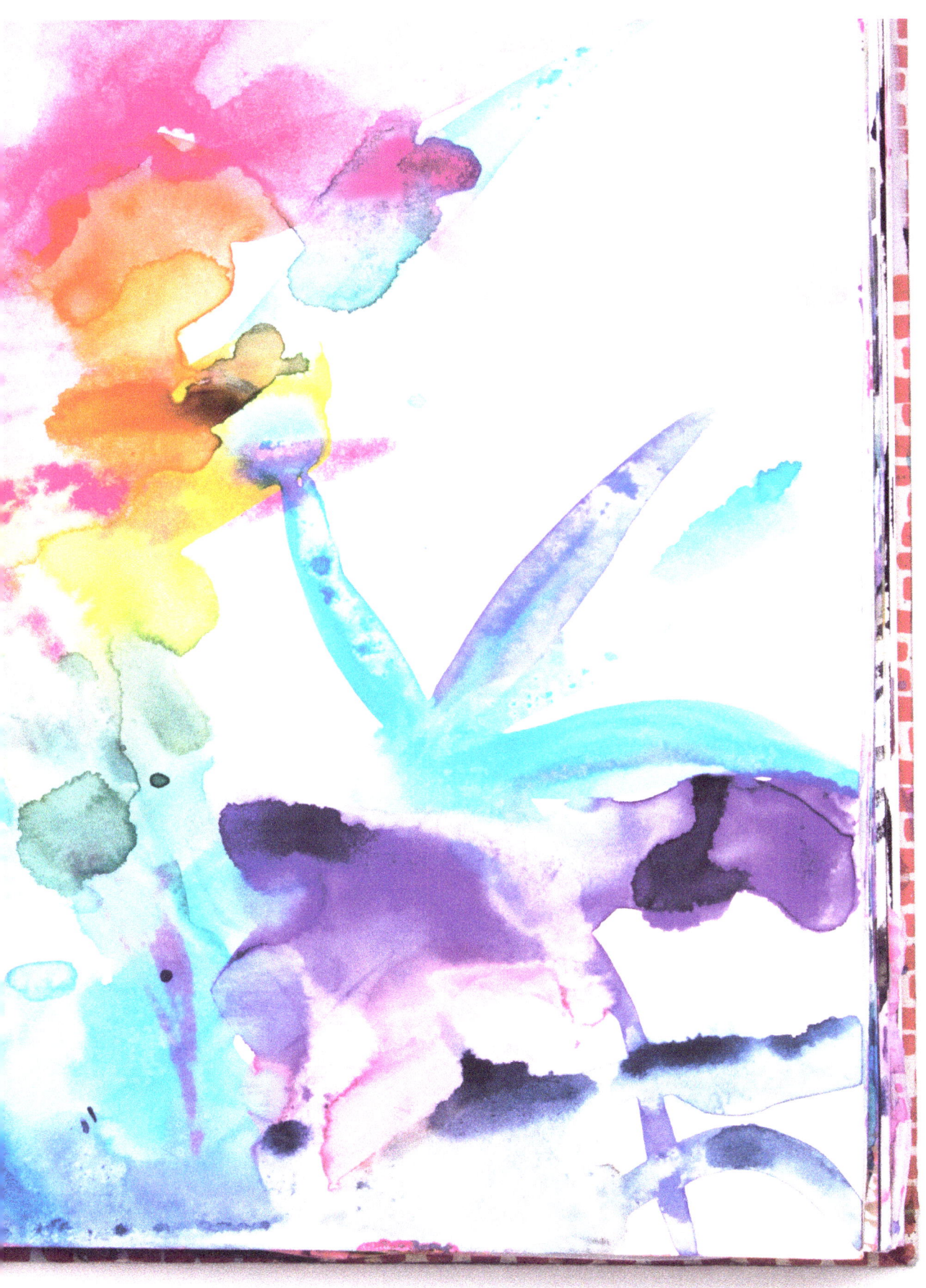

I Don't Like What I've Produced

I used to allow my self-criticism and unkind self-judgment to dictate my actions. I used to start a new sketchbook and abandon it because I was such a perfectionist and I didn't think my work was good enough. I'd want my sketchbook to be a masterpiece of brilliance. I wanted every page to be gorgeous and worthy of hanging in a gallery. I wanted to prove to myself that I was a talented and worthy artist. I wanted my sketchbook to fulfil too much.

All this pressure, all these expectations, and all this perfectionism led to a graveyard of abandoned sketchbooks.

Remember to nurture yourself rather than criticize your work. Compassion toward your art and yourself helps you to develop, grow, and learn, while pressured perfectionism gets you stuck. Lowering your standards a little and expecting a little less from yourself can allow you to achieve more. The freedom that comes with not being perfect allows you to be more in the flow. You'll find that with this mindset you will create better work and enjoy the process. The pain of not creating is so much more crippling than the pain of creating something you don't like.

Any new creative endeavor can make you feel exposed and vulnerable; it may stir feelings of doubt, fear, judgment, or criticism. Be kind and gentle with yourself as you start to create.

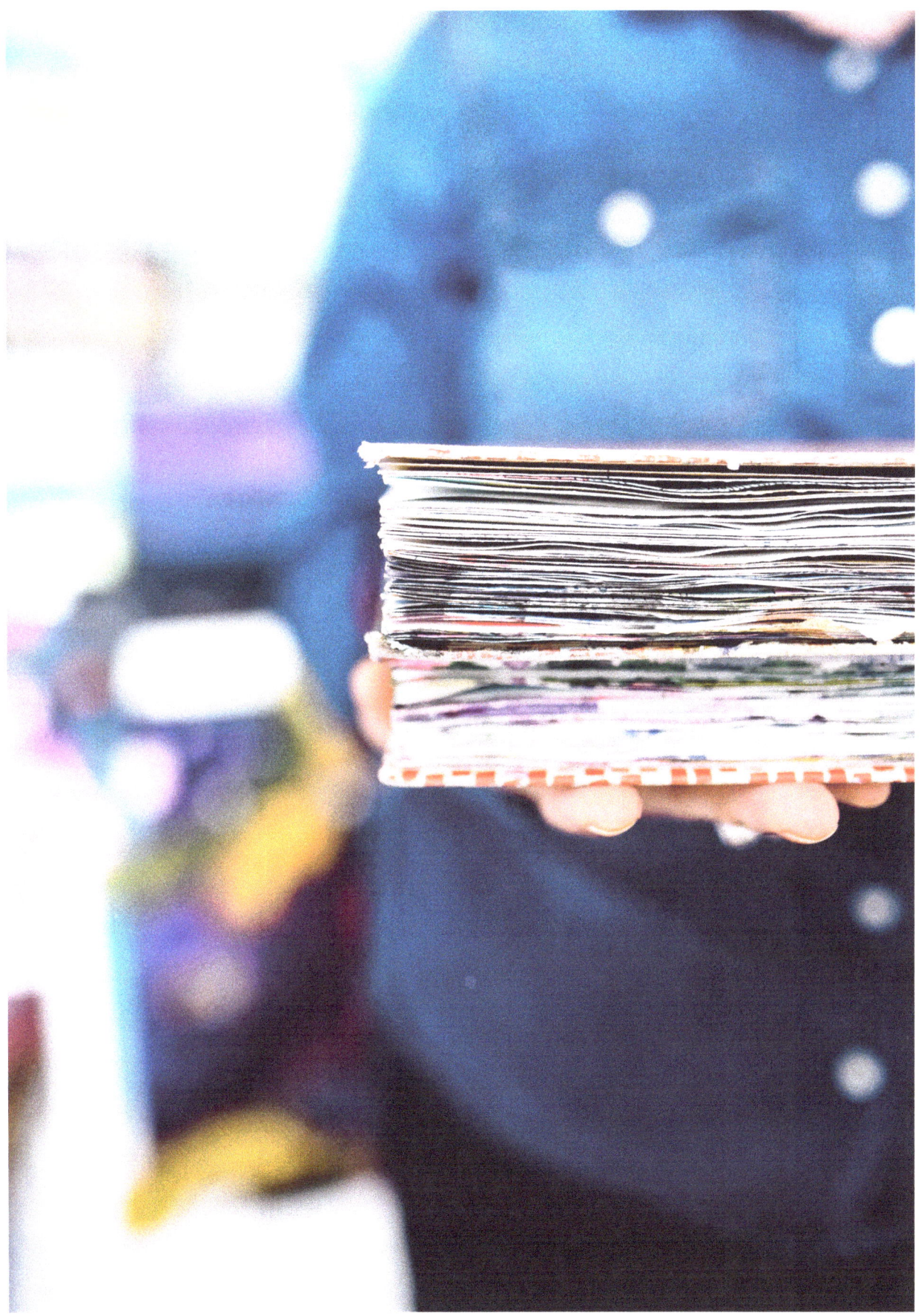

I Don't Know What To Do/Where To Start

Many times I haven't really known what to do or haven't felt inspired to do anything in my sketchbook. My foolproof response is to always do something. The power of taking a tiny action and going from there can be a way to engineer inspiration. Turn the page and just start. We can spend our lives thinking, planning, pondering, and considering. Often all this thinking and planning can be the thing that stops us from doing. So rather than thinking about starting, take a deep breath and start. There are so many ideas and prompts in this book, but only you can be the one who acts. Starting is vital; reading about starting is not enough.

Starting can be the hardest part, but by taking action you gain momentum.

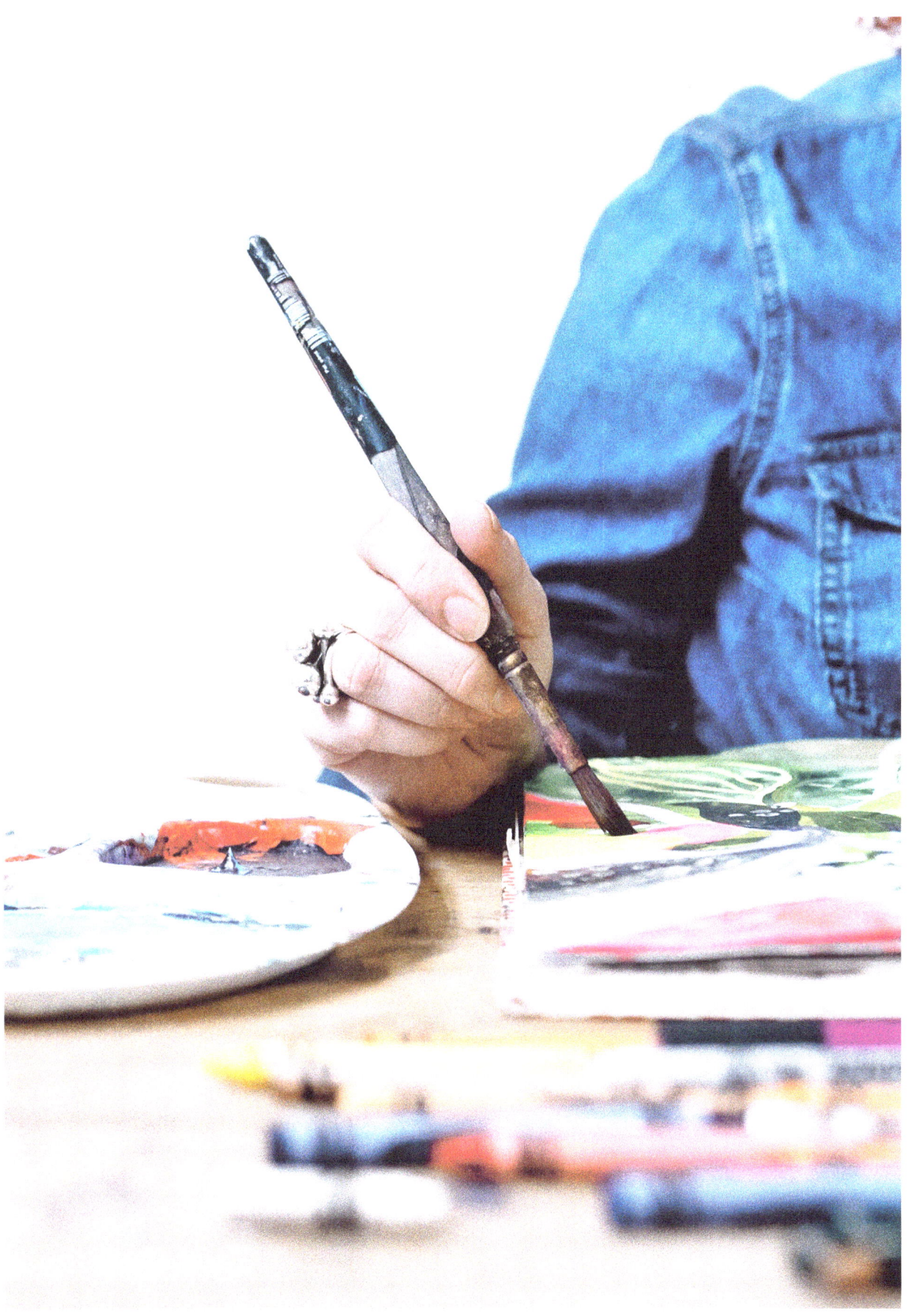

Obstacles Are Part of Being Creative

It's easy to find obstacles that stop us from starting or carrying on. Sometimes roadblocks appear once we're already underway. Try to examine and acknowledge your own blocks and obstacles. You need to know what they are in order to surmount them. Use the exercises in this book to navigate your way around your creative blocks and bumps. Listen to what you say to yourself—is it helpful?

Think of the blocks and obstacles as integral parts of being creative and know that any worthy journey has a few setbacks along the way. These blocks are part of the learning process and part of your expansion and development, so don't let them be the end of your creative road like I did for too many years.

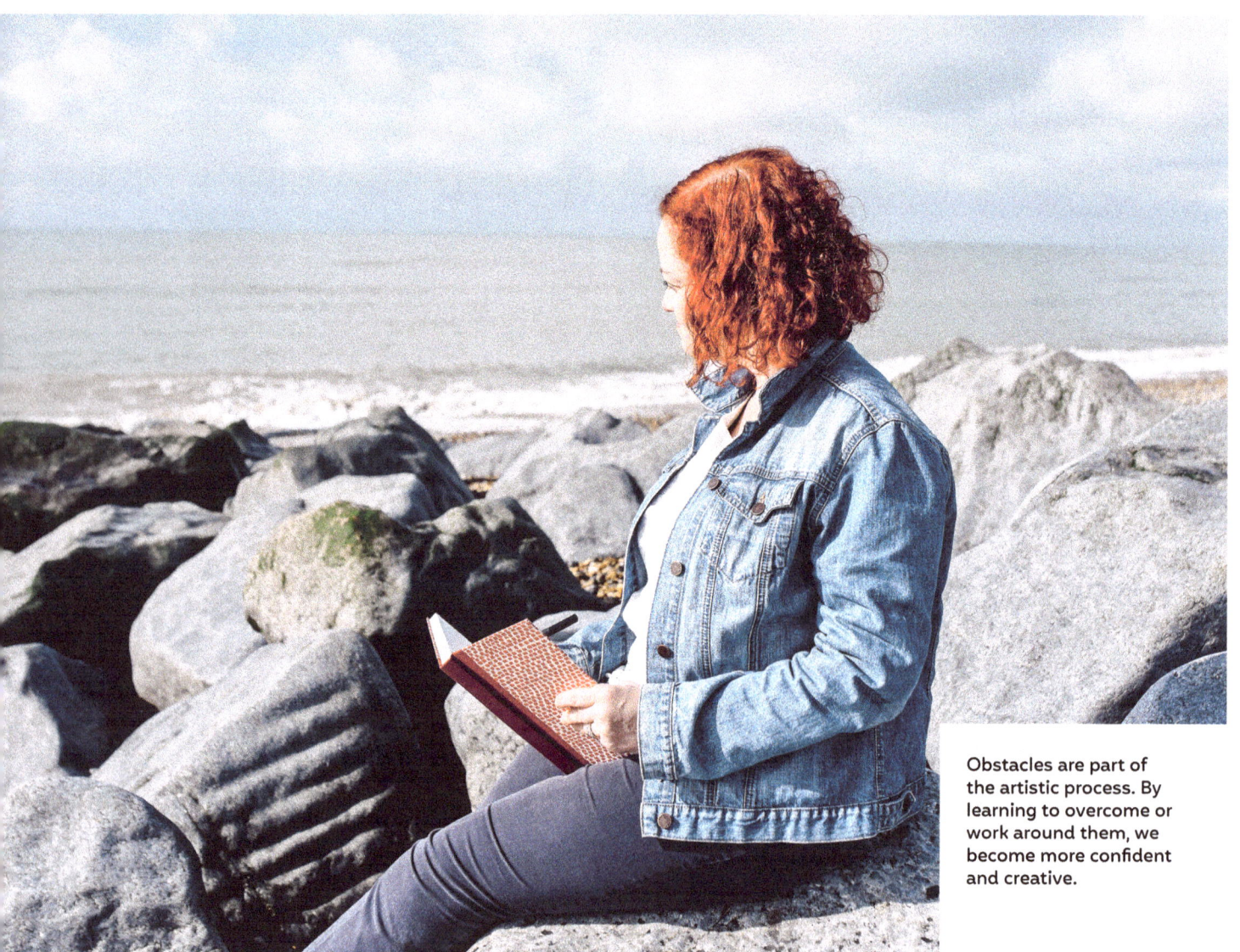

Obstacles are part of the artistic process. By learning to overcome or work around them, we become more confident and creative.

Your Motivation and Intentions

Sketchbooks have helped me to develop my confidence, uncover my inner artist, and express myself. When I first started using a sketchbook regularly, it became a safe space in which my creativity and art could flourish, a place to develop my skills, and a springboard to a more expressive and creative life. I encourage you to explore your own motivations for working in a sketchbook.

I'm a great believer in writing things down because sometimes the act of putting pen to paper can turn the intangible into the tangible. Asking ourselves questions and writing down our answers helps us articulate our intentions, allowing us to find clarity. I invite you to think about your motivation for working in a sketchbook. Write your answers in your sketchbook or, if that doesn't feel right, just explore them on a piece of paper. It is powerful to ask yourself why you'd like to develop a sketchbook practice, what you'd like to achieve, how you'd like to feel, and when and where you intend to work in your sketchbook. Use the following prompts:

- I'd like to develop a sketchbook practice because . . .
- When I'm working in my sketchbook, I'd like to feel . . .
- I'd like my sketchbook to be a place where I can . . .
- I will use my sketchbook every (frequency) for (specify) amount of time
- I will use my sketchbook at (place)

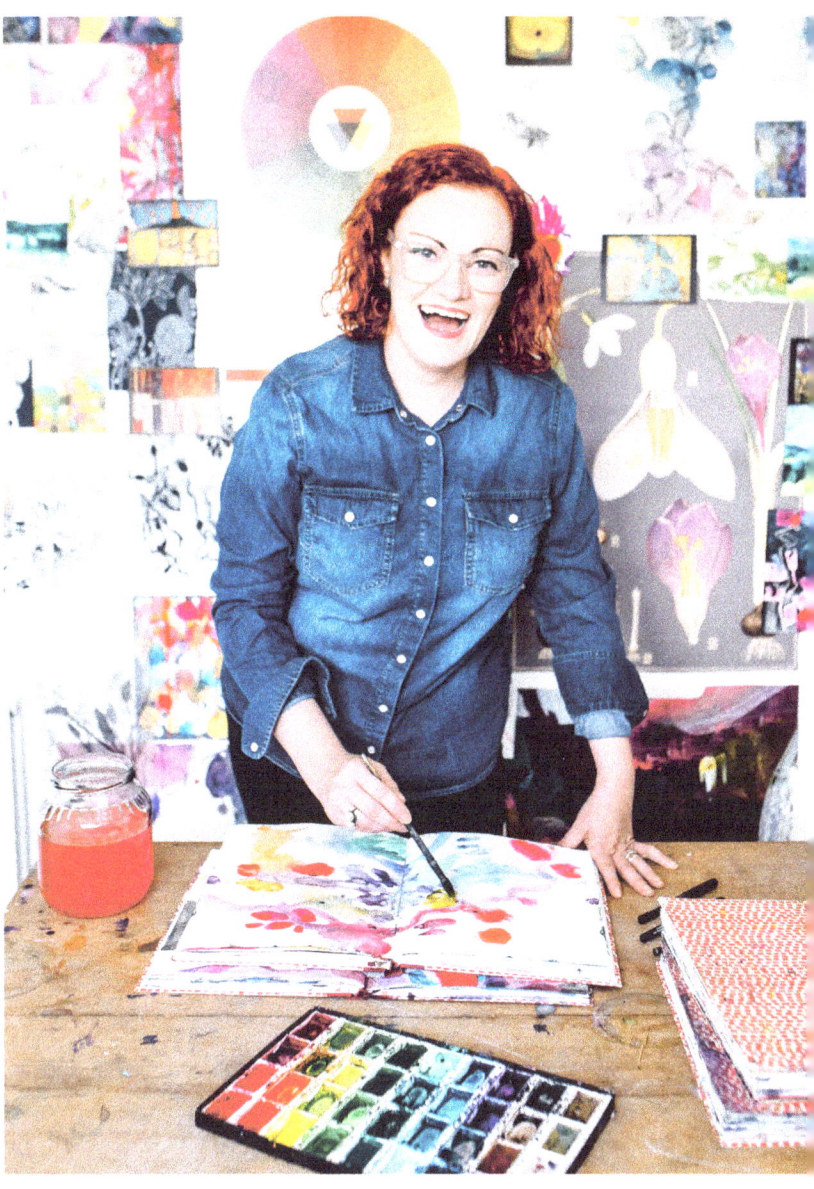

Clarity of intention is a powerful place to start.

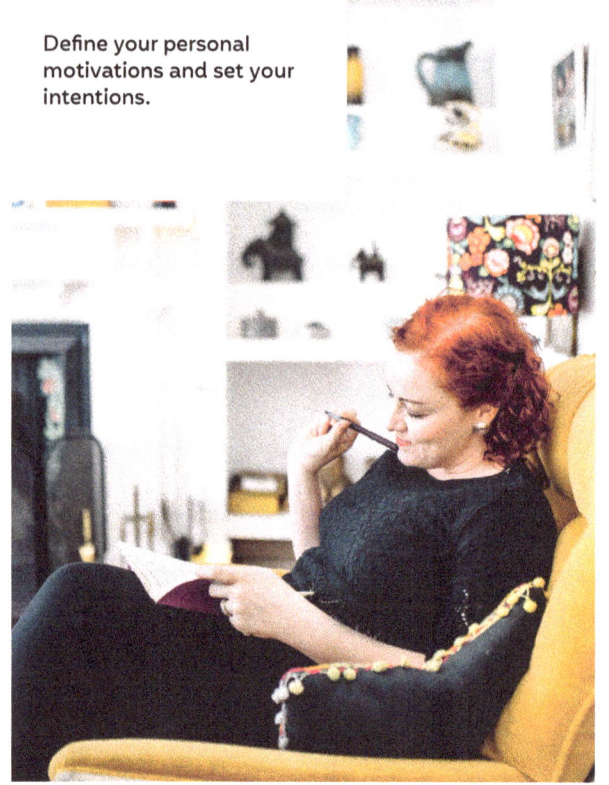

Define your personal motivations and set your intentions.

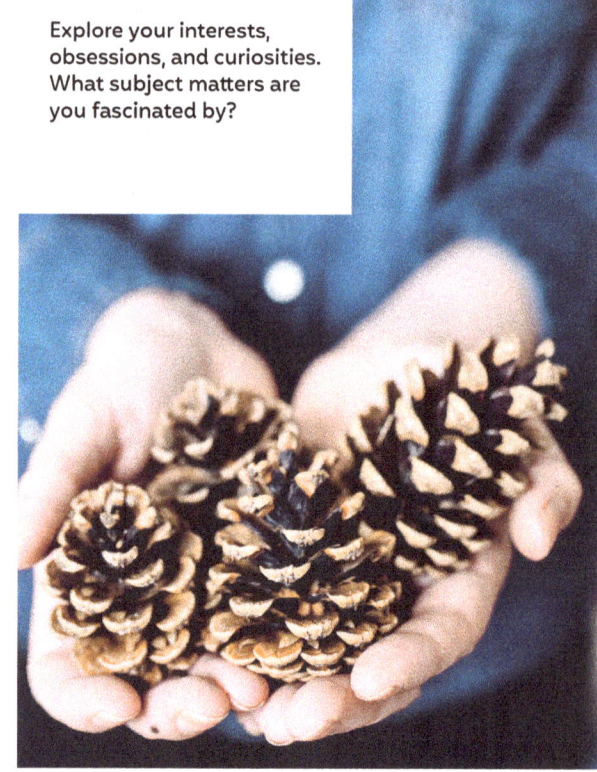

Explore your interests, obsessions, and curiosities. What subject matters are you fascinated by?

UNEARTH YOUR INTERESTS

Take a little time to complete the simple yet illuminating exercise that follows. It focuses on thinking and writing about the things that fascinate you. It asks you to identify the topics, subject areas, objects, or ideas that resonate with you and that you might like to explore in your sketchbook.

CAPTURING IDEAS ON ONE PAGE

The premise of this exercise is to capture all or some of the things that you might like to delve into in your sketchbook. Think of this as a stream-of-consciousness brain dump on to a page. You might think you don't really know the answer to this question, so spending a little time thinking and writing can be a wonderful way to get the ball rolling.

PERSONAL MAP OF INSPIRATION

Ask yourself this simple question: What would I like to explore in my sketchbook? Then sit quietly and think about your answers. Write down everything that comes to mind. Do not edit yourself. It doesn't matter if your list

sounds like a disparate collection of weirdness. Weird is wonderful. I now believe that my "weirdness" is the most interesting part about me. My lifelong obsession with patterns is one example of my weirdness (I can still remember all the carpet and wallpaper patterns in a house we left when I was five.) Then there are my all-consuming love affairs with random items from the natural world (shells, feathers, pinecones, leaves, seaweed, fish scales, and so on). All these things come out in my art and my sketchbook. Unearth your quirks and idiosyncrasies, then embrace them, nurture them, celebrate them, and use them.

Think of this writing, thinking, and note-taking exercise as a starting point for capturing your tiny curiosities. It's a way to record your interests, whether they are fleeting fragments or full-fledged ideas. It's a treasure map of the things you'd like to explore in your sketchbook. You list subjects that interest, fascinate, or intrigue you or pique your curiosity. Spend at least 20 minutes writing down the tiny and large things that spark your interest.

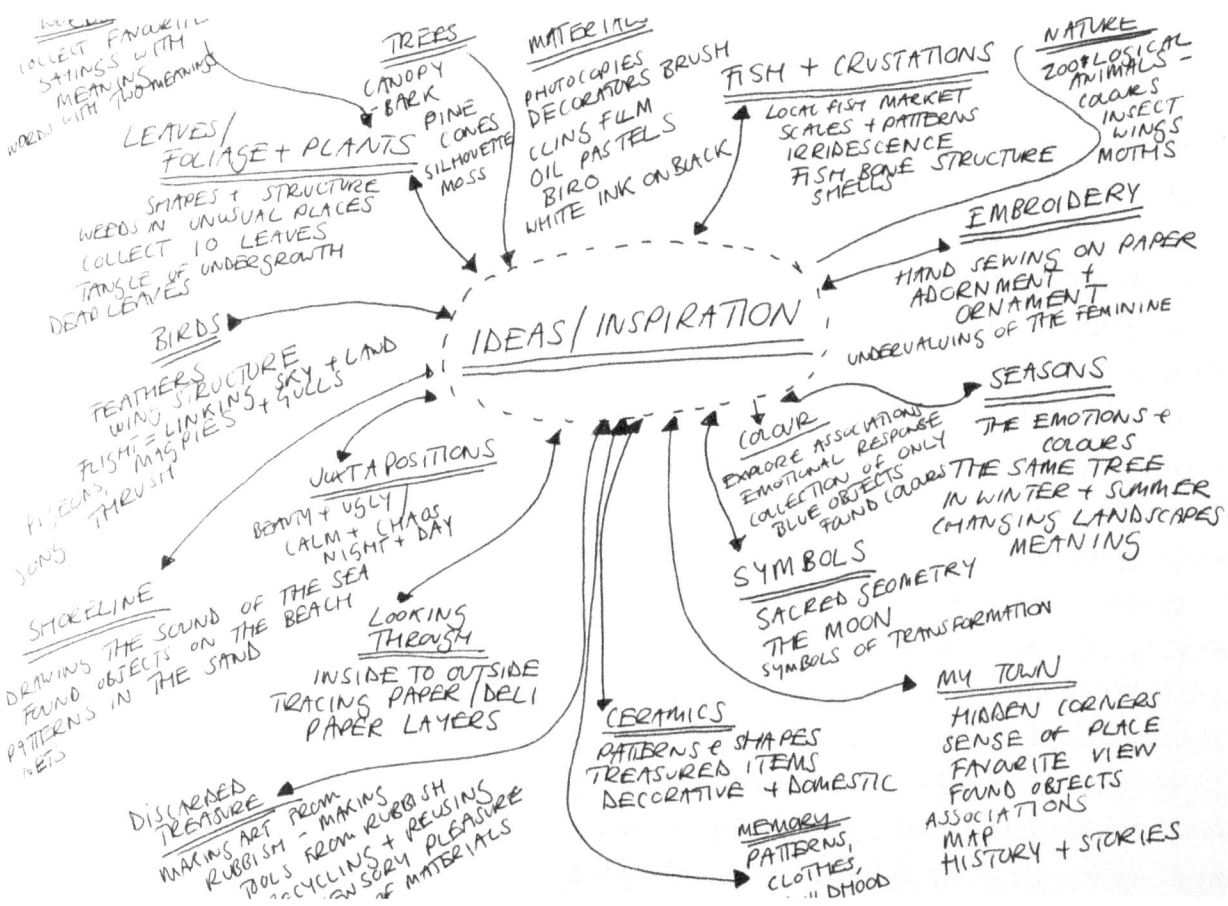

Here is an example of one of my inspiration maps. Yours will look completely different and contain things that are special to you. We are all unique and have our own set of influences, interests, and inspirations. Listen to your inner whisper, your inner wisdom, and write about it. Writing out these ideas will allow you to follow their unique threads.

BEING MINDFUL ABOUT YOUR INTERESTS

This exercise is something that you can return to, add to, or do again from start to finish. You may find that after you do this exercise, when you are just going about your daily routine, new ideas spring to mind. It's as if the act of writing these things down primes your brain to seek out inspiration at other times. When you are mindful about seeking out inspiration, you'll find that it is all around you.

QUESTIONS TO ASK YOURSELF

Complete this exercise in your sketchbook or on a blank piece of paper—your choice. I tend to do mine on a large piece of paper to allow me freedom and space to write as much as I like.

Ask yourself some or all of the following questions to get your ideas flowing:

- How would you describe the art that moves you?
- What art subject matter are you most drawn to?
- What did you enjoy creating or drawing as a child?
- Consider your creativity up to this point. What have you enjoyed?
- Is there an artistic approach that you have always wanted to try?
- What art materials interest you?
- Which subject areas excite you?
- Which subject areas fascinate you?
- What are you intrigued by?
- What kinds of objects do you like to collect?
- What sort of places do you like to visit again and again?

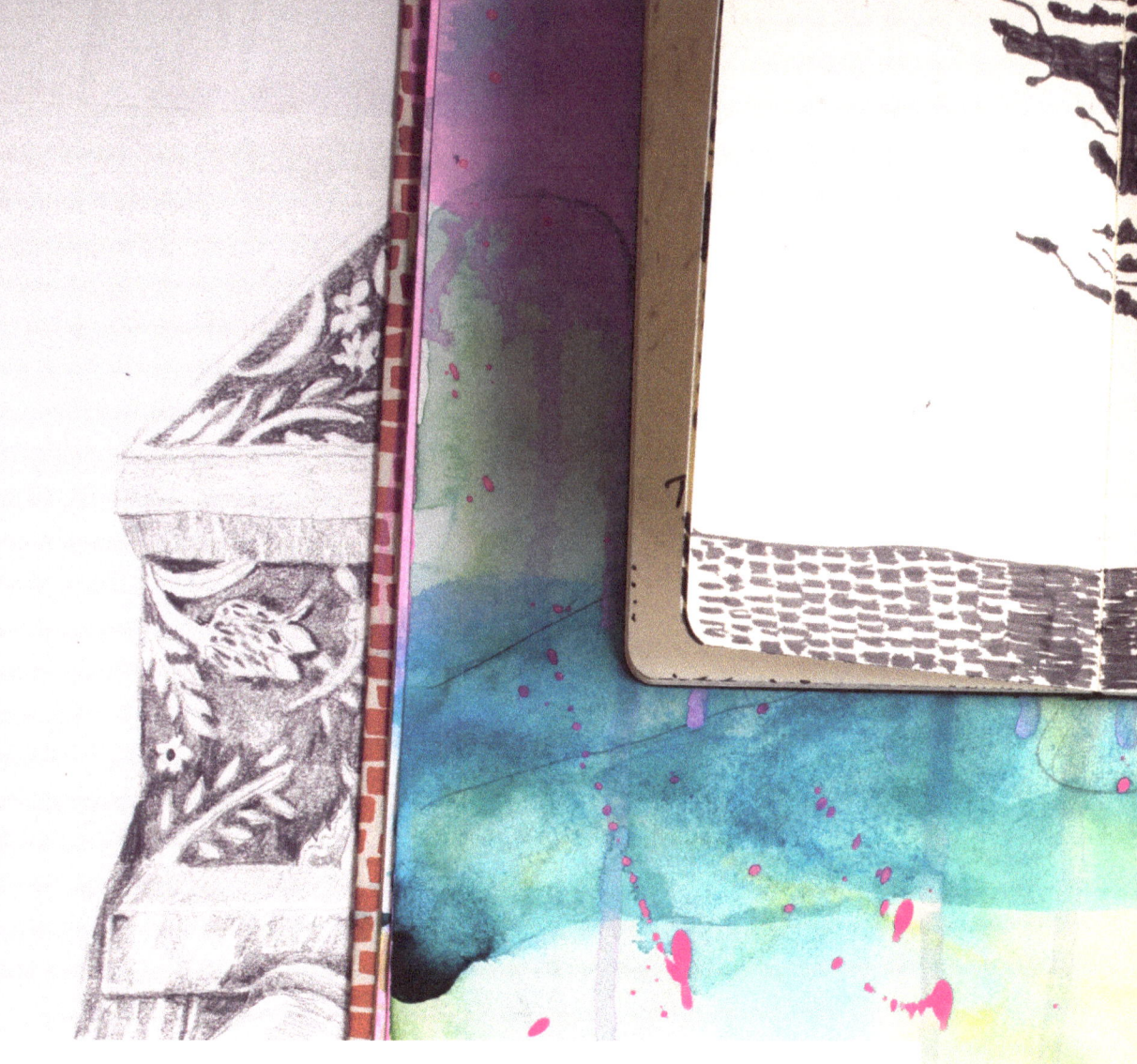

GETTING GOING

This chapter provides everything you need to get started in your sketchbook. It invites you to consider the type of sketchbook that best suits you and the various materials you can use. The variety of exercises are designed so that you can use them as jumping-off points and then adapt them to your own style.

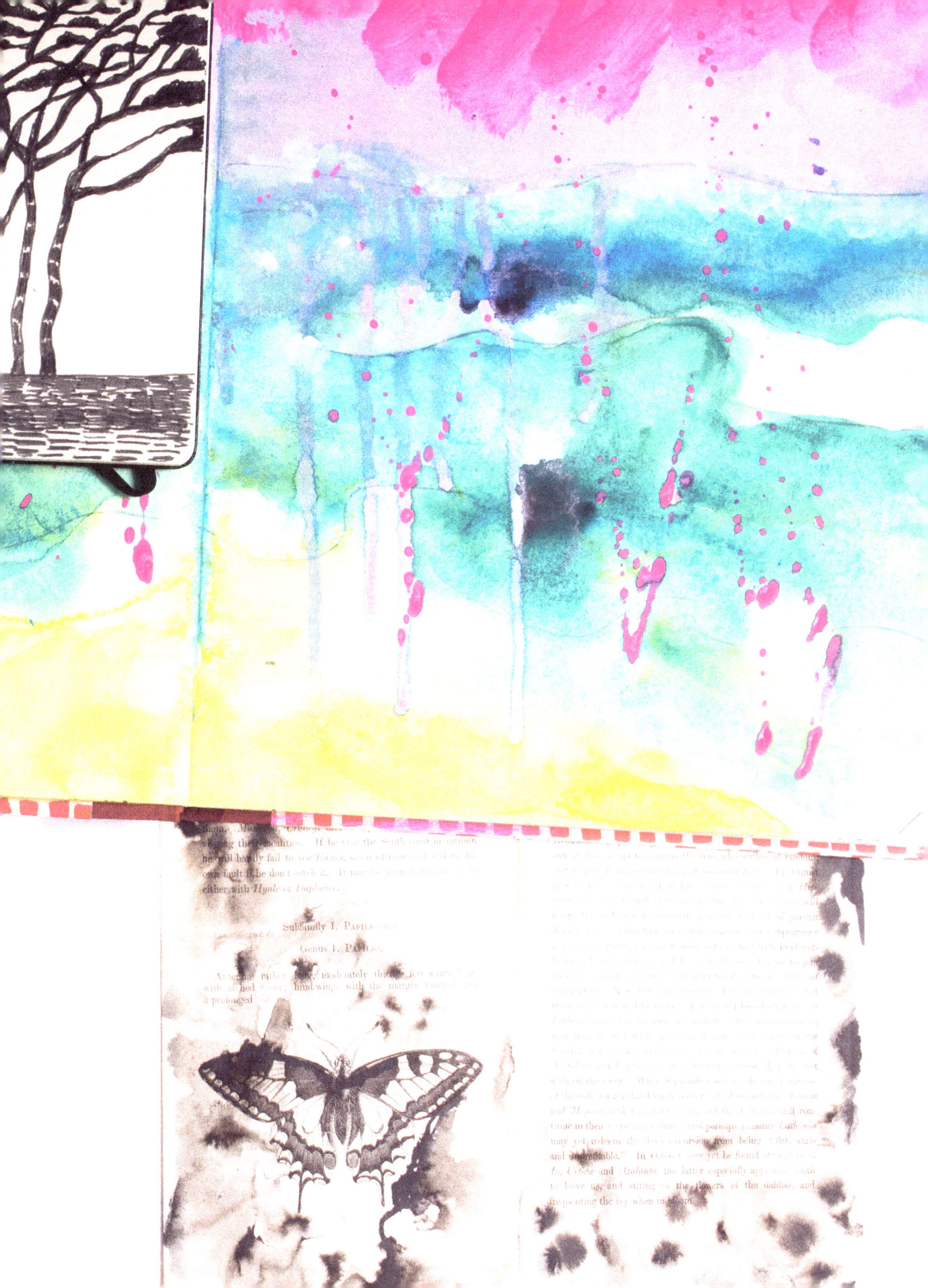

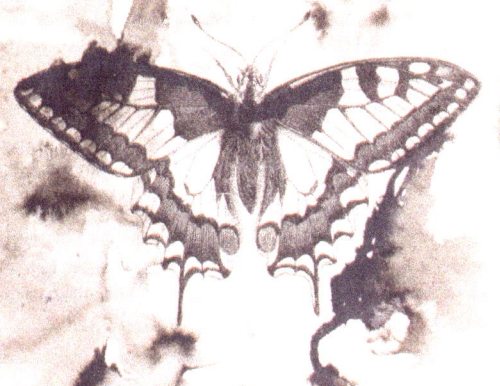

visiting these localities. If he visit the South coast in autumn he will hardly fail to see *Edusa*, which of course it will be his own fault if he don't catch it. It may be worth his while to try either with *Hyale* or *Daplidice* ...

Subfamily 1. PAPILIONIDÆ

Genus 1. PAPILIO

Antennæ rather long, moderately thick; fore wings long with arched costa; hind wings with the margin toothed and a prolonged tail ...

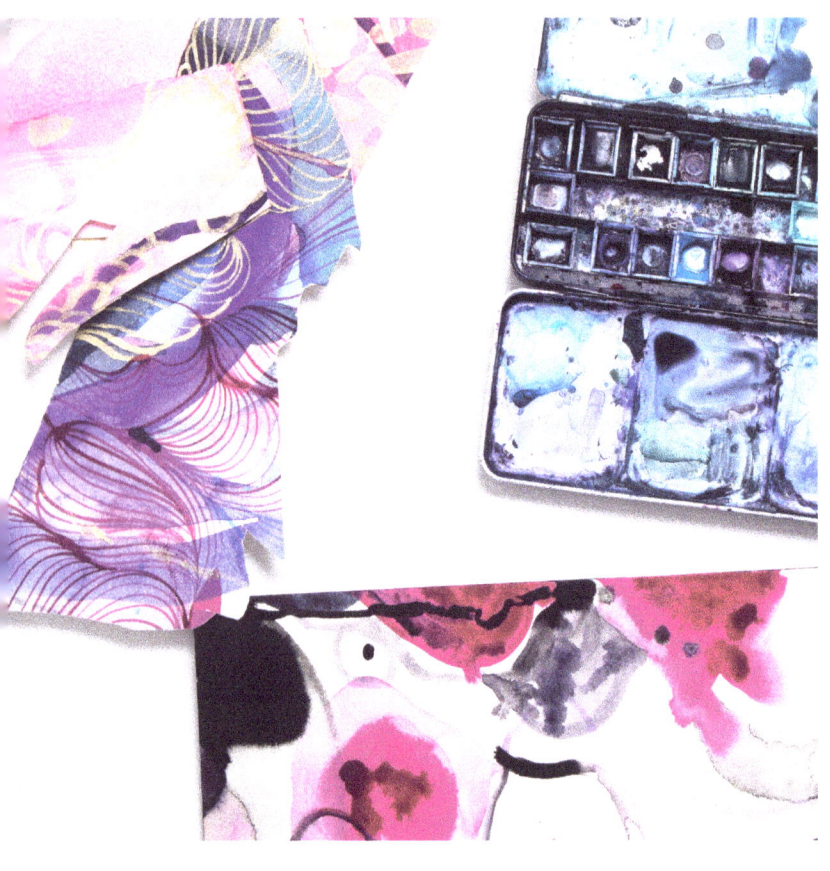

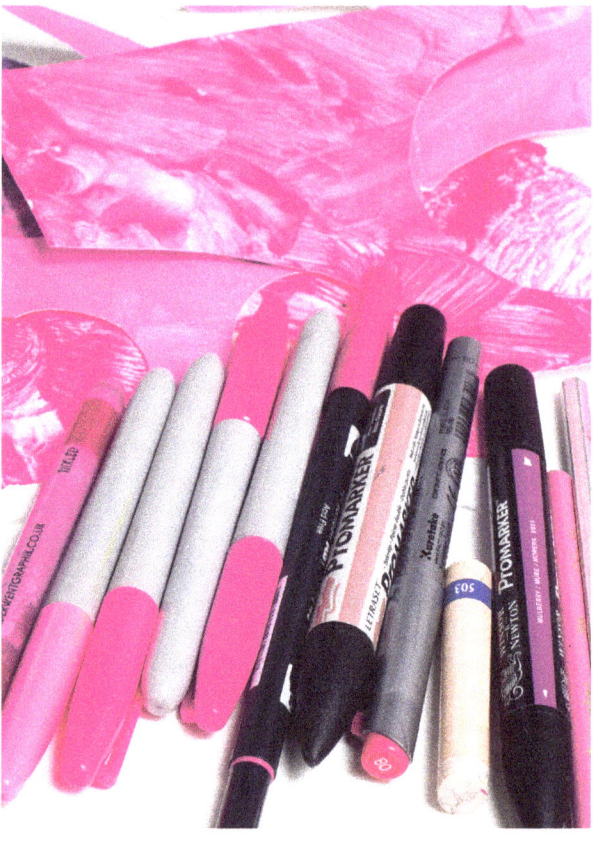

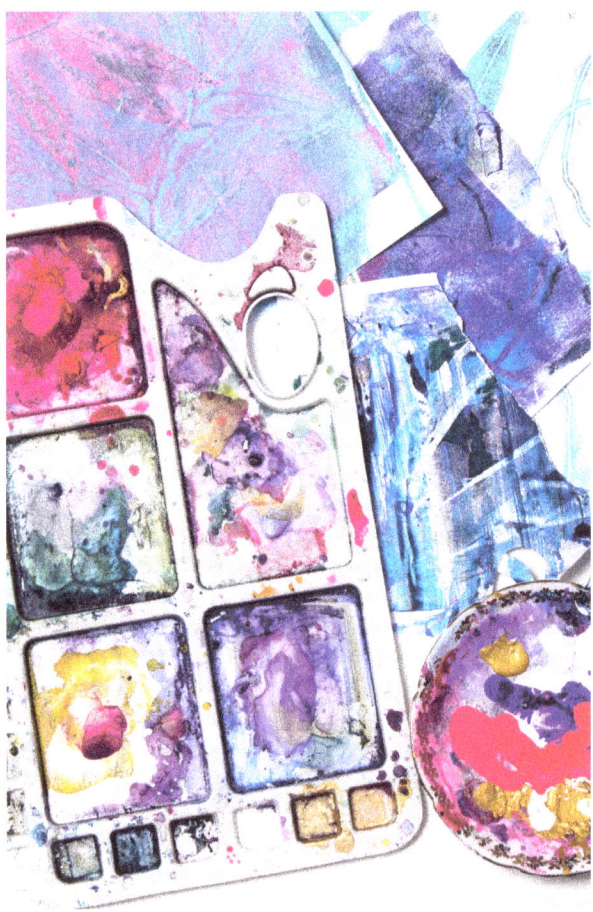

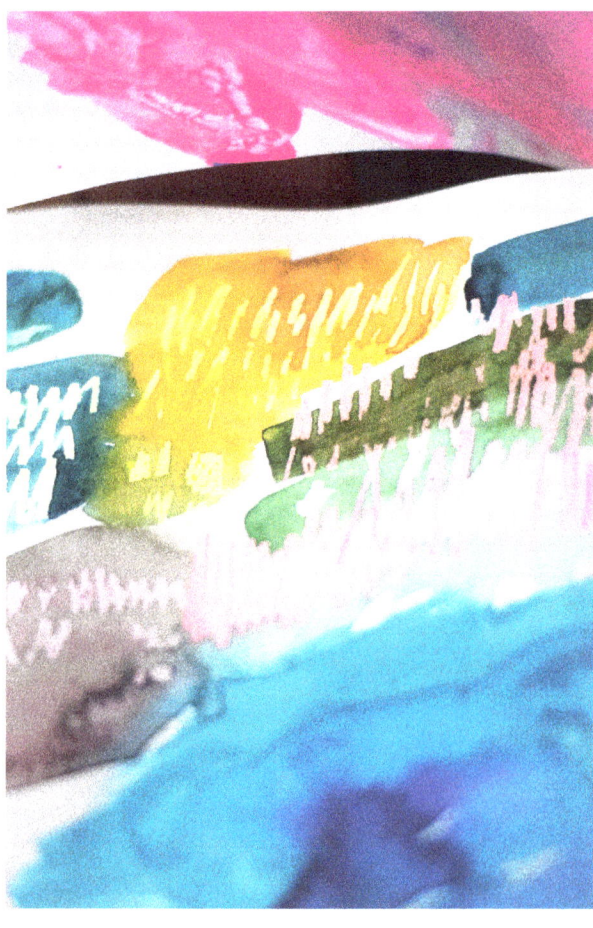

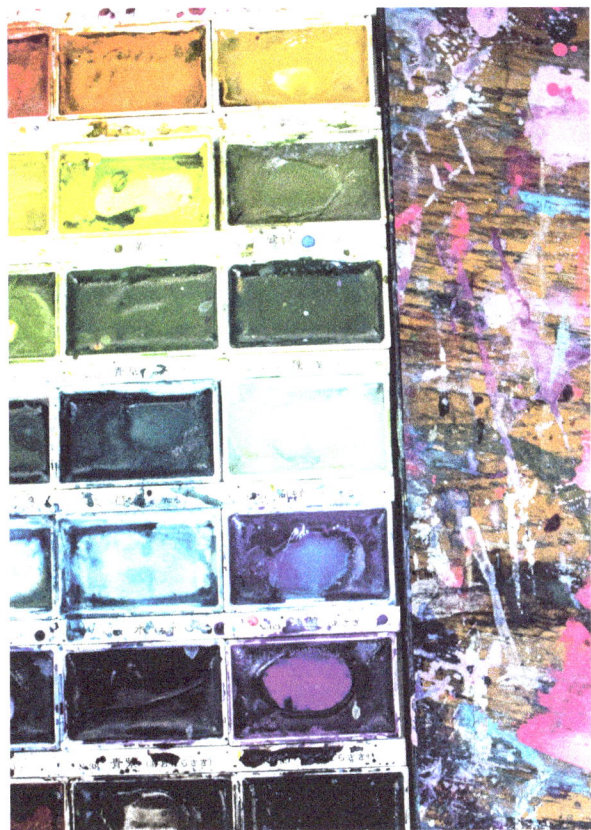

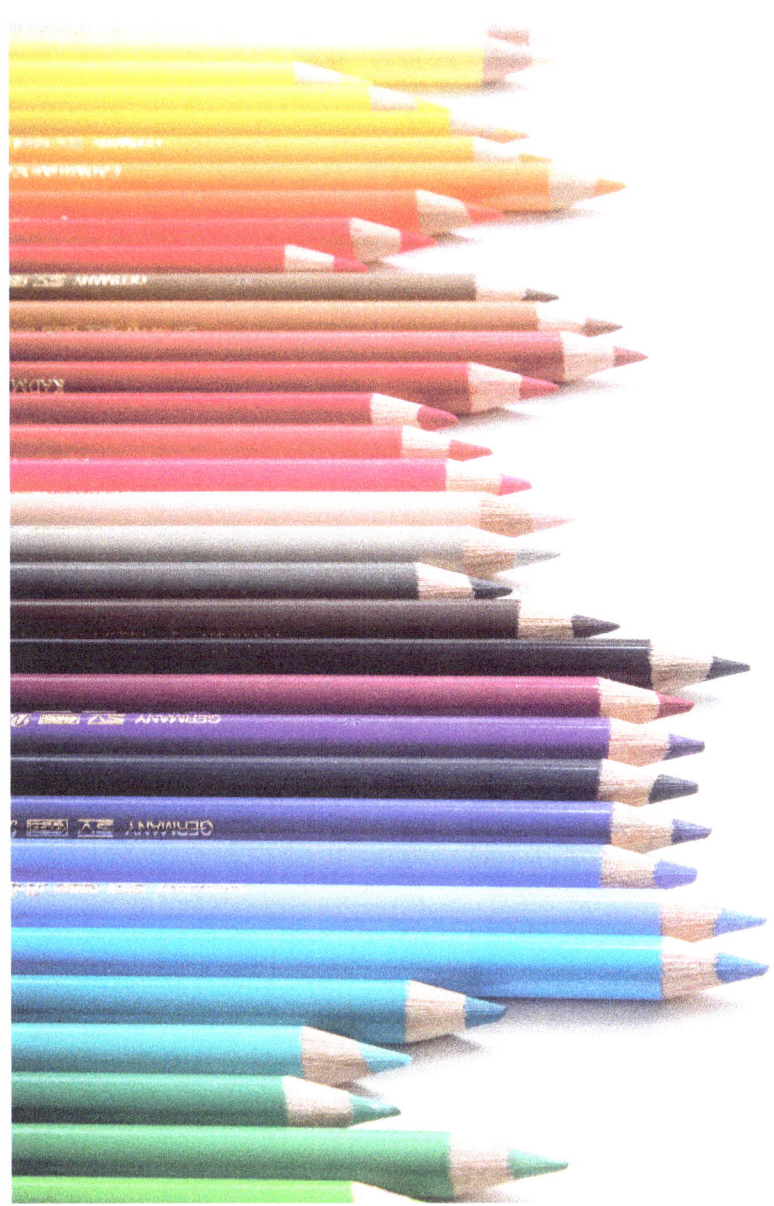

◀ ▲ I find real joy and creative alchemy in mixing media and art supplies to create striking or unexpected results. I often mix collage elements with hand-drawn details, pens with paint, and crayons with watercolor. Throughout this book, I suggest ways to experiment by combining the materials you have on hand to make art that is personal to you.

TYPES OF SKETCHBOOKS

Let's explore the different types of sketch-books available and what to think about when selecting one. I help you select a sketchbook that is perfect for you and that you will relish using. Sketchbooks can be called many things, such as journals, notebooks, visual idea books, art books, and visual diaries. It doesn't matter what you call it as long as the name resonates for you.

Consider the Medium

If you are going to use a lot of wet paint in your sketchbook, you will need a book with heavy-weight paper that can handle the amount of liquid and paint you'll throw at it. Use paper that is at least 200 gsm (grams per square meter or g/m^2), or approximately 137 pounds.

Think About Where You'll Use It

Consider where you will be when you use your sketchbook. I mostly use my larger sketch-books at home or in my studio, so their overall weight and size are not important factors. But if you plan to carry your sketchbook with you on a daily basis, then you'll want to use a lighter-weight, more portable one.

▶ Sketchbooks are available in myriad types, sizes, and formats. When selecting the best type for you, consider where and how you intend to use it.

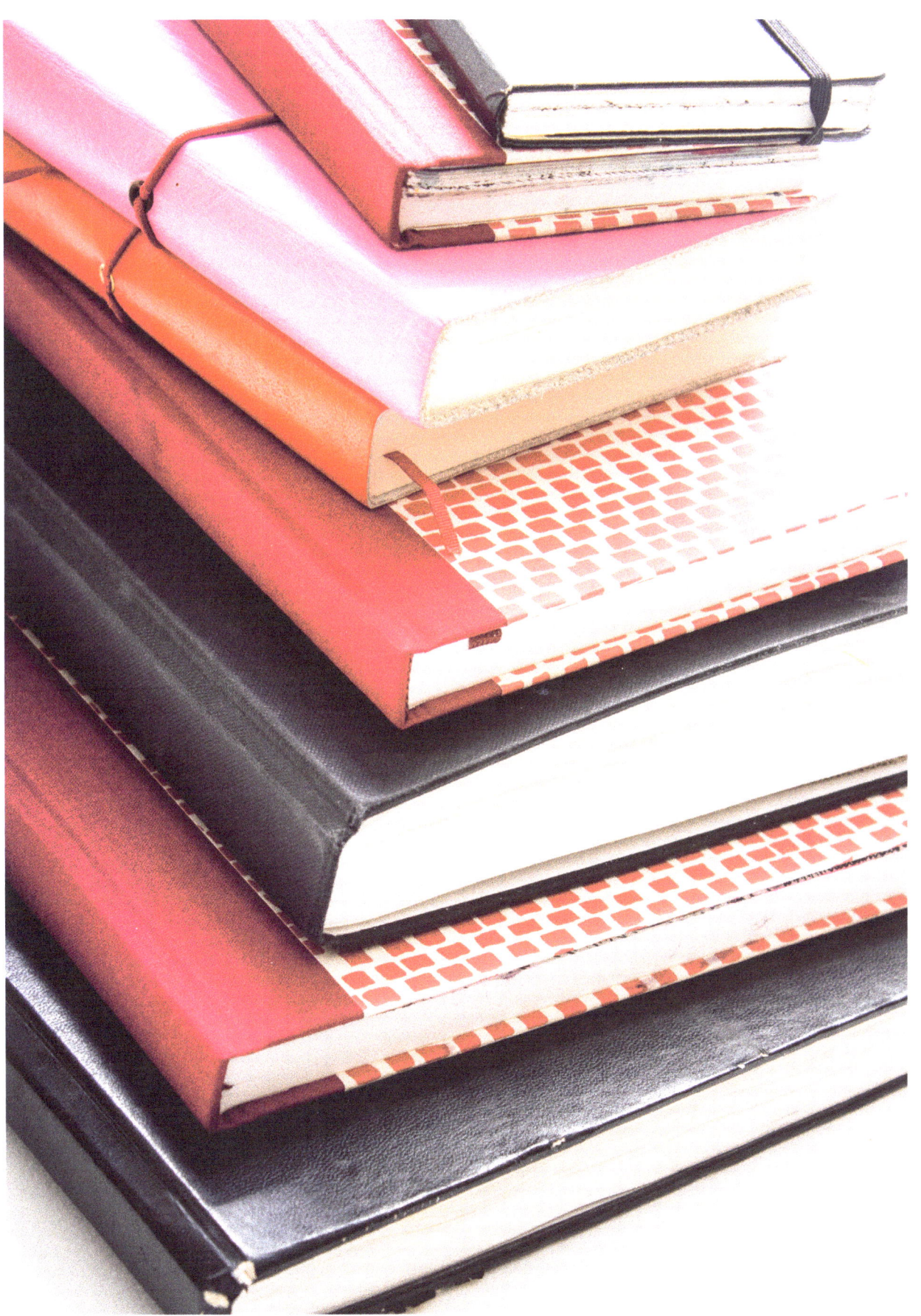

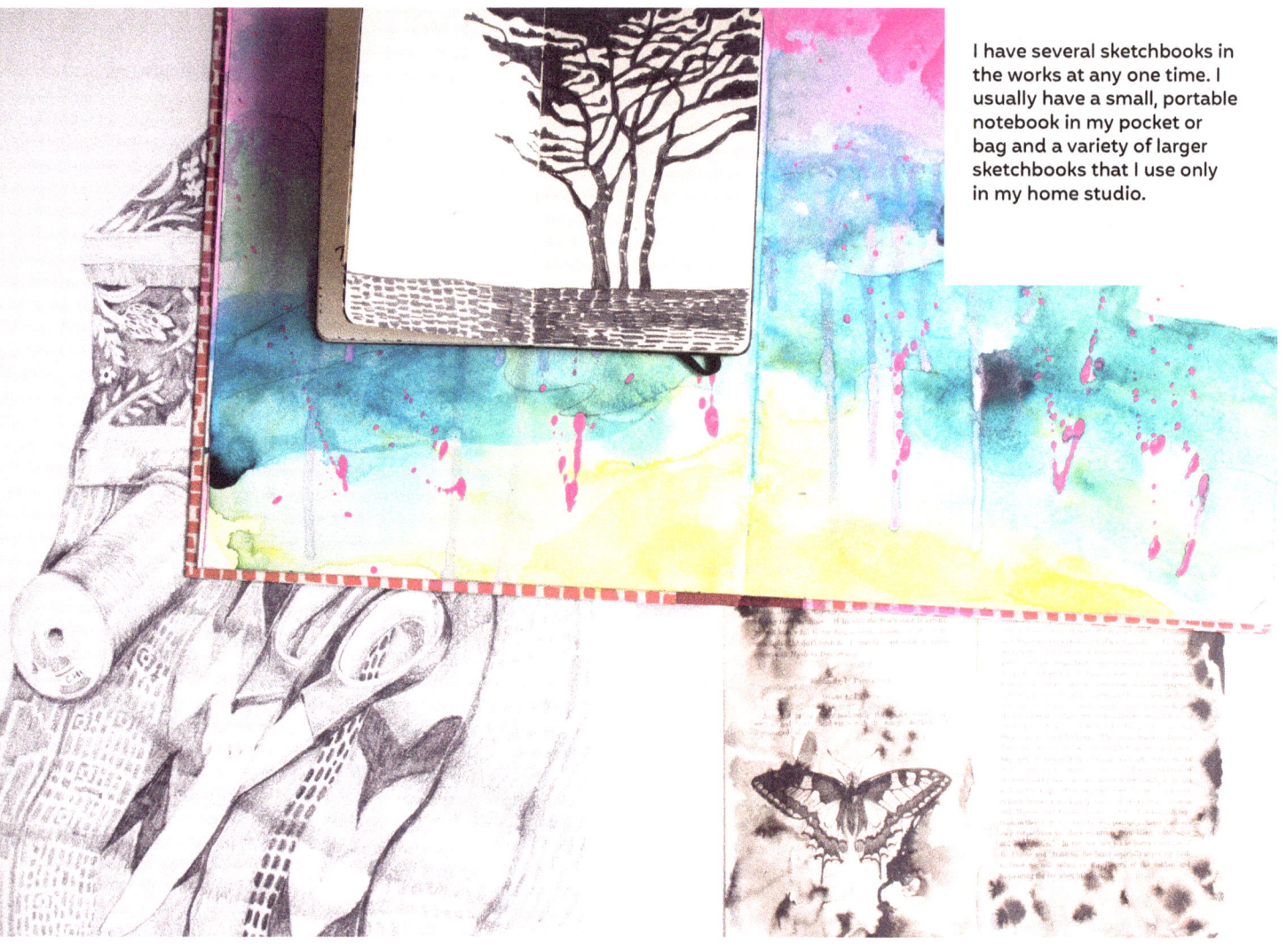

I have several sketchbooks in the works at any one time. I usually have a small, portable notebook in my pocket or bag and a variety of larger sketchbooks that I use only in my home studio.

Portrait or Landscape?

Consider the orientation of your sketchbooks. I like to work in a portrait (vertical) format. Many other artists prefer to work in a landscape (horizontal) format. Think about your preference when purchasing a sketchbook as this will influence where the binding is. Bindings may be spiral bound or stitched and glued like a hardcover book. Spiral-bound books allow you to easily lay the pages totally flat and turn them with ease. If you like to work across double-page spreads, however, you may find the spiral wire disruptive to your flow.

Look for a Comfortable Sketchbook

Find a sketchbook that feels good to use, is comfortable in your hands, and is worthy of sharing your creative journey. Avoid books that you think are too formal or too good to use. If you want to save your sketchbook only for your best work, you won't feel comfortable putting it through its artistic paces.

MATERIALS AND ART SUPPLIES

Consider the art materials that most appeal to you, the ones you really enjoy using. In the same way that we all have our own distinct lexicon of marks, we all have a special affinity or natural attraction to certain materials.

When working in your sketchbook, be conscious of which materials make you feel excited, at ease, and expansive, and which materials make you feel restricted or awkward. Try completing the same exercise with different materials. Experiment and see what works for you.

Many of us love experimenting with new products. But instead of buying new products in the hope of boosting creativity, always begin with the materials you already have on hand. I am as guilty as the next person in believing that a certain new paint or new type of ink will elevate my artistic practice. Shopping for new supplies can easily become a substitute activity for just getting started with the perfectly good supplies you already have.

The following are some of the supplies I enjoy using. You might have a completely different selection of favorite supplies, and that's great. I encourage you to embrace the materials you love using and adapt the exercises accordingly.

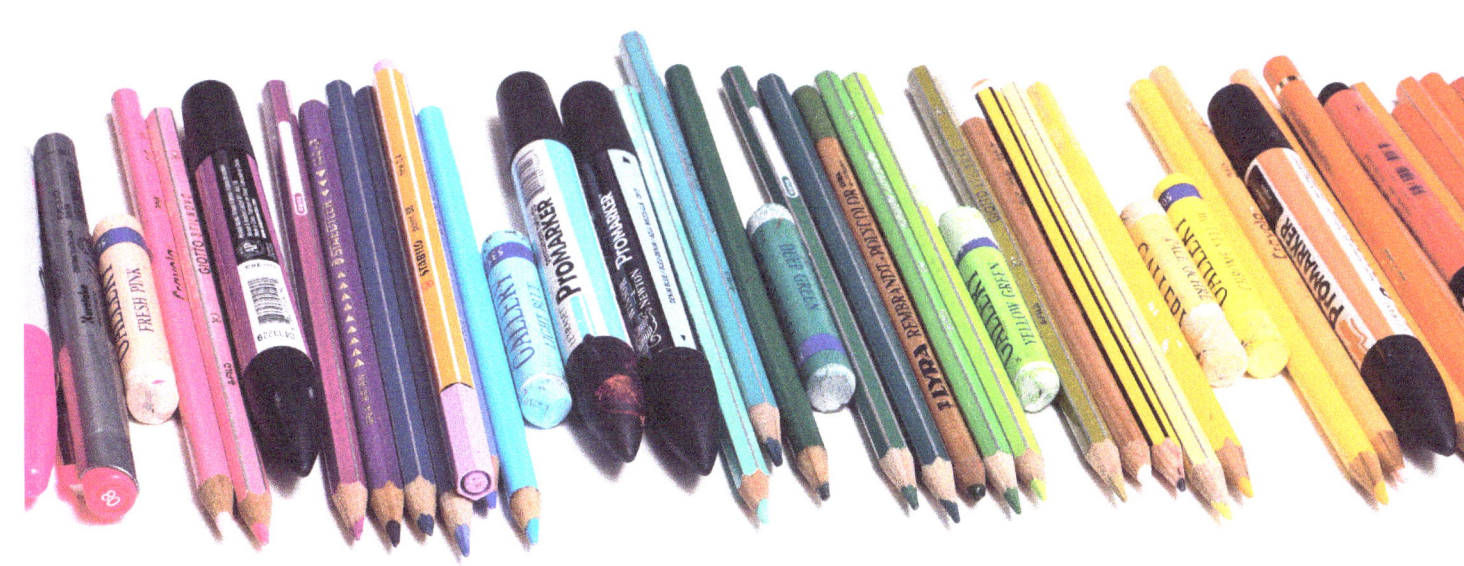

There is a world of possibility when it comes to art materials and supplies.

Pencils and Graphite

There is something wonderful about the humble pencil. H (which stands for "hard") pencils are hard, precise, and great for detailed work. Softer B (black) pencils are for smudgy, darker, and thicker lines. I enjoy using water-soluble graphite pencils, which can be used with or without water. Add water to the drawn line and it will turn your marks into an ink-like wash. You can also dip your water-soluble graphite pencil straight into the water and draw with the wet flowing line.

Pens

I use a lot of black fine-line pens in my sketchbook, either on their own or to draw over collage and dry paint. As a child, I loved felt-tip pens and still love the process of coloring with them. When I'm not using a felt-tip pen (also called a marker pen), I sometimes use a blue ballpoint pen.

Pencils are versatile art tools.

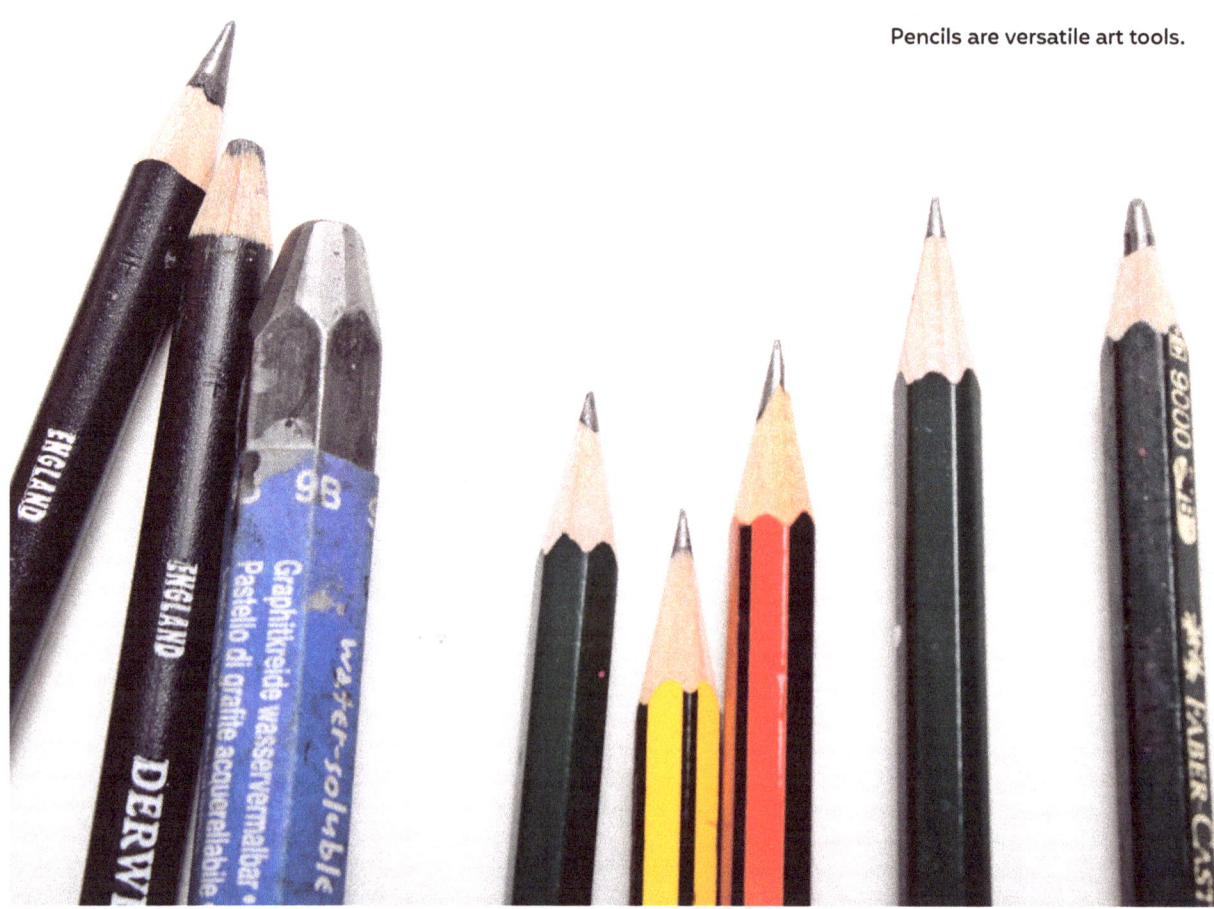

Paint

I frequently use watercolor paint in my sketch-book and art. There is something about the unpredictability of this kind of paint that I find alluring. I love the way the color mixes with the water on the page and creates unexpected patterns. I also enjoy using gouache paint, which is more opaque than watercolor. Acrylic paint comes in a stunning array of colors and textures and can be used in techniques that require you to have distinct layers of paint over something.

Ink

I enjoy the fluidity of ink. One way to use ink is to simply brush clean water over a sketchbook page and then drip ink onto it to create expanding dots, circles, and happy accidents.

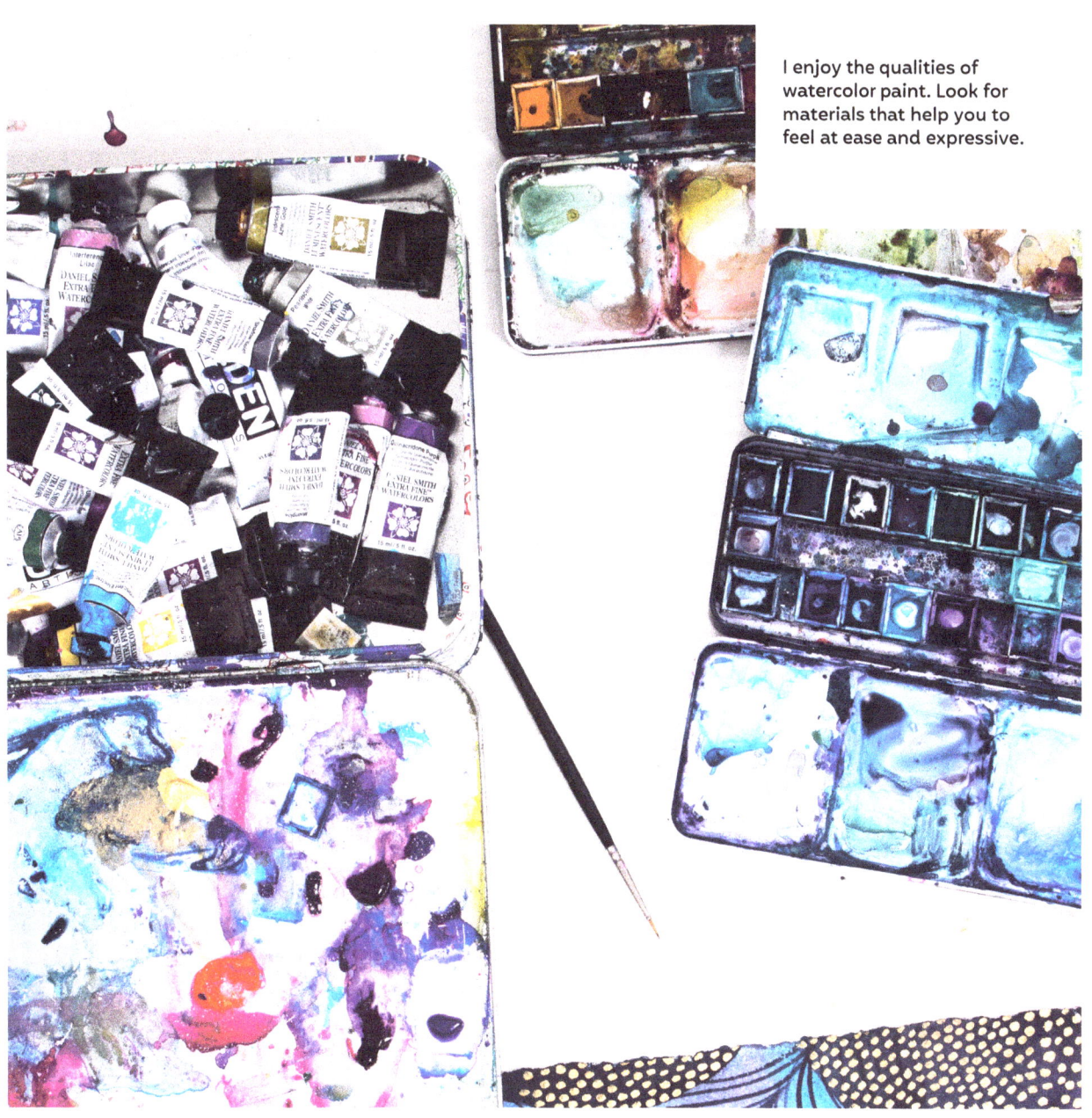

I enjoy the qualities of watercolor paint. Look for materials that help you to feel at ease and expressive.

Collage Materials

I have a collection of interesting papers including old book pages, pages from magazines, found papers, and abandoned art works. I also create, print, and draw on scrap pieces of paper with the intention of incorporating them into my sketchbook. To paste them into the sketchbook, I use a PVA-based glue, which is inexpensive and works with all sorts of paper.

Brushes

Most of my brushes are inexpensive and come in a variety of sizes and shapes. Using a variety of brushes on one page adds visual interest. For example, I often use decorator brushes to create big, bold marks in tandem with tiny brushes to add details, dashes, and dots.

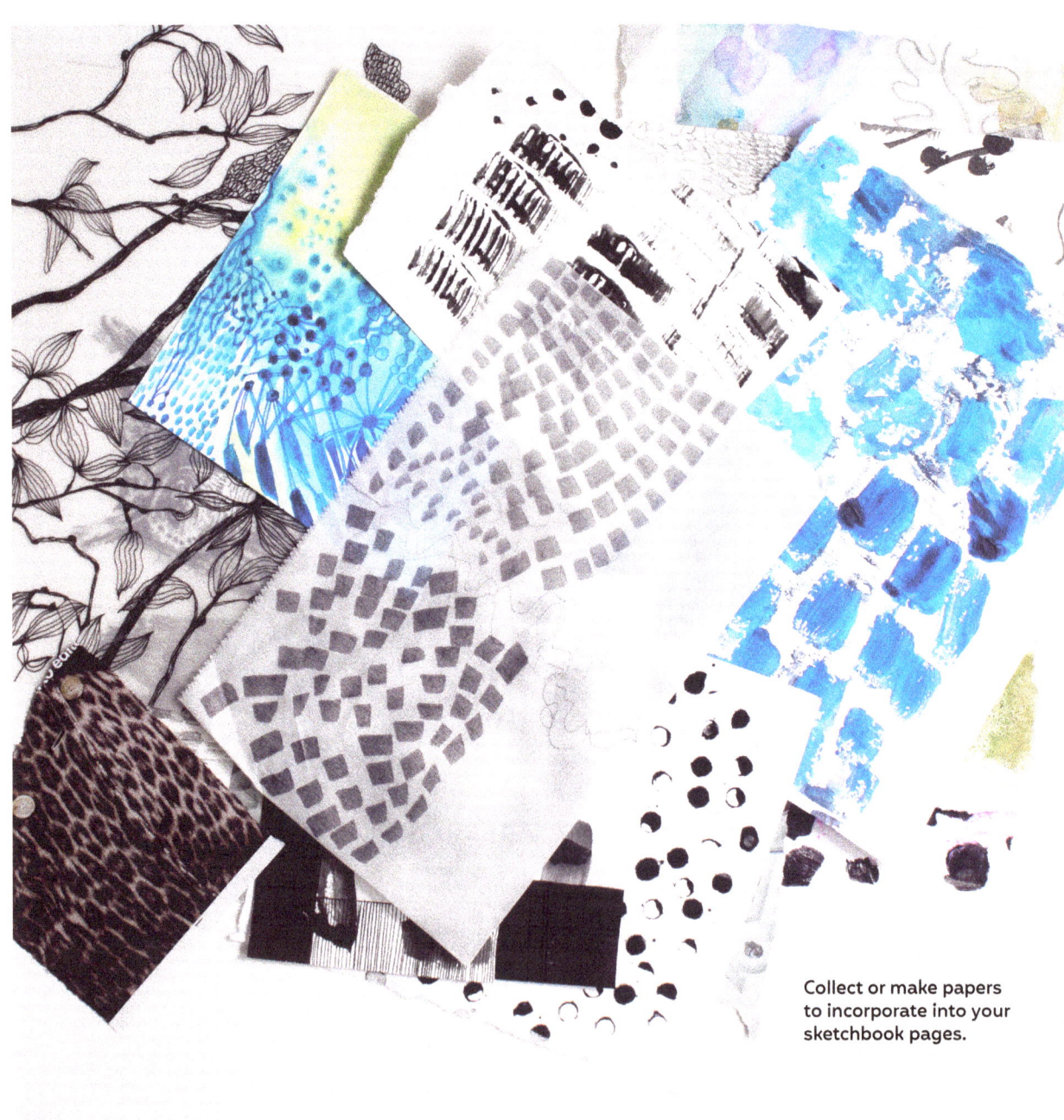

Collect or make papers to incorporate into your sketchbook pages.

COLOR

My sketchbook is colorful. I love using the power and beauty of color. To harness the magical qualities of color, it helps to know a little about color theory.

The Color Wheel

The color wheel organizes colors in a circle according to how they relate to each other. Artists often reference a color wheel to see which colors work well together.

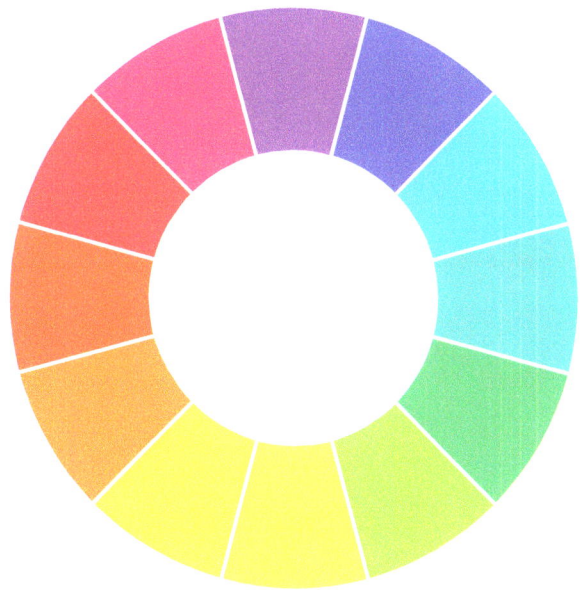

PRIMARY COLORS
The three primary colors are the building blocks. They're called primary because they can't be made from mixing other colors together.

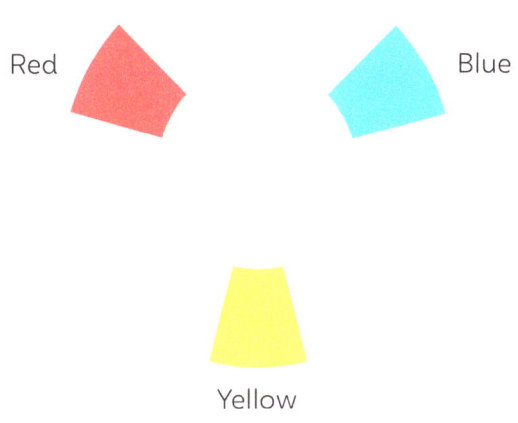

Red

Blue

Yellow

SECONDARY COLORS
When you mix two primary colors together, you create a secondary color:

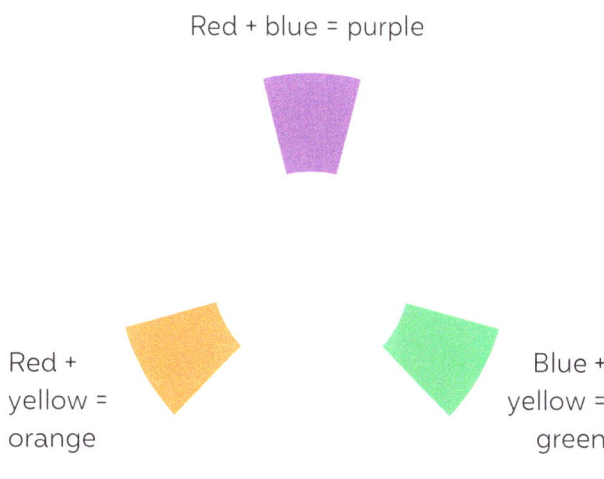

Red + blue = purple

Red + yellow = orange

Blue + yellow = green

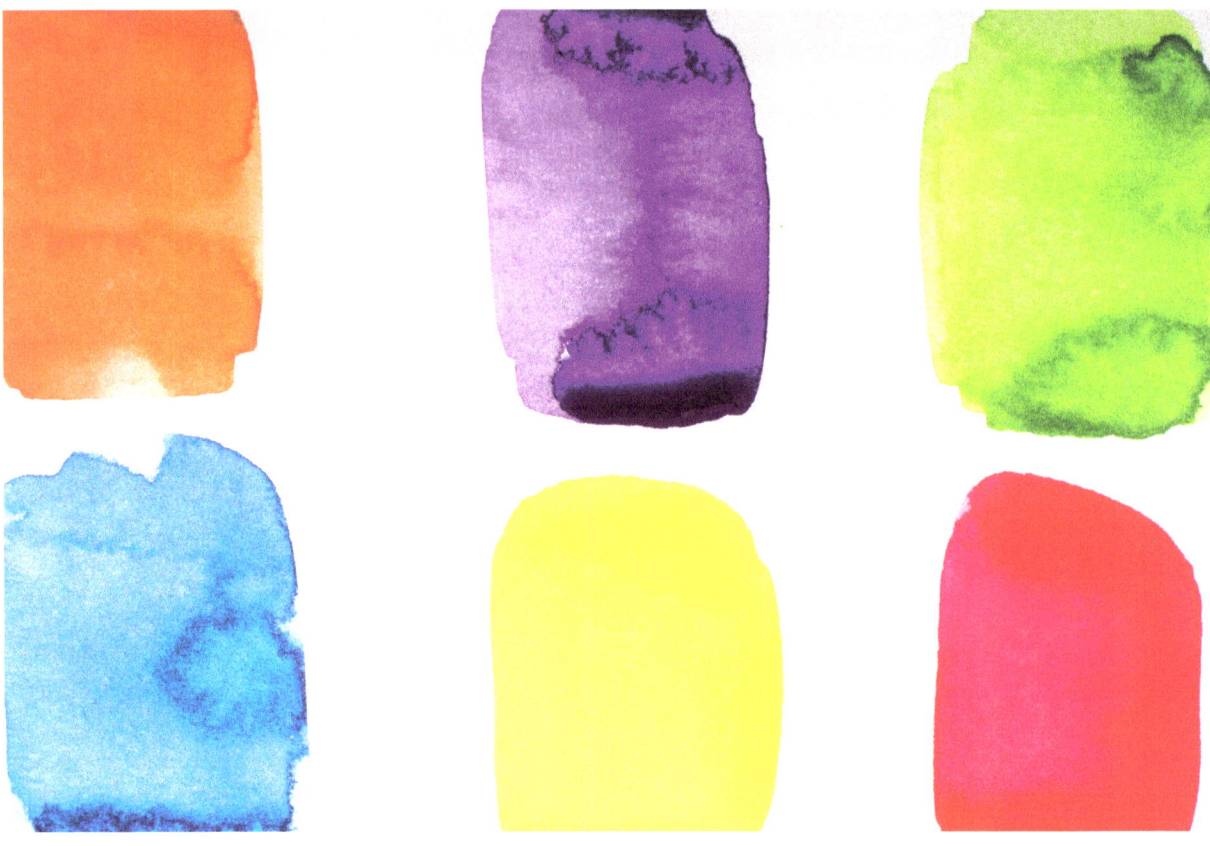

OPPOSITES ATTRACT

Complementary colors are pairs of colors that are opposite each other on the color wheel. When complementary colors are used together, they create a dynamic effect. Because they are high-contrasting opposites, complementary colors seem to pop and fizz when placed next to each other, bringing out each other's best qualities:

Blue + orange
Yellow + purple
Red + green

▲ **Experiment with using opposite pairs of colors in your sketchbook.**

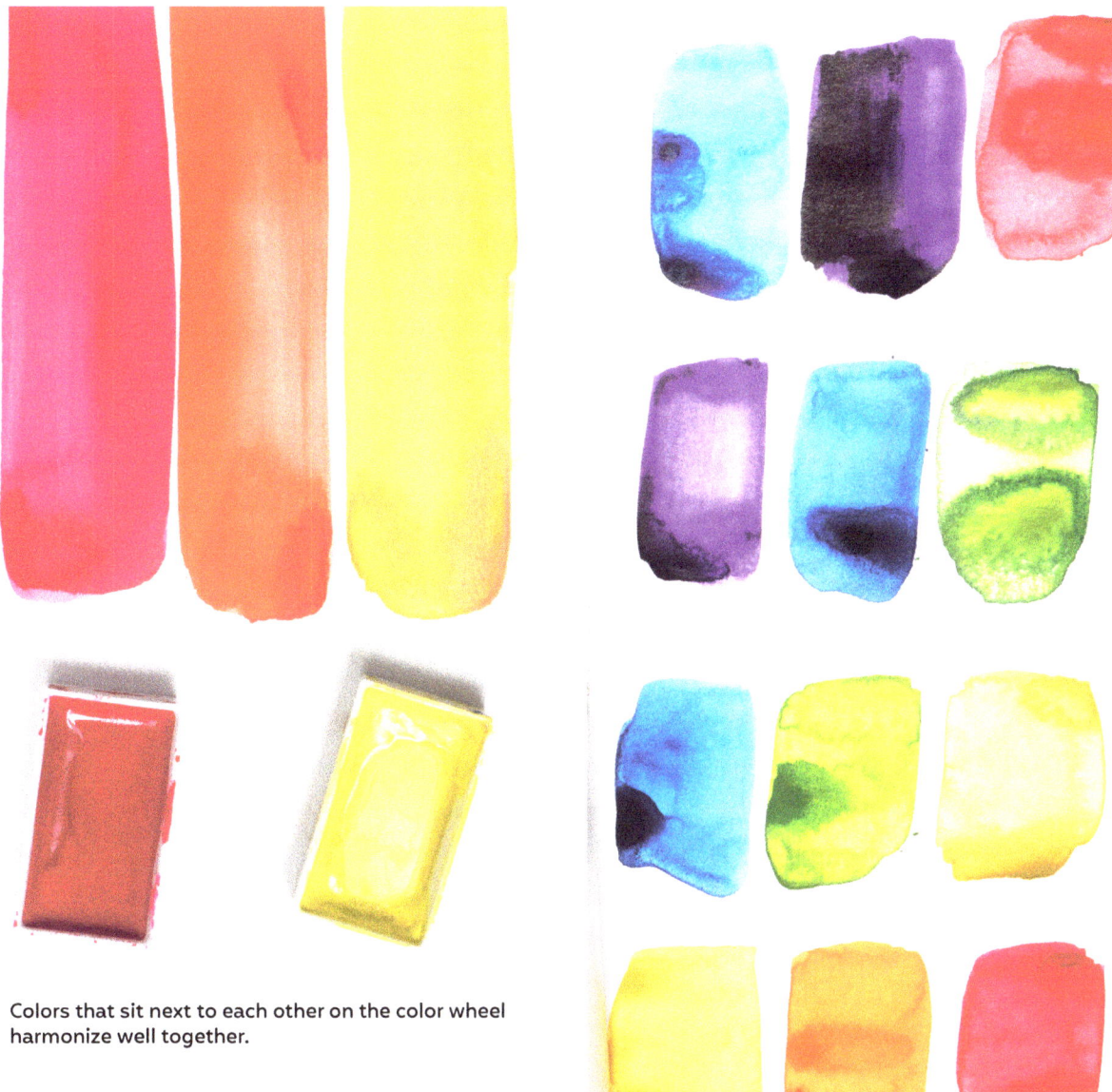

Colors that sit next to each other on the color wheel harmonize well together.

Here are examples of harmonious trios painted in watercolor paint.

HARMONIOUS TRIOS

Analogous colors, or harmonious colors, are groups of three colors that sit right next to each other on the color wheel. They tend to harmonize with each other nicely but can lack contrast:

Red + orange + yellow
Purple + blue + green
Green + yellow + orange
Blue + purple + red

DYNAMIC TRIOS

If you pick three colors that are equally spaced on the color wheel, they always work well together:

Red + yellow + blue
Orange + green + purple

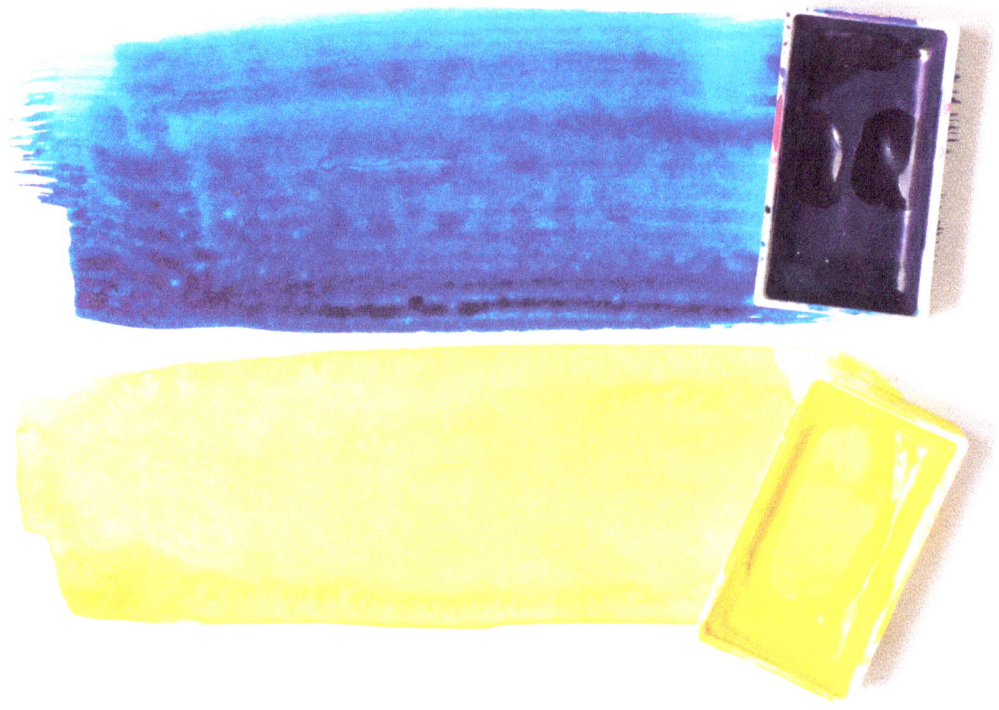

COLOR TEMPERATURE

It can be helpful to think about the temperature of colors as either cool or warm. The colors that are closest to yellow on the color wheel are the warmest, with yellow being the warmest of all. Warm colors that contain a lot of yellow tend to come forward on the page, as if they are moving toward you. Cool colors—those closest to blue on the color wheel—tend to recede or appear to go back in space. This is because our eyes perceive warmer colors first, before cooler tones.

If you were to paint a yellow blob next to a blue one, the yellow blob might look as if it were coming toward you while the blue one might look as if it were receding. You can use this trick if you are painting a landscape or want to create depth. Use warmer colors in the foreground and cooler colors in the background to create the sense of near and far.

▲ **Warmer colors tend to come forward and look closer, while cooler shades tend to recede and look farther away.**

VIVID AND MUTED

Think about how you use both vivid and muted tones in the same artwork. Be aware of the intensities and saturation of the colors. Consider pairing bright and bold colors with more muted and subtle colors to create contrast and variety.

If you are drawn to the bright and brilliant colors, use them with more subdued hues for greater impact. When you use only super-bright colors together, their combined impact is likely to be dulled and diminished. Bright pink used next to a bright orange doesn't stand out and look as extraordinary as it might if the pink were used next to a subdued gray or dull olive green.

A page that uses only highly saturated hues with no muted colors to counterbalance them can look a little naïve. Conversely, a painting that uses only very muted tones may lack dynamic energy, but adding a splash of bright color can draw the eye and act as a focal point.

Using both bright and muted colors in tandem can help your work to appear more nuanced and interesting. These six images were created by painting stripes of acrylic paint in my sketchbook. The sketchbook was upright and standing on my desk so the color from above dripped and blended into the colors below.

You can usually create a more muted shade of any color by mixing it with a little of the color that is opposite it on the color wheel.

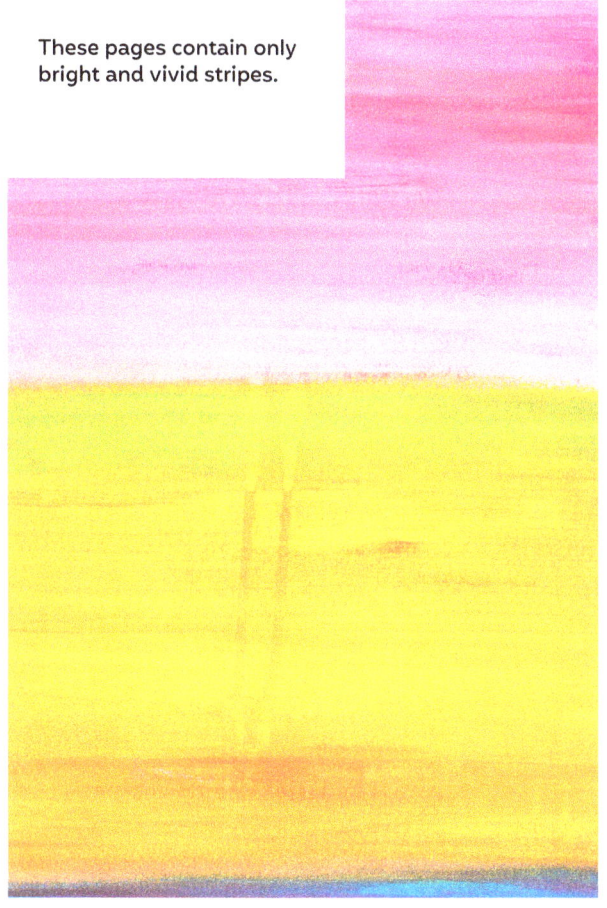

These pages contain only bright and vivid stripes.

These pages contain only muted color stripes.

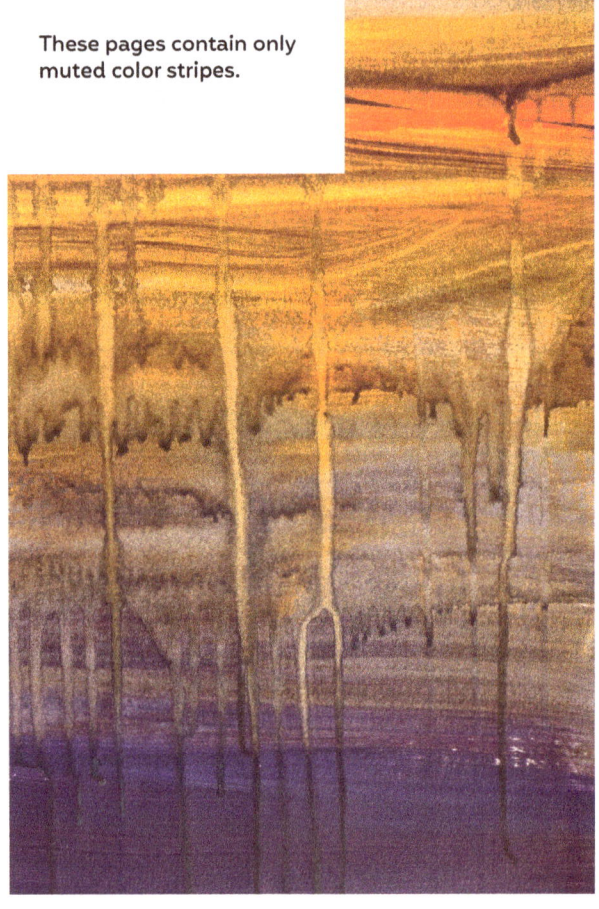

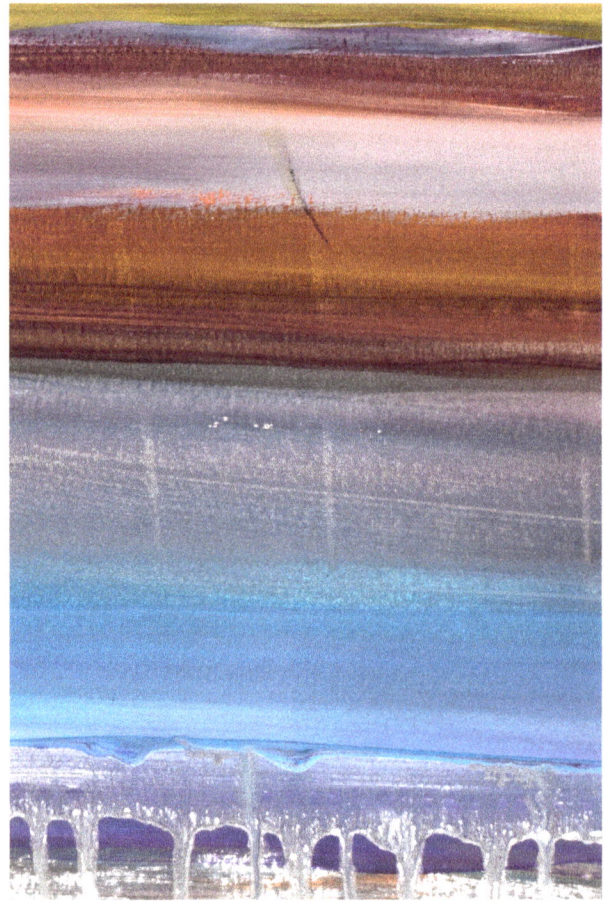

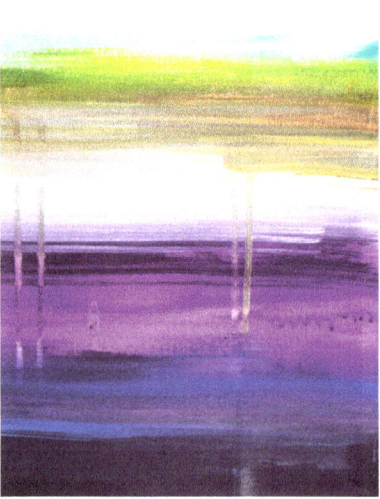

▲ These pages contain both vivid and muted color stripes.

Color Experiments

Here are a few ways to experiment with color:

- Mix your own secondary colors.
- Find paintings by artists you admire that use complementary colors.
- Create your own color wheel in your sketchbook.
- Create a page or several pages in your sketchbook that are based on complementary colors.
- Paint stripes to see how different colors react when placed next to each other. Create several pages of stripes: one with only bright and bold colors, one with only muted colors, and one that combines both bright and muted tones.

THE JOY OF DRAWING

I'd love for you to fall in love with drawing. Here's a collection of art exercises to get you going in your sketchbook. The exercises are designed to be flexible so that you can adapt them and make them your own.

Mark-Making Exercise

I believe that everyone can draw. Drawings are made up of lines and marks. Simple mark-making exercises can be very powerful and are an easy way to free you up and get you started. Making marks on paper might sound like a childish thing to do, but it's a valuable exercise. It puts you in a place of inquiry and allows you to develop your own visual language.

Get to know the types of marks that appeal to you and are personal to you. We all have a lexicon of expressive marks and unearthing your own can be a rewarding experience. The lines and marks that come naturally to you are the handwriting of your art. Our natural way of making marks on the page is the essence of our art.

Try this exercise with a pencil: How many different marks can you make with the pencil on one or two pages of your sketchbook? Think about the speed of your mark making and the pressure you exert. Also consider the scale, size, and range of tones. Experiment with using your nondominant hand.

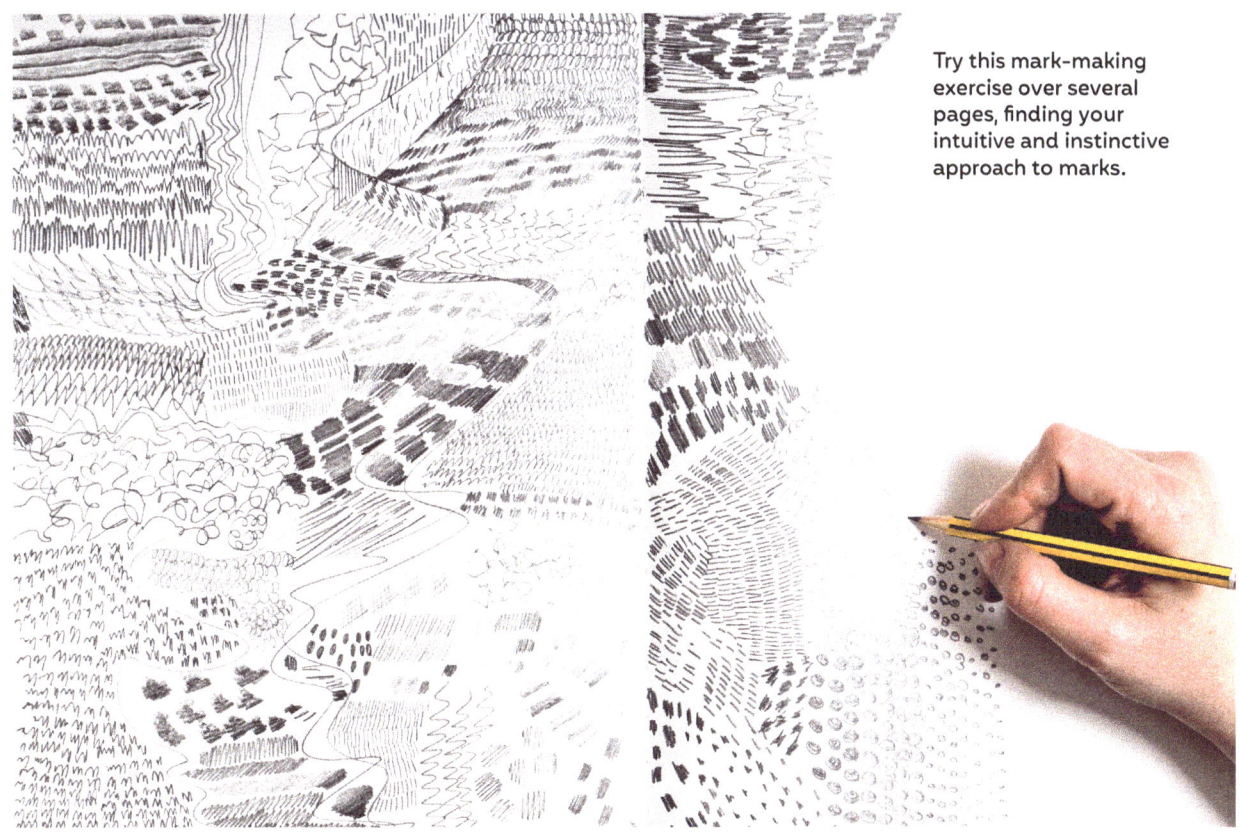

Try this mark-making exercise over several pages, finding your intuitive and instinctive approach to marks.

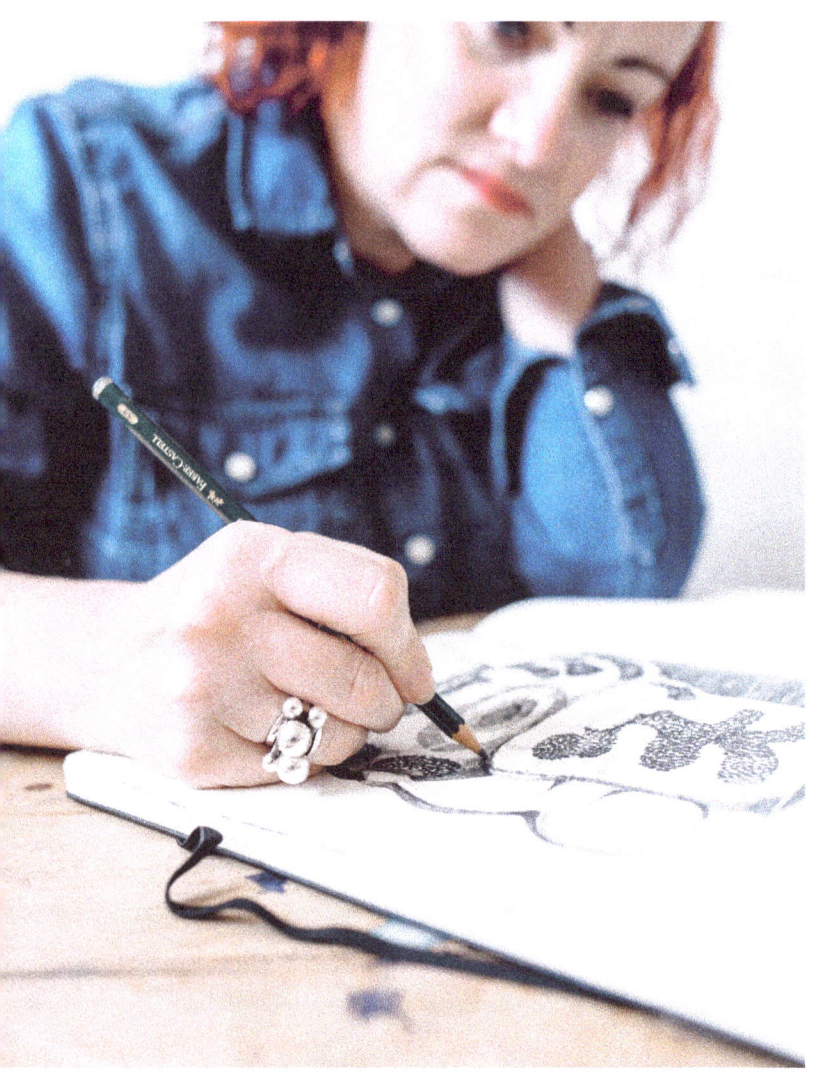

When you draw something in front of you, you are interpreting your subject matter, understanding it, and developing your own response to what you see.

Exploratory Drawing

Drawing is not necessarily about producing a perfectly realistic rendition of what you see. Rather it is a way to interpret the world. Drawing is not so much about the thing you are drawing, but more about how you interpret the thing you are drawing. The importance comes from you and your personal lens.

When you draw something, you see it differently and you explore it. When drawing something, you must spend time really looking at the object or subject. It's not just about seeing the shapes and lines of what's in front of you, it's about determining its intrinsic nature and purpose and discovering your response to it.

As you begin to draw, you may feel awkward or apprehensive, yet with most things in life, the more you do something, the more confident and at ease you become. Try to approach the page with a sense of curiosity and possibility. Asking yourself questions as you make your art is a good way to stay conscious and connected to what you are making. Consider the following questions:

- What is it about this subject matter that interests or excites me?
- What about the subject's essence would I like to convey in my drawing or painting? Is there something about its shape, form, texture, shadow, or silhouette that particularly appeals to me?
- Which materials are best suited to my subject matter?
- What do I want to learn through doing?
- How do I want to feel as I create?
- What do I actually feel as I create?

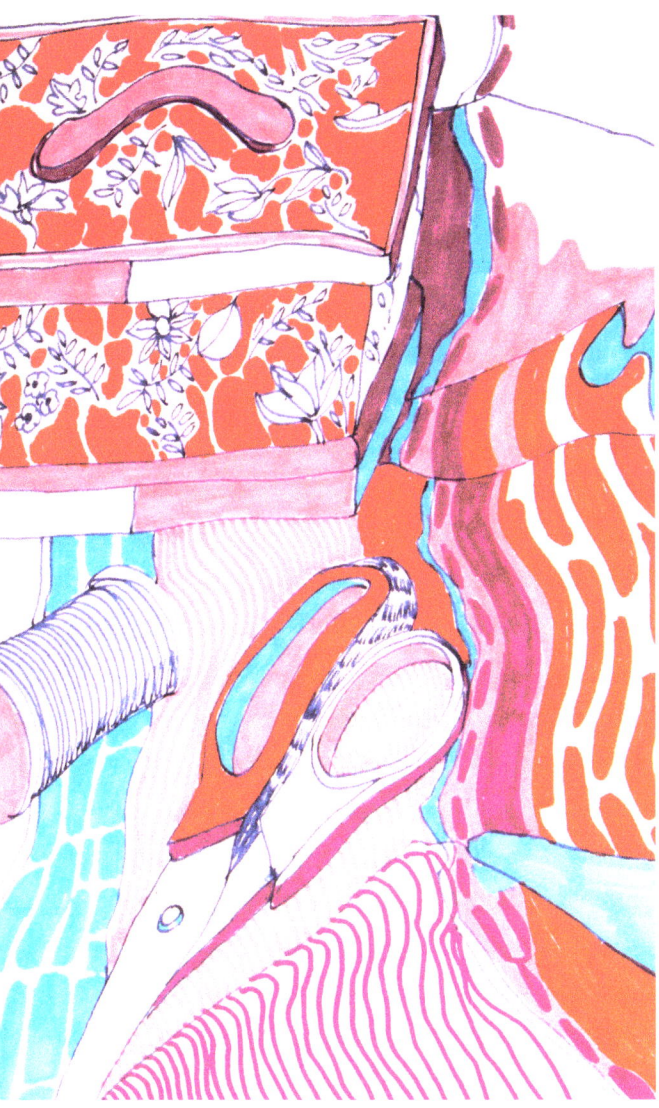

Select objects to draw that have meaning to you. Here I have drawn my mother's button box and sewing materials. This drawing is made with fine line and felt-tip pens.

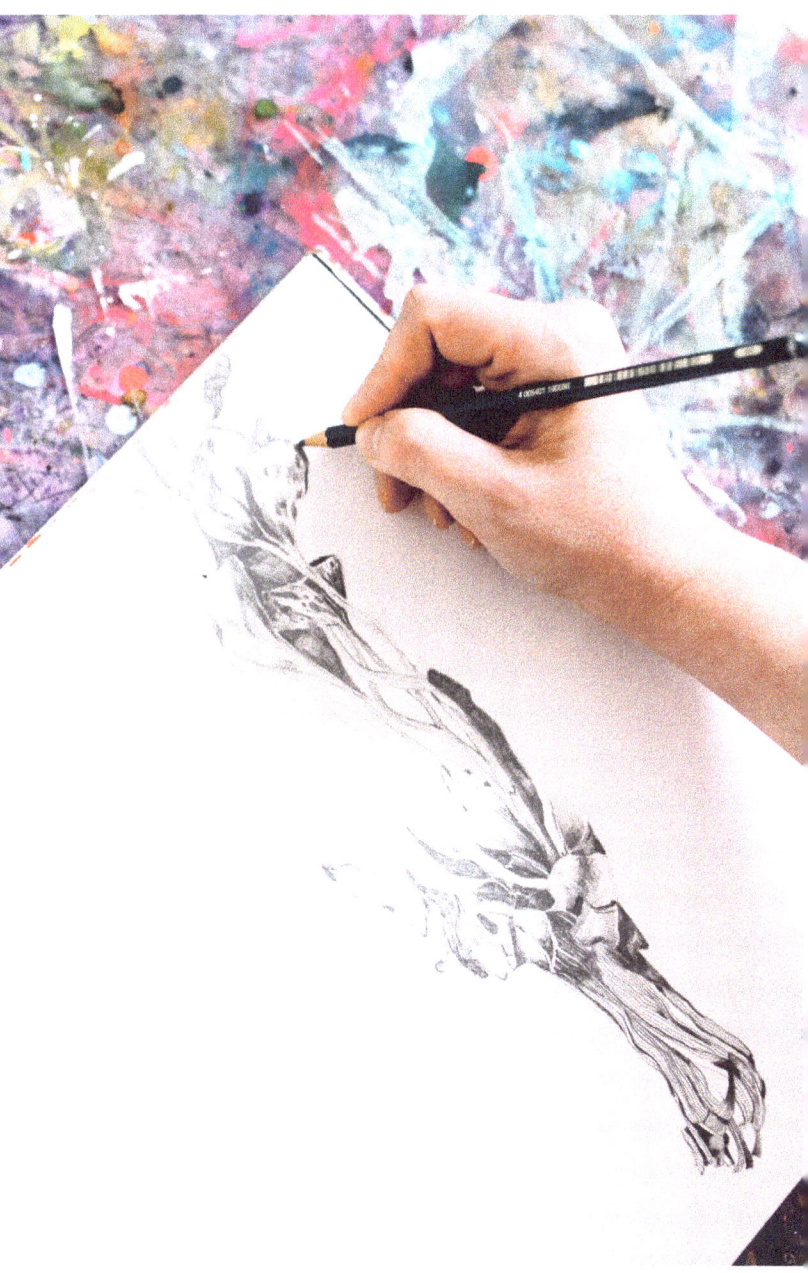

When you draw something, you are making a connection with it. As your pen or pencil dances around the paper trying to represent what you see, you have an opportunity to understand the thing you are looking at better than you did before.

Selecting Something to Draw

Select your objects or subject matter carefully as they are important. What you draw or paint should matter to you in some way. It's very hard to draw things that you have no interest in or connection with.

The item or items you select to draw should have something in their essence that interests you, intrigues you, and appeals to you.

Be mindful when you select something to draw or paint. Selecting your subject is an important part of the process.

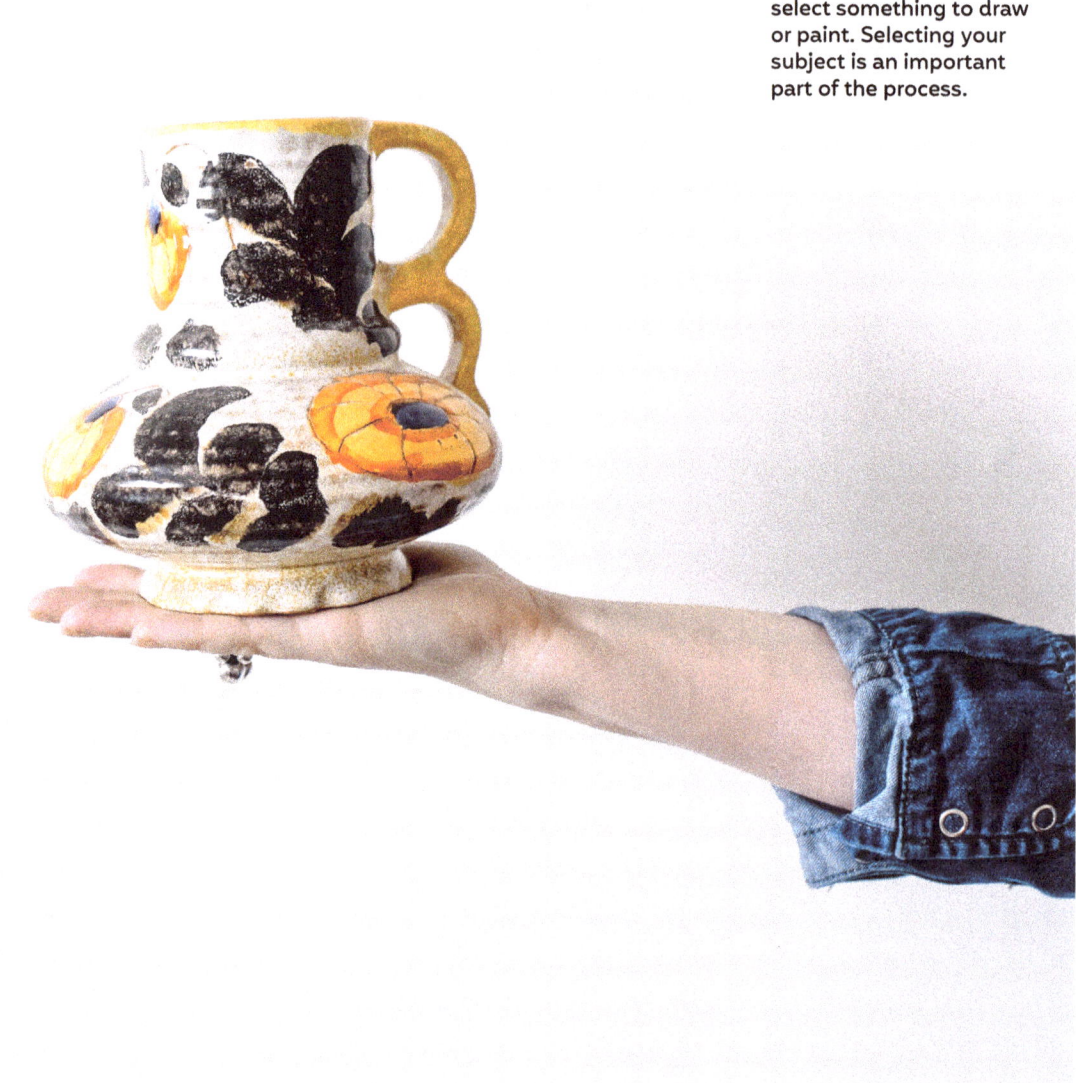

More Looking Than Drawing

Spend more time looking than drawing, even if you are completing the super-quick exercises. By being mindful and slowing down to see and study your subject, you are more likely to capture what you are trying to draw.

Taking the time to look closely helps us draw what is in front of us rather than what we think is in front of us. I tend to draw items as I think they should look, instead of how they look. When I spend more time focusing and really observing, my drawings better reflect the reality of what I am drawing.

Drawing helps you see and understand your subject matter with new eyes.

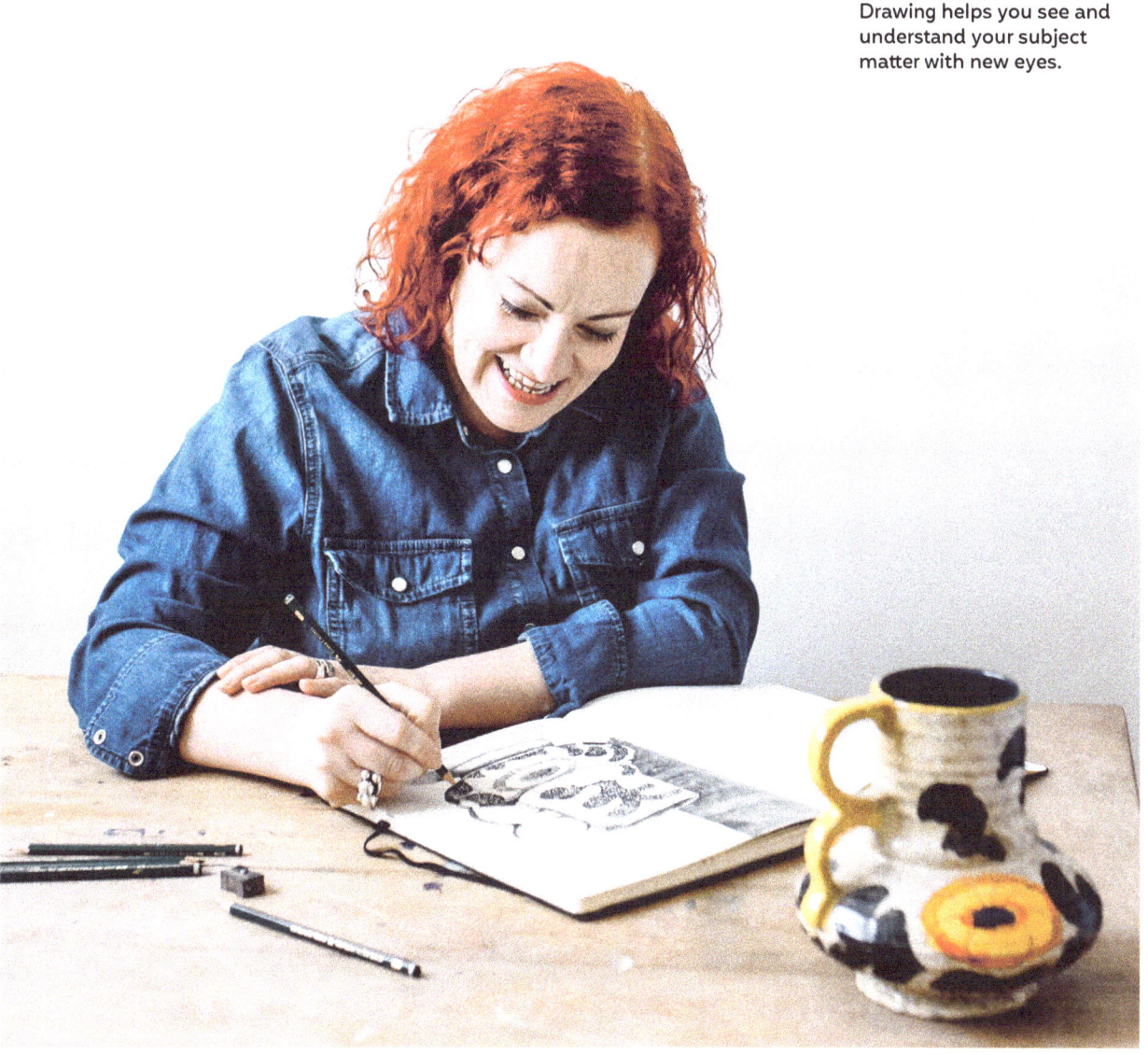

Ways to Start Drawing

There is an energy and vibrancy about a quick drawing, an off-the-cuff quality that can be very liberating. A speedy drawing can have a certain beauty and an immediacy. When you practice quick drawing, try drawing several images on one page or do one drawing over and over again. Approach the same drawing with a variety of art tools, such as a pencil or thick felt-tip pen. If you haven't drawn in many years, you may feel reticent to start. I am cheering for you! I encourage you to take action, dive in, and start drawing.

The following are simple exercises to try on your subject of choice. They are designed so you have the freedom to experiment with them and make them your own.

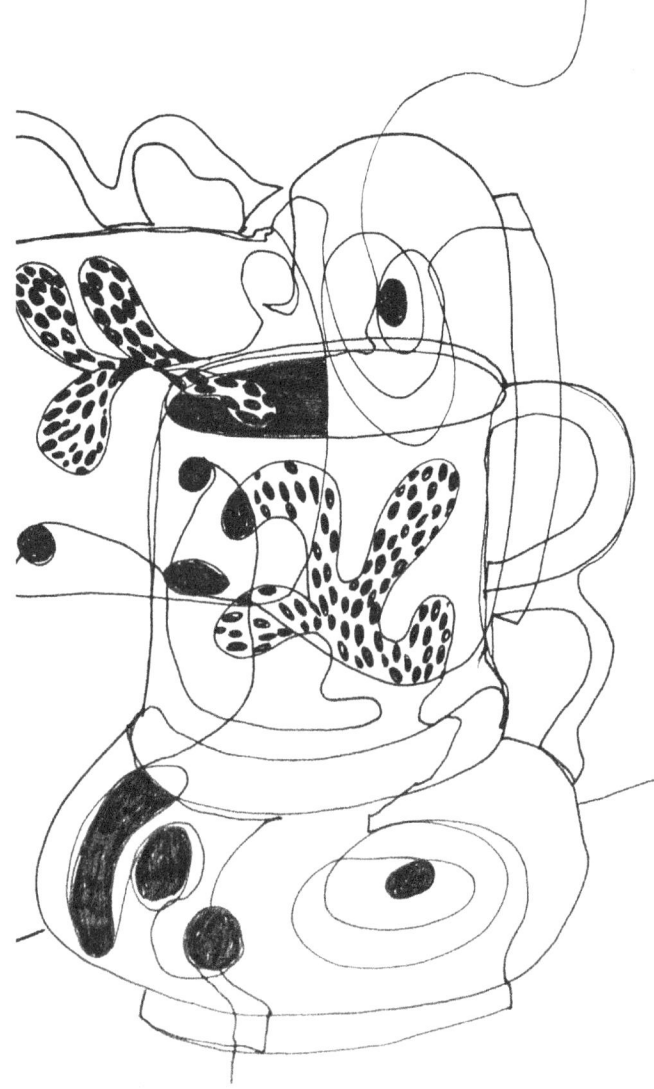

Drawing is not just about the result; it is also about the practice, the experience, being in the moment, the actual doing, and all the lovely learning that happens along the way.

Don't Look at the Page

This is a super-quick exercise in which you draw the object without looking at the page. Instead, focus on your subject matter. Don't let your pencil or pen leave the page—it should follow your eyes as you look at the contours and outlines of the object. Your drawing may look weird and distorted at first, but this technique helps to free you up, allowing you to really examine and understand what you are drawing, and not worry about the end result.

You can't be too precious about a drawing if you're not allowed to even look at the page as you draw. The drawing can capture the essence of your subject and create an interesting starting point that you may add to and develop or leave just as it is.

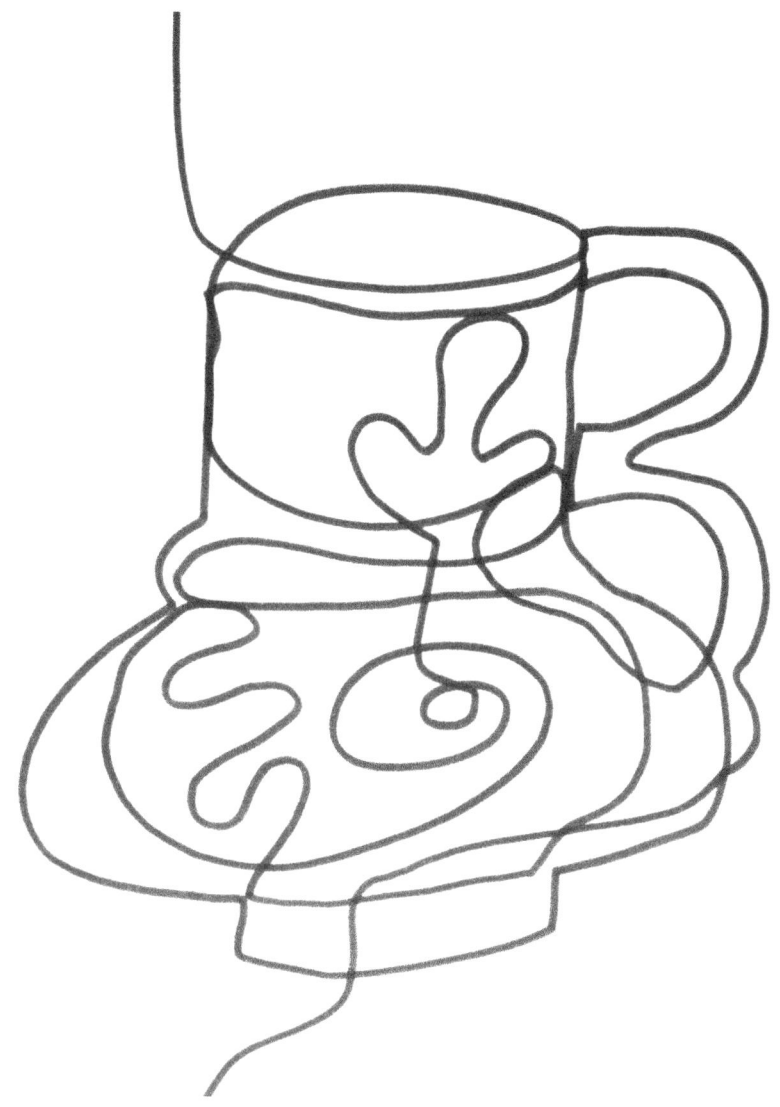

Quick, simple drawings are a good way to find your rhythm and not overthink what you are creating.

Draw the Space Around the Object

It is useful to think about the area around your subject—the negative space. We often assume we know what a certain object looks like, so we draw how we *think* it looks rather than what we actually see. Drawing the space around the object is one way to capture its true form.

By drawing the space around the object instead of the object itself, you bypass your assumptions. You are not drawing the thing, you are drawing the space that the thing sits in, which encourages you to draw from observation rather than assumption.

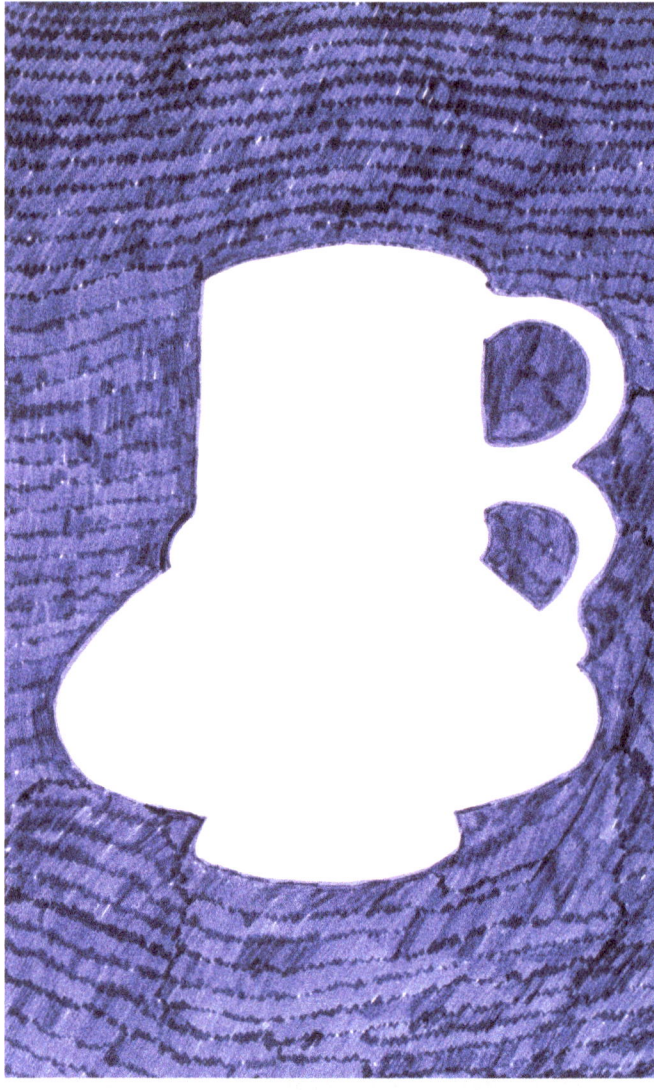

Drawing the space around your object can lead to dynamic and complex results.

Timed Sketches

Setting time limits can be particularly helpful when getting started. Because you only allow yourself a limited amount of time, this technique takes the pressure off. The lower the expectations, the freer and more expressive you become. Draw the same subject with different time limits and then compare each drawing. Try the following:

- 1 minute
- 5 minutes
- 20 minutes
- 1 hour

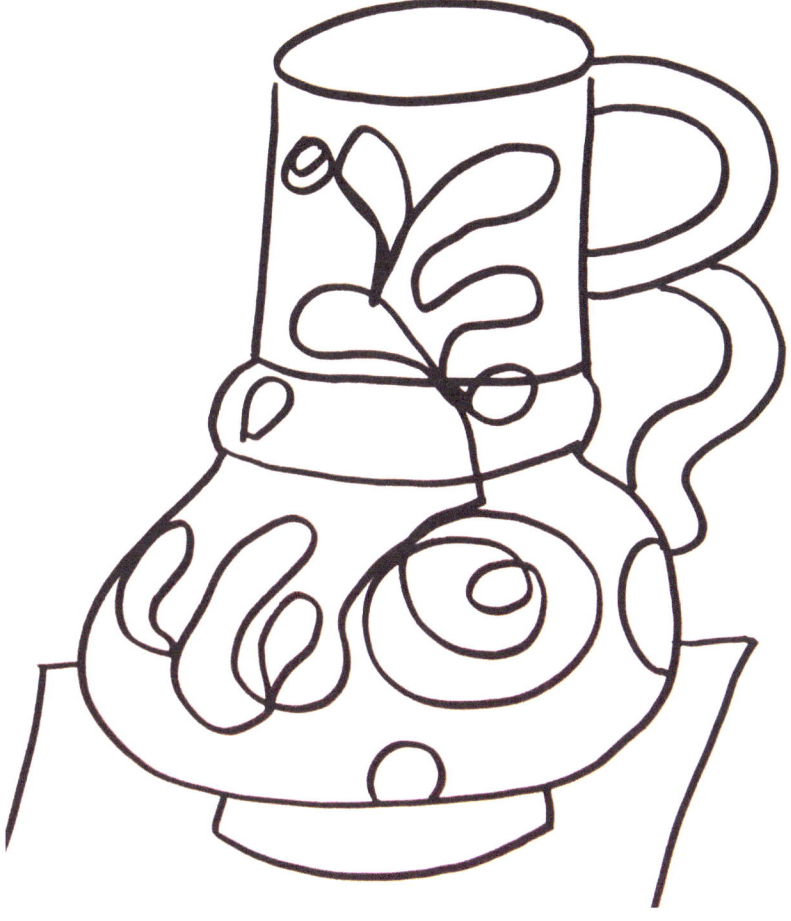

This drawing took less than a minute. Two drawings that took longer are on the next page.

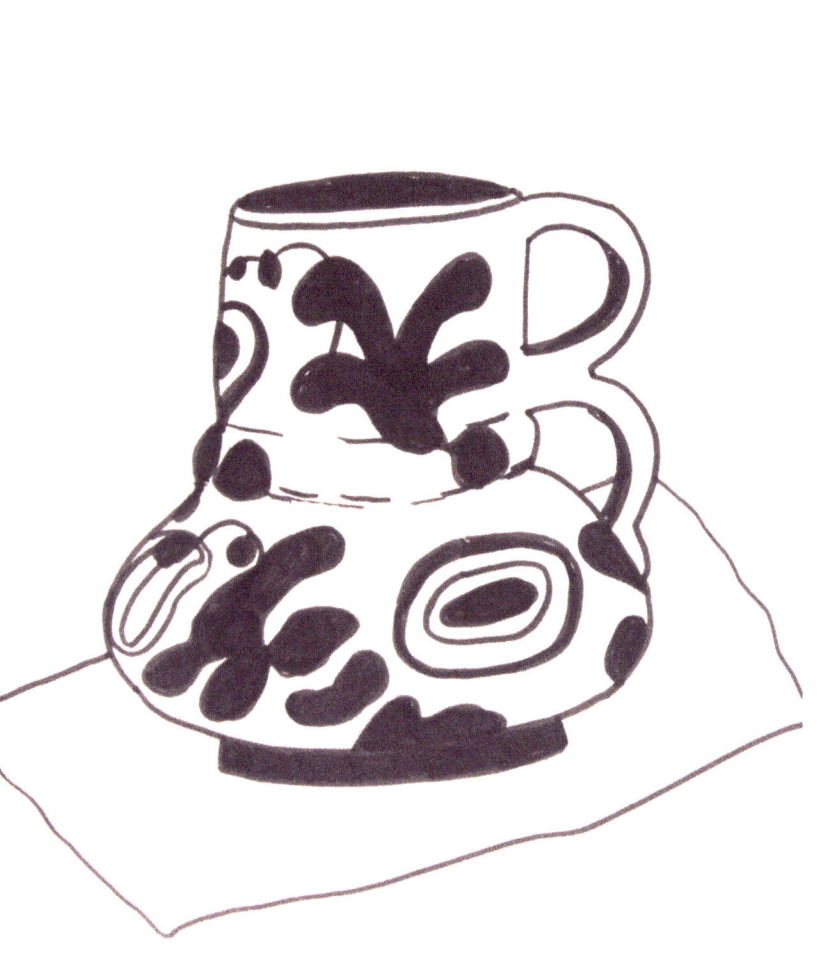

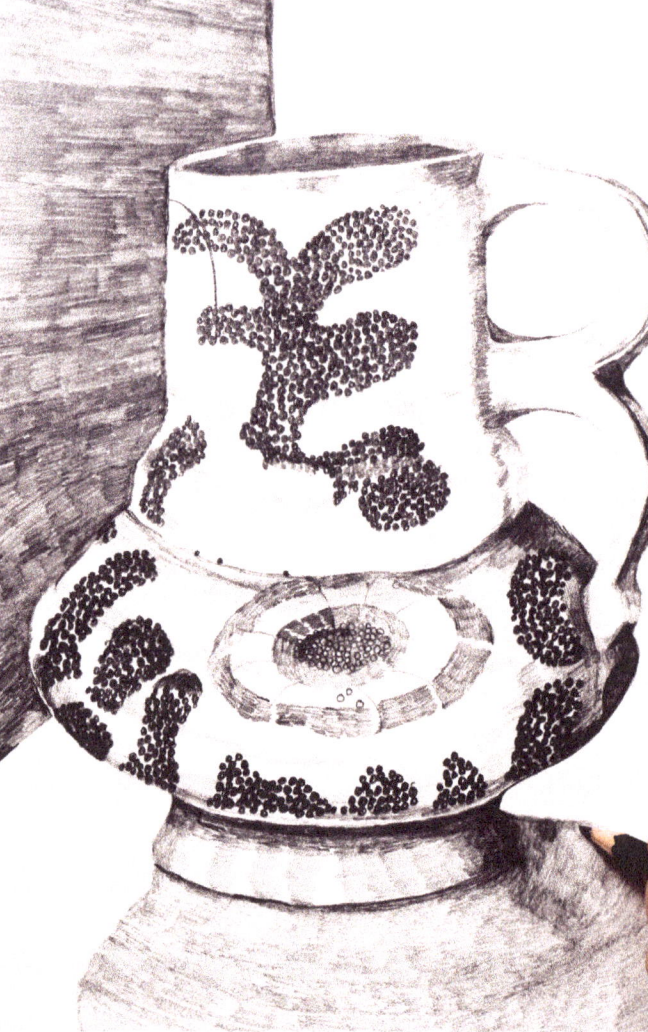

This drawing was completed in fewer than 5 minutes.

This drawing was completed in 1 hour. Try drawing the same subject in different time allowances and compare the drawings.

Developing Your Drawings

There are many ways to adapt these simple drawing exercises to make them your own. Here are a few examples:

- Try the same exercise using different materials or combining materials that you have, such as felt-tip pens, pencils, biro pens, ink and a brush, or watercolors.
- Draw the same subject again and again on the same page.
- Try doing more than one of these exercises on the same page.
- Complete one drawing and then turn your sketchbook to a different angle and draw a second similar drawing over the top of the first.
- Draw your subject at a massive scale so only part of it fits on the page. Then draw it much smaller on the same page.
- Add color to highlight certain aspects of your drawing.

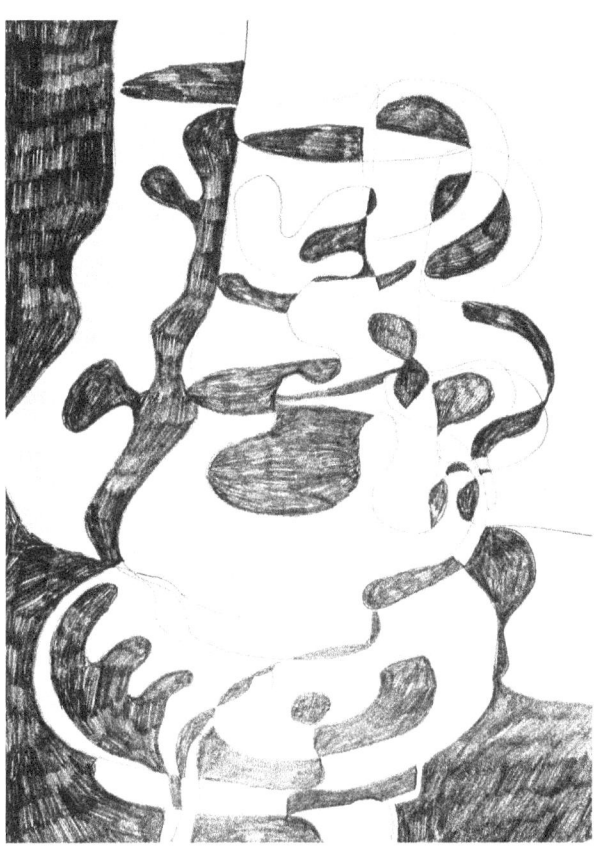

Draw a couple of quick one-line drawings on top of each other. Look for the interesting shapes that are created by the two drawings. Select areas to shade or color to create a composition.

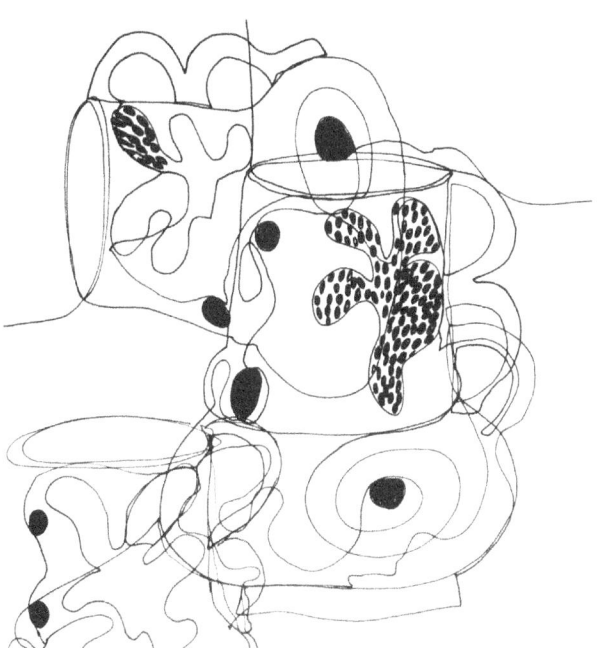

Experiment by drawing the same thing multiple times on one page. Turn the sketchbook sideways or upside down and draw over the top of another drawing at a different angle.

REVEL IN VISUAL VARIETY

When working in your sketchbook, consider how you create variety and variation on one page or on a double spread. Difference, contrast, and variation can be what makes a page interesting, dynamic, and full of energy. There are so many ways to incorporate visual variations. Here are some:

Light and Dark

Consider the tonal differences in the art pages you create. Incorporate a variety of light, mid-tone, and dark areas. For example, if you are using a pencil, alter the pressure to experiment with making a variety of tones. When using colored materials, consider the tonal value in addition to the actual color.

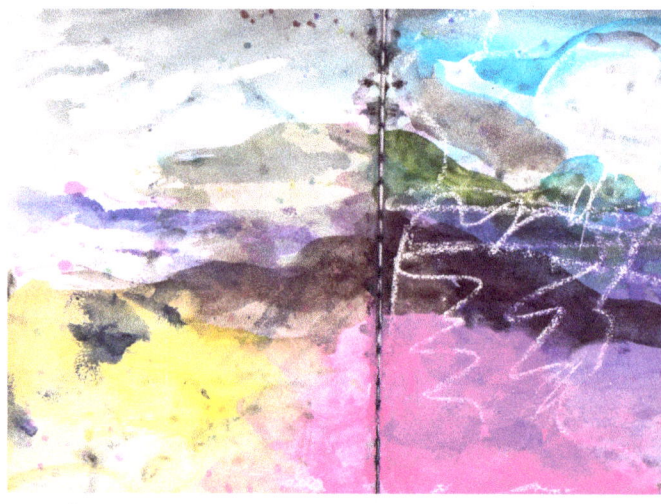

Our eyes are visual sensors that are particularly sensitive to light and dark. Tonal differences and contrast on a page help our eyes to travel around the page.

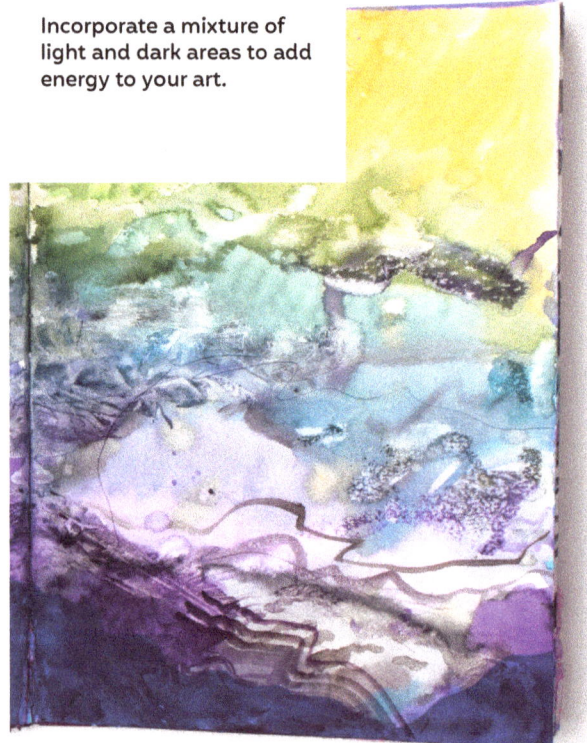

Incorporate a mixture of light and dark areas to add energy to your art.

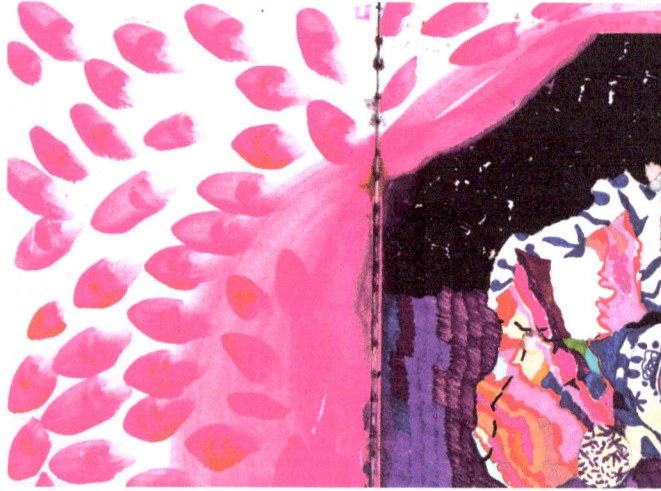

The light and dark values of a piece of art are its most important visual aspects.

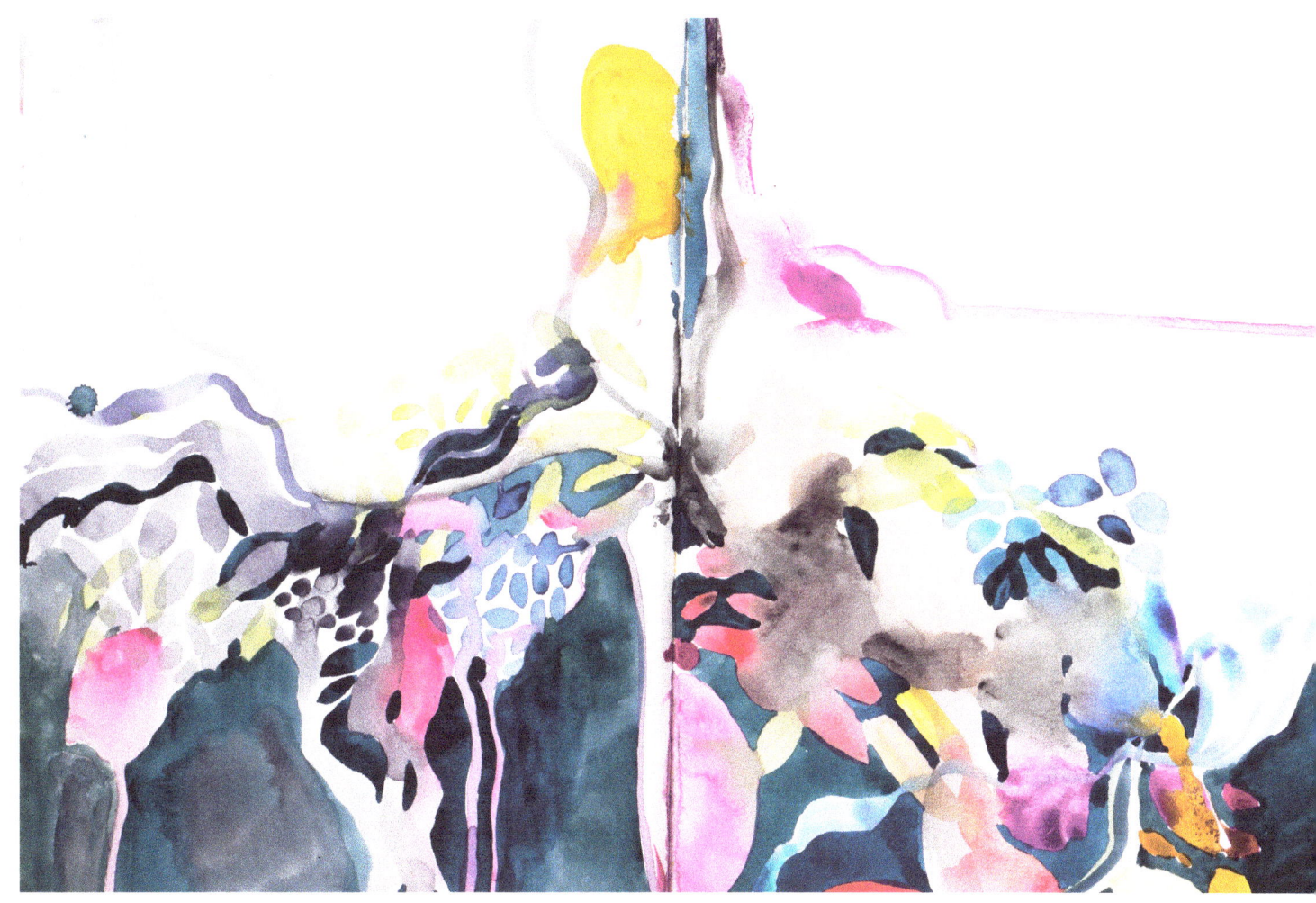

Big and Small Marks

It can be useful to use a variety of different marks, both big and small, to create interest and variation. Try using a big brush and a small brush on the same page. Contrast quick marks with slower, more deliberate marks.

▲ Vary the marks to create visual interest. Test the difference between marks made in different ways. Explore a diversity of ways to make the same mark, fast or slow, large or small, with heavy pressure or gentle pressure.

Delicate and Bold Areas

If you have a particularly bold area on a page, you may want to consider also having an area that is softer, more delicate, or fainter.

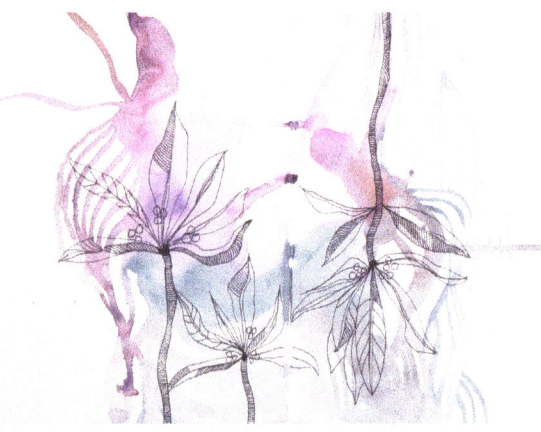

Be conscious of how you use bold and delicate areas. On these sketchbook pages, the delicate watercolor washes are contrasted with more definitive pen drawings.

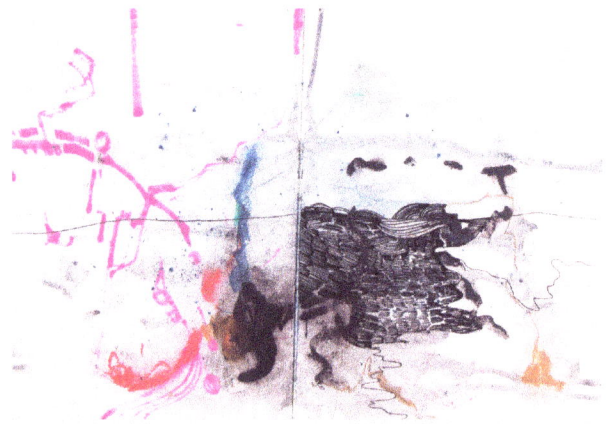

On this double-page spread, the dark, bold sections are surrounded by softer areas.

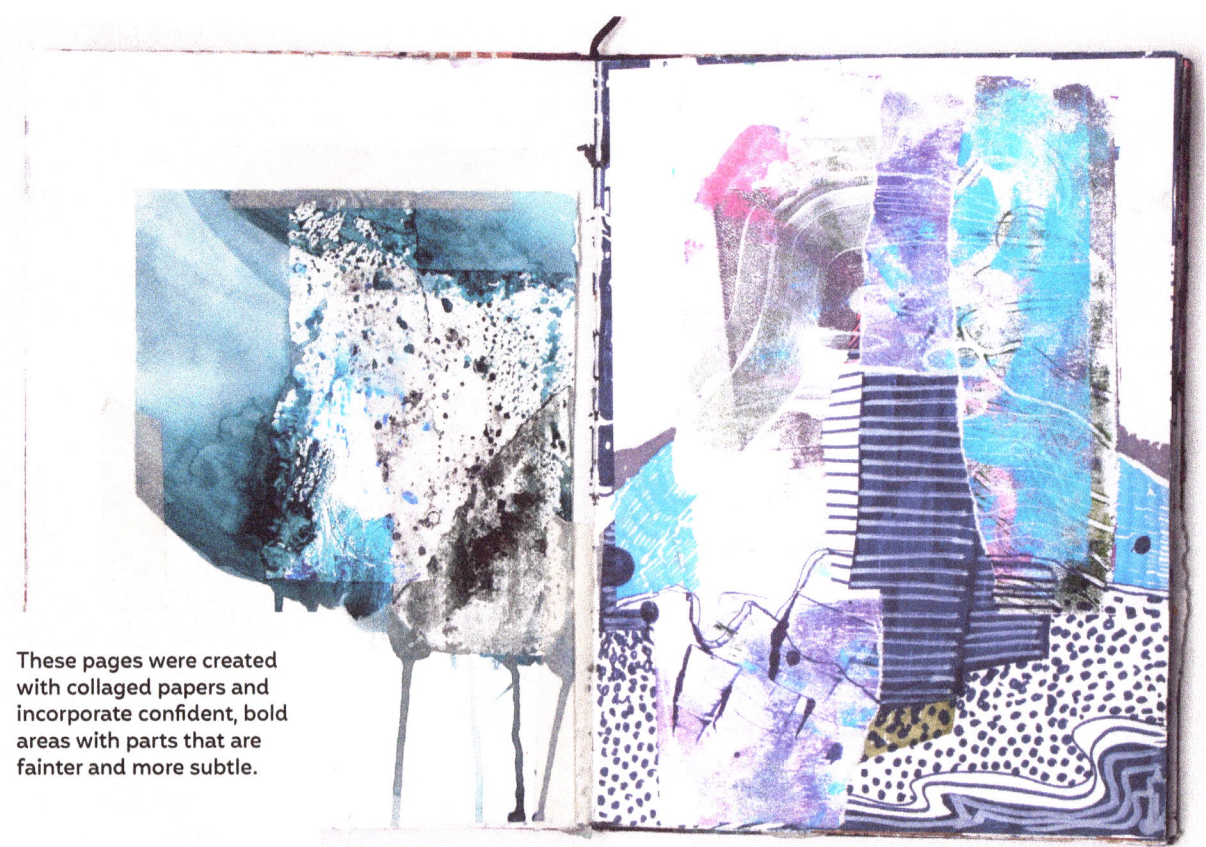

These pages were created with collaged papers and incorporate confident, bold areas with parts that are fainter and more subtle.

Busy and Quiet Areas

Incorporate quiet areas, which are more restful, to allow the intense areas of your work of art to breathe.

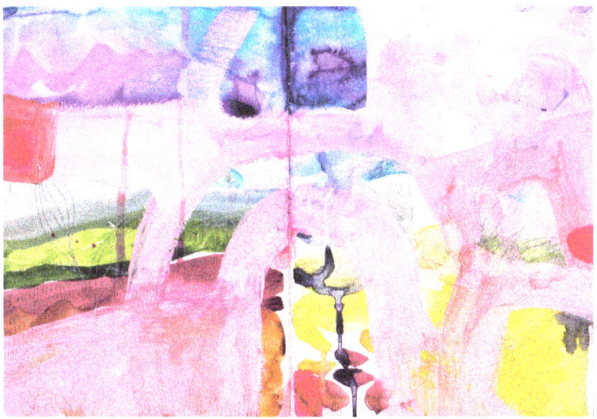

Contrast the busy areas on your page with quieter sections that feel more restful. This provides breathing space and contrast. On this page that was created with a base of bright watercolor blobs, a layer of pale pink acrylic paint over the top creates a quieter foil for the more intense areas.

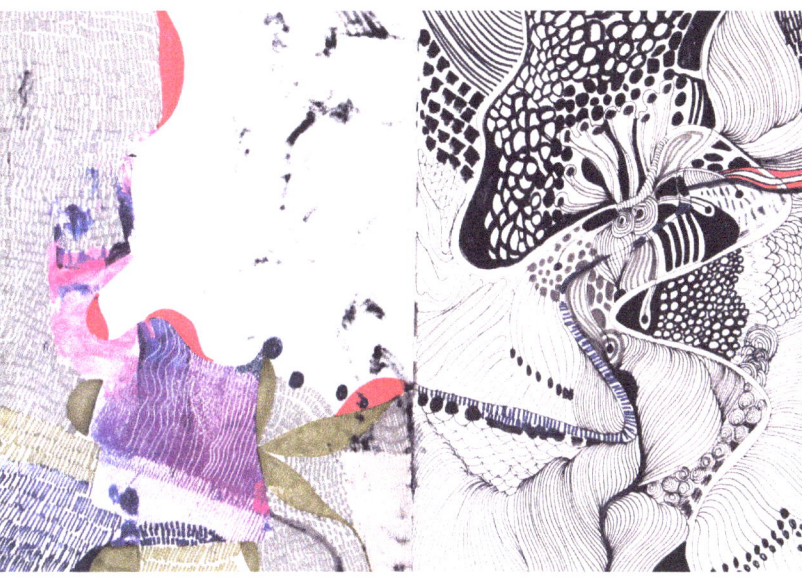

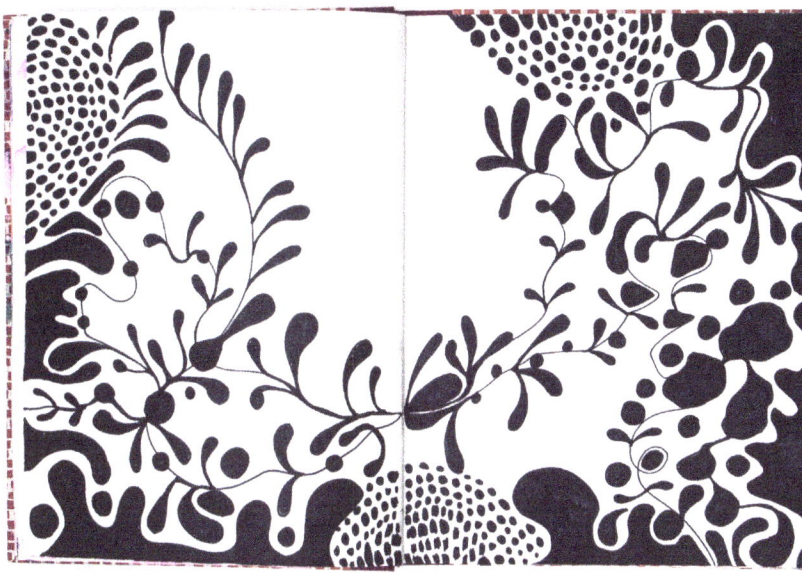

▲ A white space or quieter area in the center of a page can act as an invitation to look into the page, a space through which you can enter the artwork.

Variety of Tools and Materials

Using a variety of tools and materials and their contrasting properties can bring energy and interest to your artwork.

Curves and Straight Edges

Another way to bring contrast is to be mindful about your use of curved, straight, or angular lines and shapes.

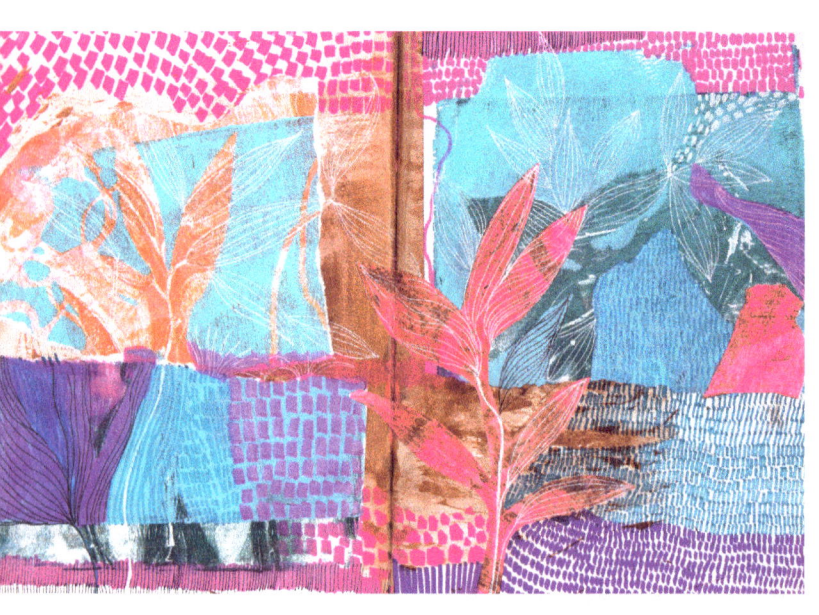

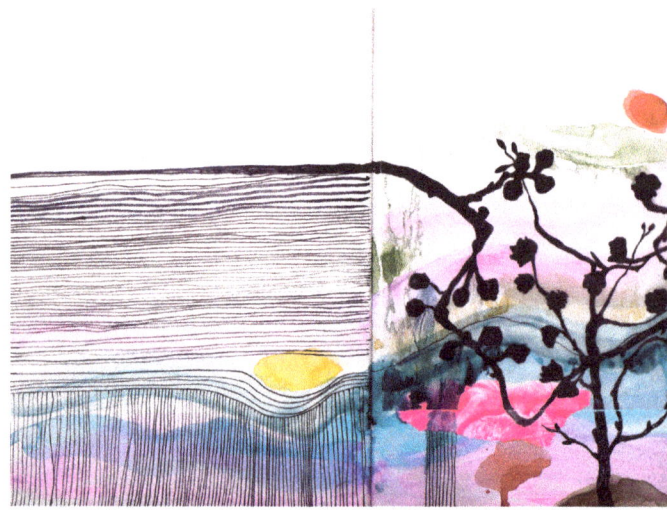

Experiment by including organic and geometric shapes on the same page.

These pages were made using acrylic paint, collage, a white pen, and colored felt-tip pens. Try mixing unusual combinations of art materials on one page.

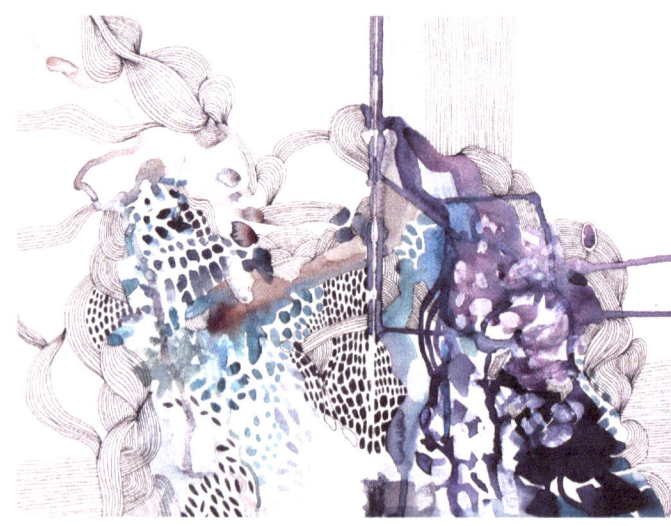

Incorporate both straight and curved lines into your artwork.

Variety of Colors

You can incorporate visual variety by using color in several ways. Try using black and white with color on the same page. Use both warm and cool tones, and muted and vibrant tones, on the same page. Employ colors that are opposite each other on the color wheel on the same page.

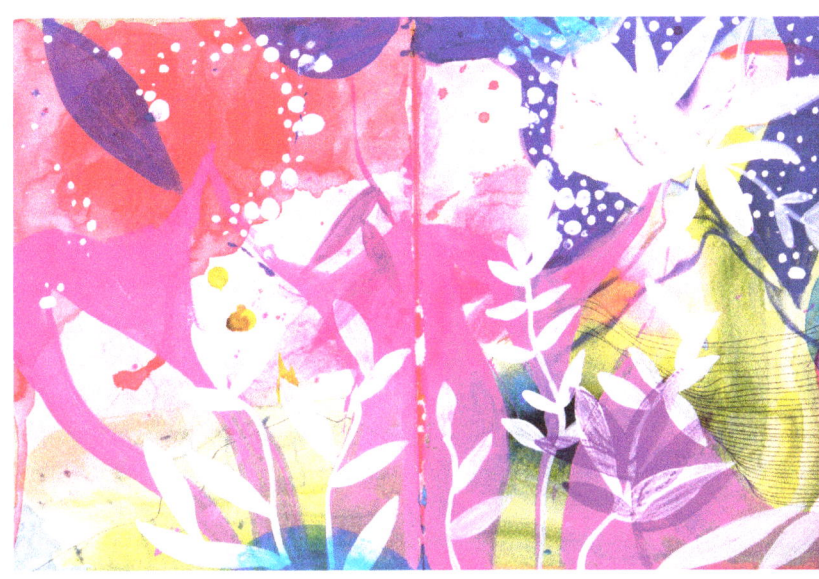

The base for this page is green and red, which are opposites on the color wheel.

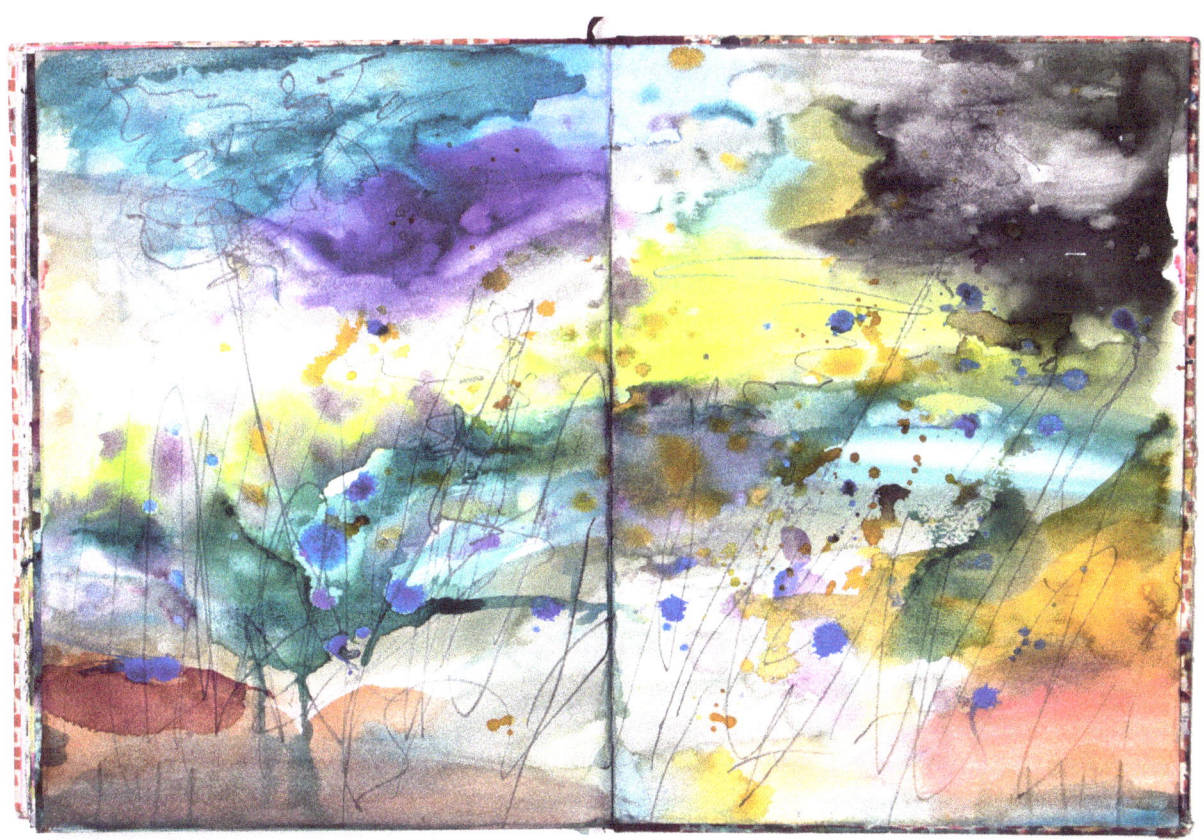

Blue and orange are opposite each other on the color wheel, as are purple and yellow. Try using a color with its opposite.

GETTING RID OF THE WHITE PAGE

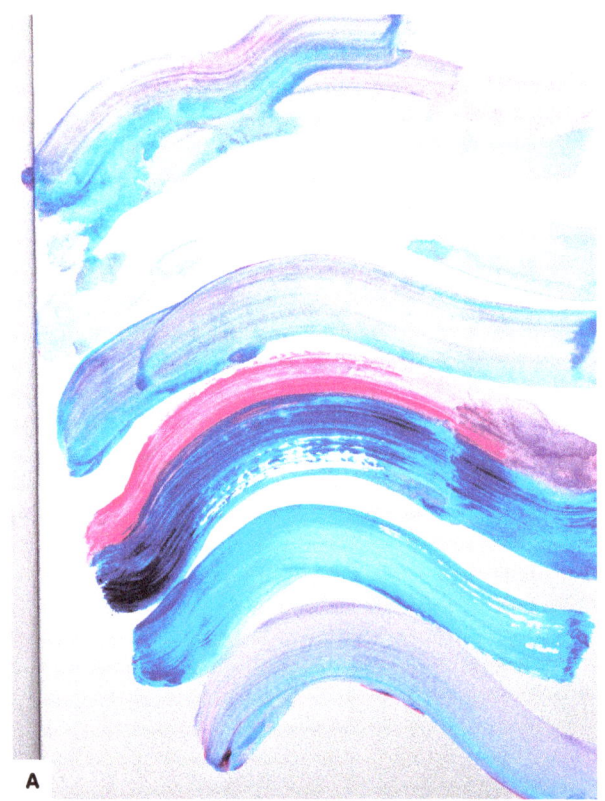

It is not uncommon to find a blank white page a little daunting. If this is the case for you, try some of the following ways to get rid of the expanse of white. These simple methods create a few marks or a little color on the page that you then draw or paint over. These approaches add a little interest, put something on the page for you to respond to, and act as a starting point that takes away the whiteness.

Leftover Paint

Often when I have leftover paint in my palette, I use it to make a few dabs or random marks on blank pages in my sketchbook. These marks provide visual interest to work into or around when you use your sketchbook next.

A Get rid of a blank page by making random marks with paint. Achieve a rainbow effect by using a big brush and picking up two or more colors simultaneously on the brush tip.

B Allow your original marks to dry and work over them. Think about how you could feature some of the original marks on the page. Here I drew a quick tree shape and painted around the pencil to create a tree shape with the negative space.

C Consider building up many different layers in your artwork. Let each layer dry and add more detail or use a different brush.

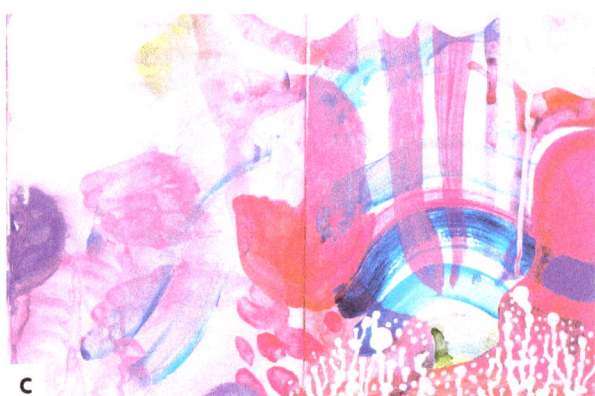

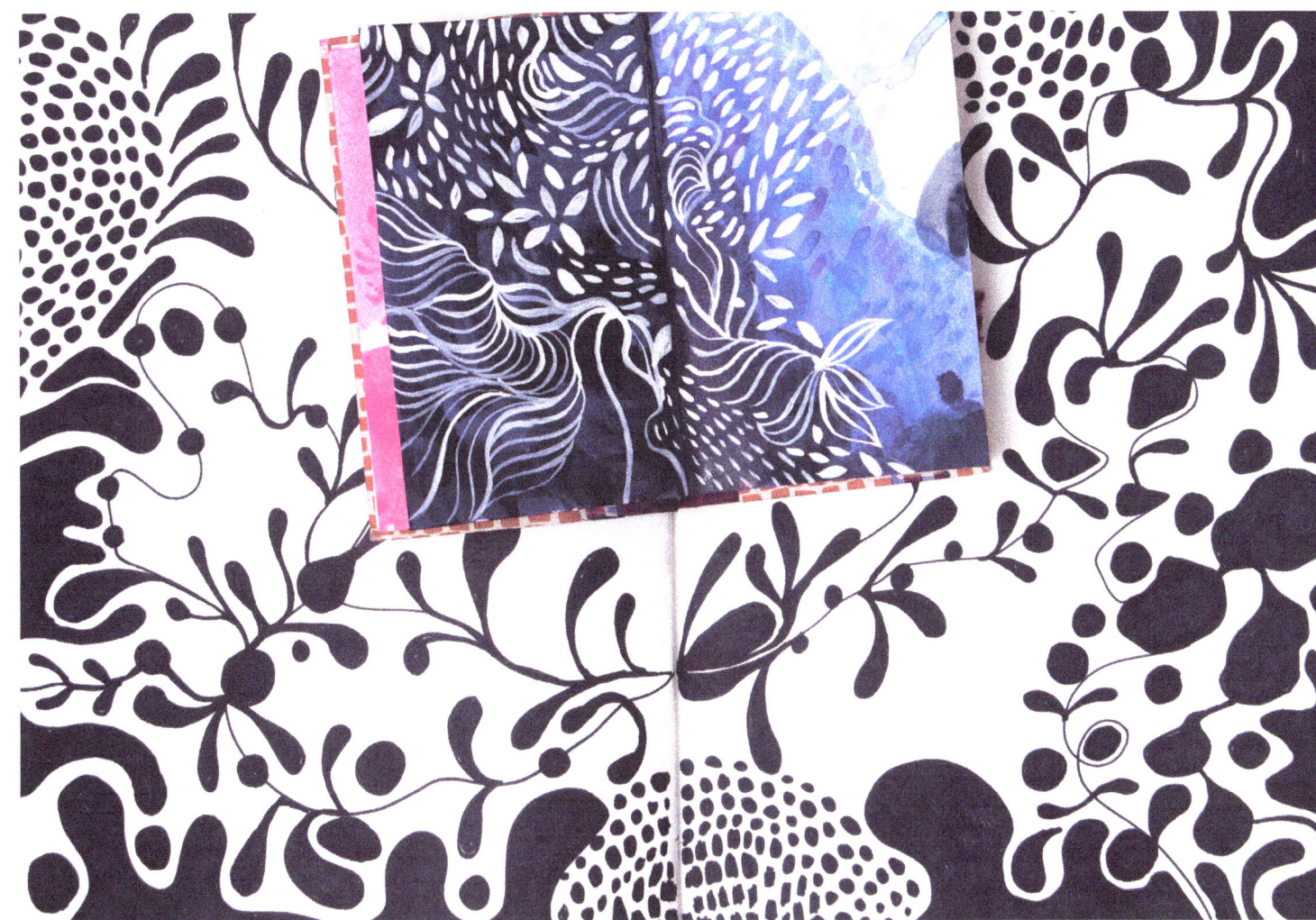

Here are two sketchbook pages that were started with random lines. The larger one features patterns drawn with a black felt-tip pen. The smaller one features white ink on dark blue ink. The starting point for both pages was a few lines. In the black and white pages, a wiggly line was drawn down the page and across the page. This helped structure the pattern.

Some Random Lines

I might just draw one or two completely random lines across a page in a bit of a scribble. Try closing your eyes and drawing a few lines. Or listen to your favorite music while drawing lines. Then consider how you might like to develop your lines. Try drawing three lines with three different art materials. I might cover five or six pages this way, and then when I come back to my sketchbook, I often find the smallest beginning of something to respond to.

Collage

Collage or glue an interesting scrap of paper onto a blank page and then work over it.

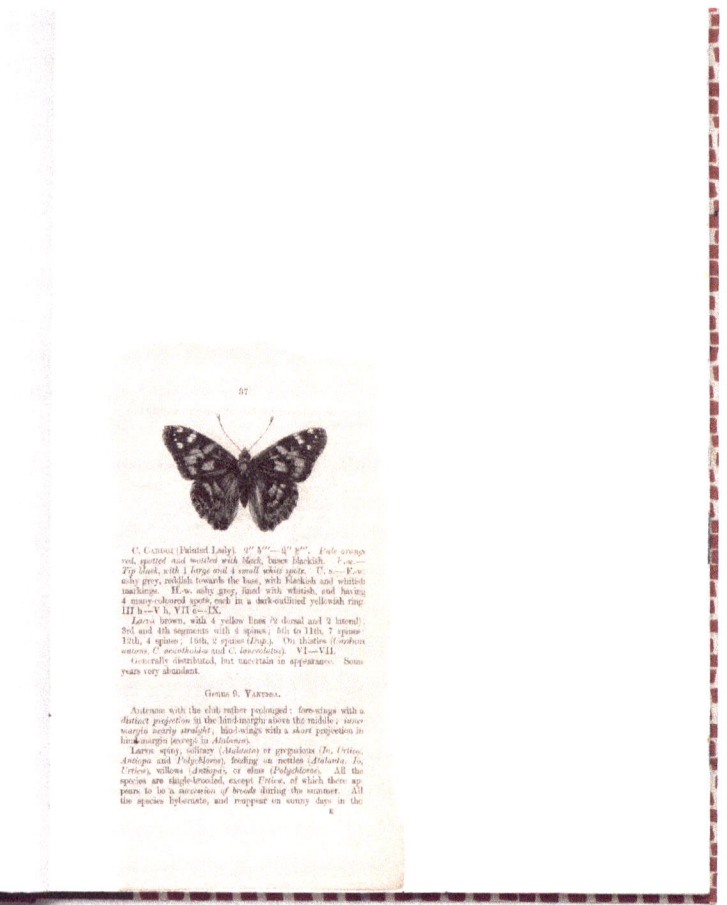

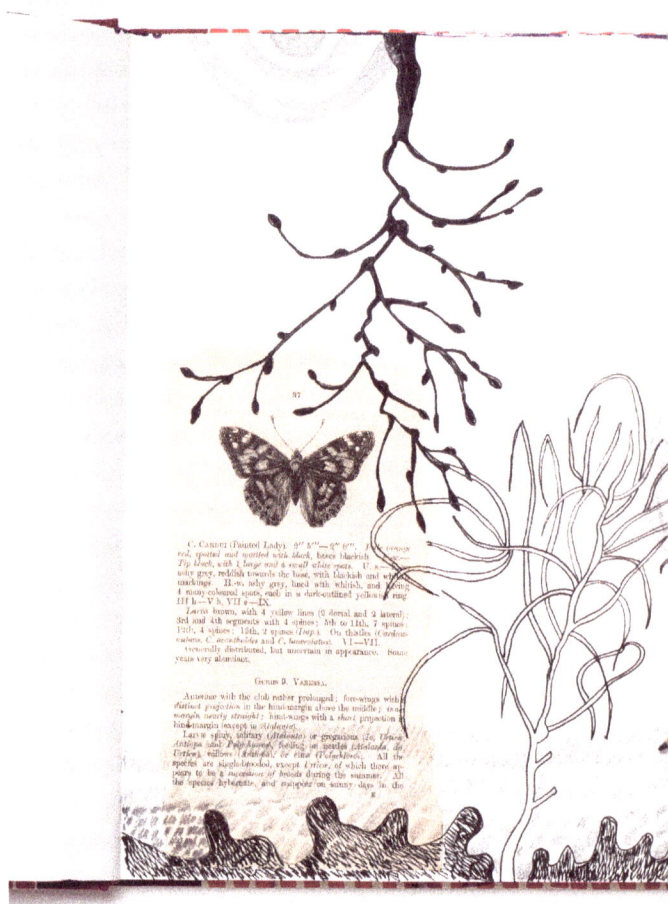

Select an interesting fragment of paper to glue into your sketchbook.

Respond to the collaged element by using it as a starting point or springboard.

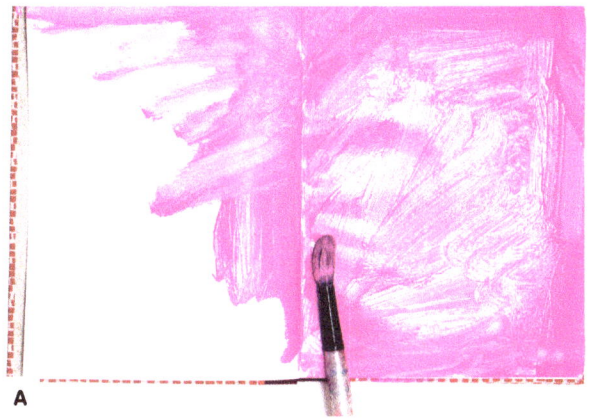

A

Colored Ground

I often paint a page pink or green and then draw or work over it. It is worth experimenting with colored backgrounds or grounds (the first or foundation layer) and see what they do to your artwork. Try different paints and colors and see what works for you. For example, use a white pen on a black page or experiment with different opacities of paint, such as starting with watercolor, letting it dry, and then painting over it with acrylic paint.

A Experiment with using different background colors. Paint your page and let it dry.

B Work over the colored area in your chosen medium. Here I used a black fine-line pen over a pink page.

C Experiment with different colored backgrounds and learn about the effect they can have on your finished work.

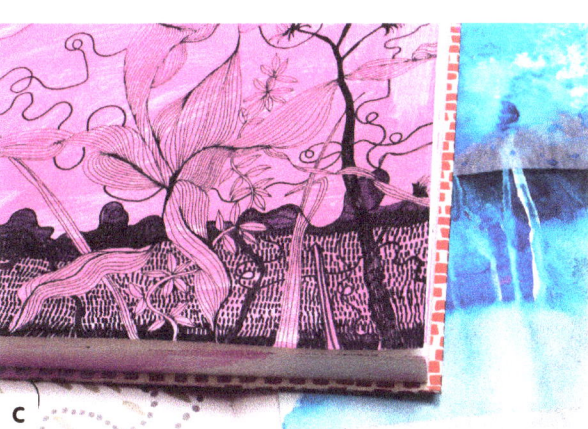

B

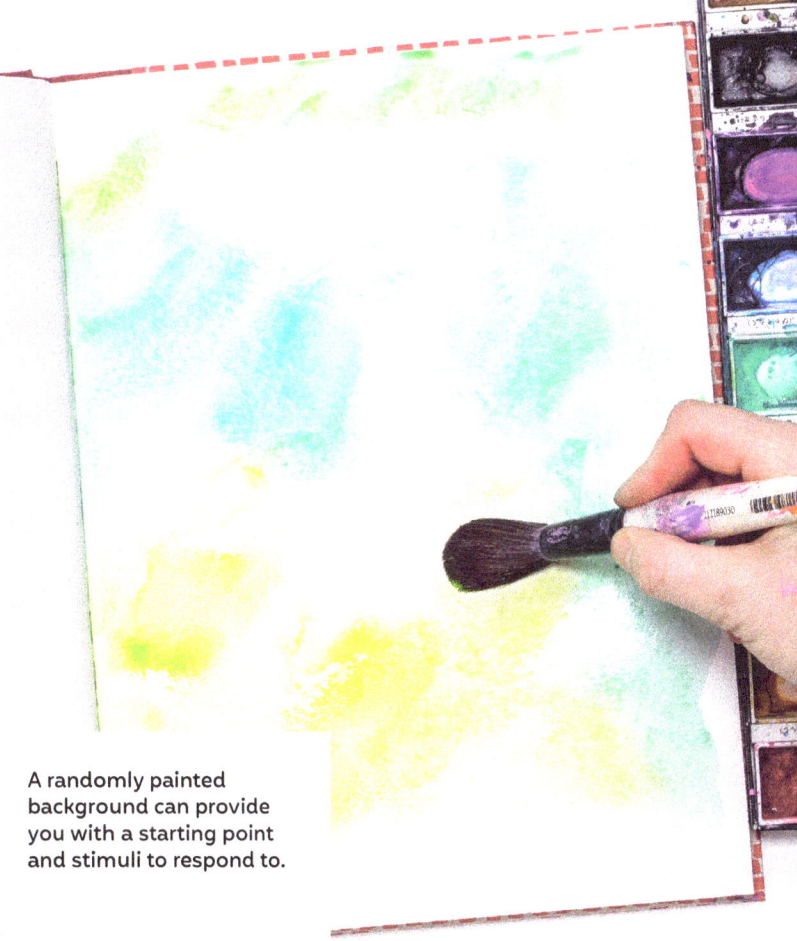

A randomly painted background can provide you with a starting point and stimuli to respond to.

C

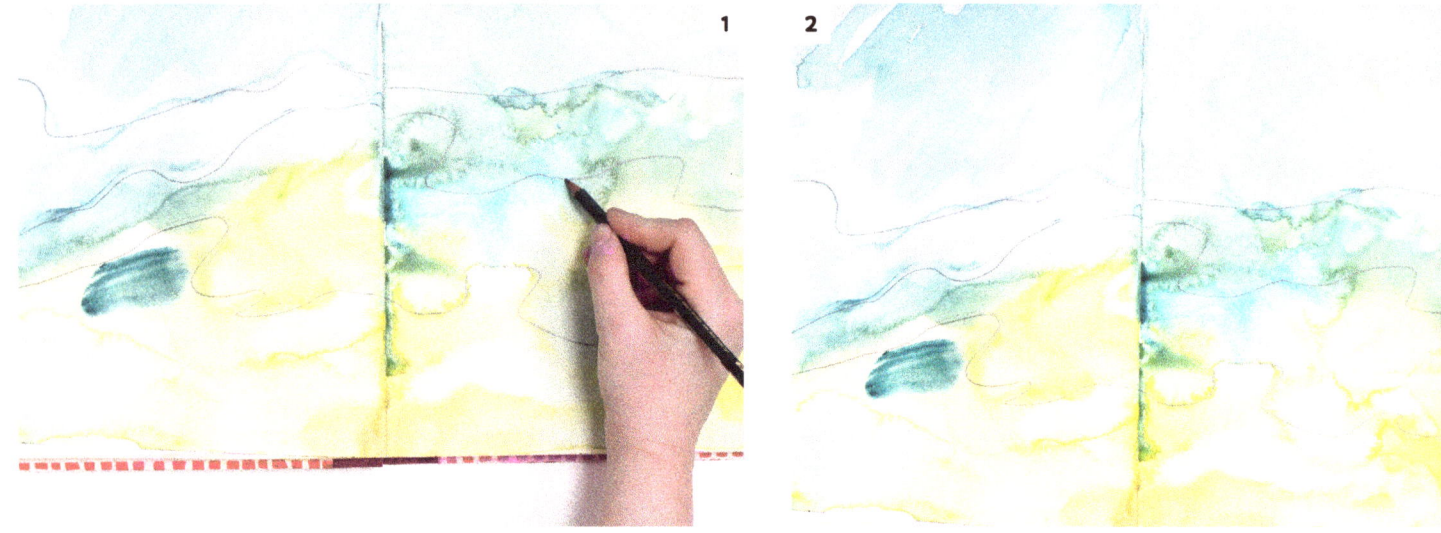

1
2

Add a color or colors to a page as a background and then draw in some random lines. Ask yourself how you could develop this starting point. The example here reminded me of rain on hills, so I developed it into an impressionistic landscape.

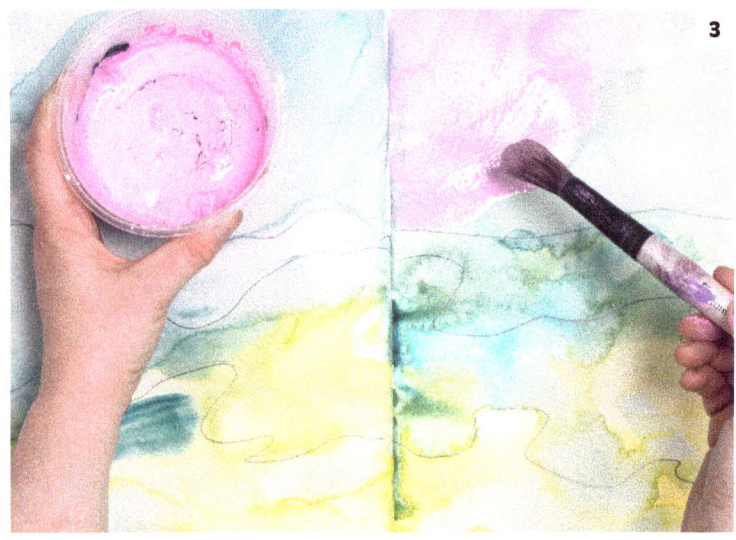

3

Add layers of your chosen medium to build up your sketchbook page.

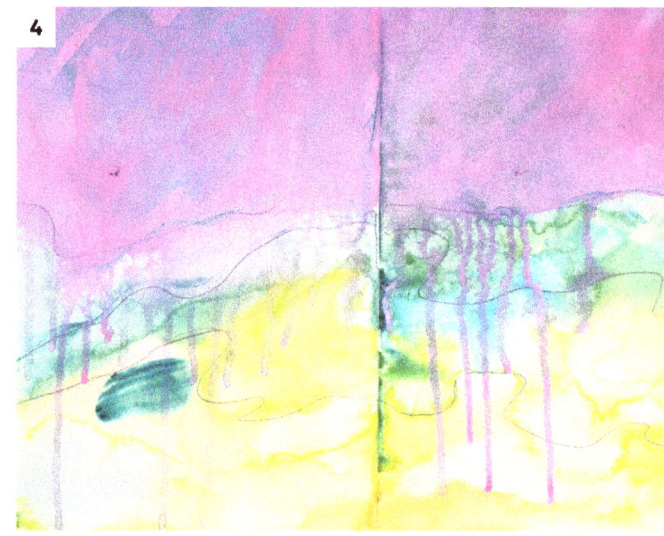

4

Experiment with spraying water on acrylic paint and moving your sketchbook around to create deliberate drips.

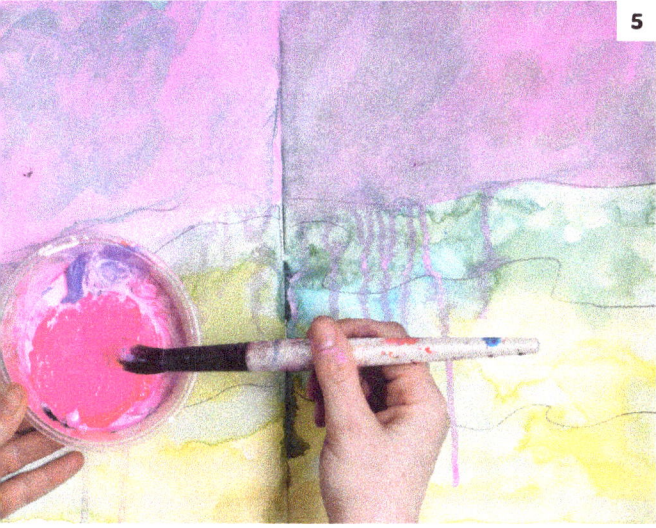

5

Once one layer is dry, build impact and visual interest by accentuating certain areas.

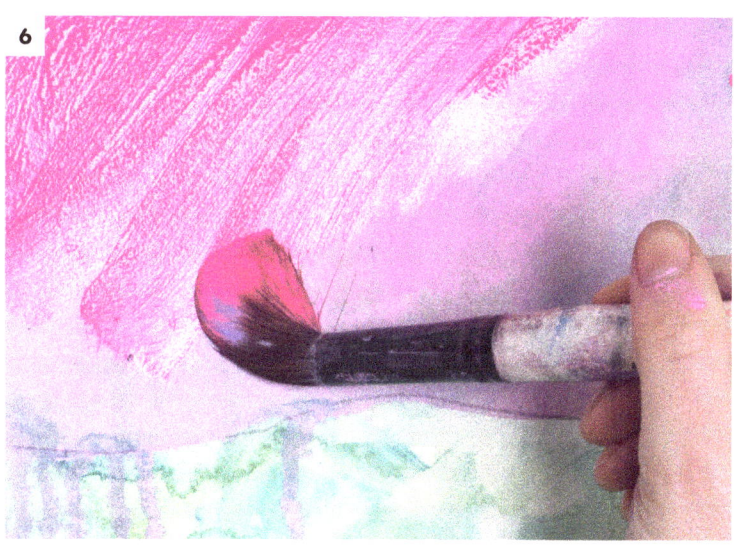

6

Select a brush to correspond with the type of effect you are after. A big, fat brush will create bold and gestural marks.

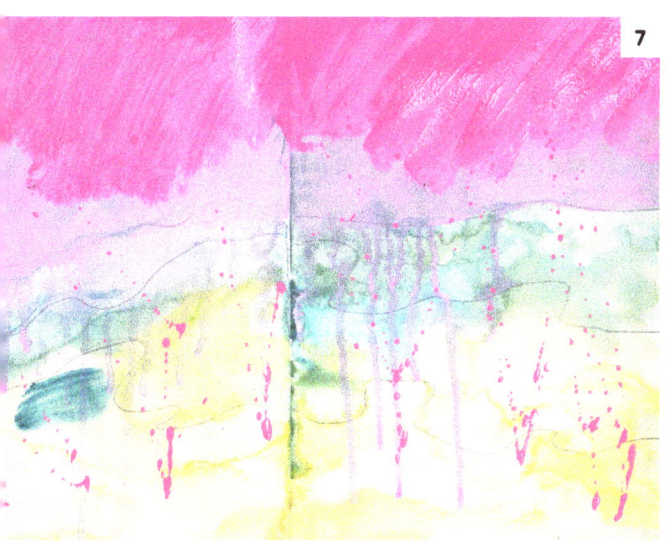

7

Experiment with drips and splashes to create movement. Here I went rather overboard on the splashes. If I were to redo this page, I would limit these and ensure they were not as uniform.

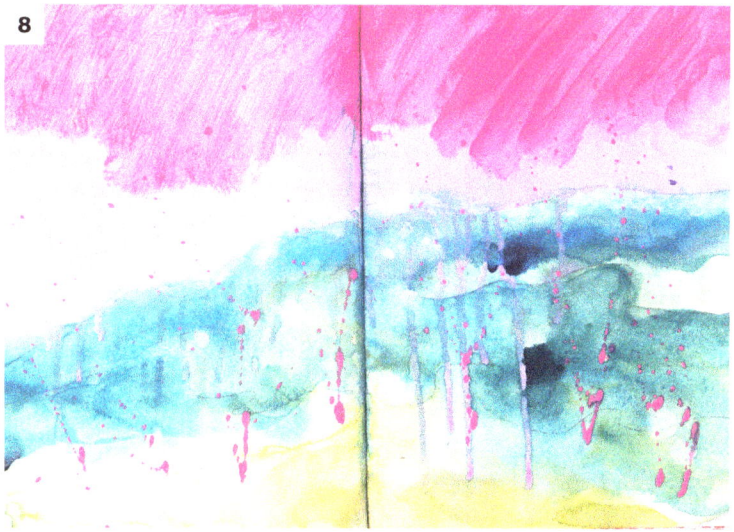

8

Think about the value tones of your page. In the example here, everything was looking very midtone, so I added dark blue watercolor paint and a little white paint on the horizon to vary the tones.

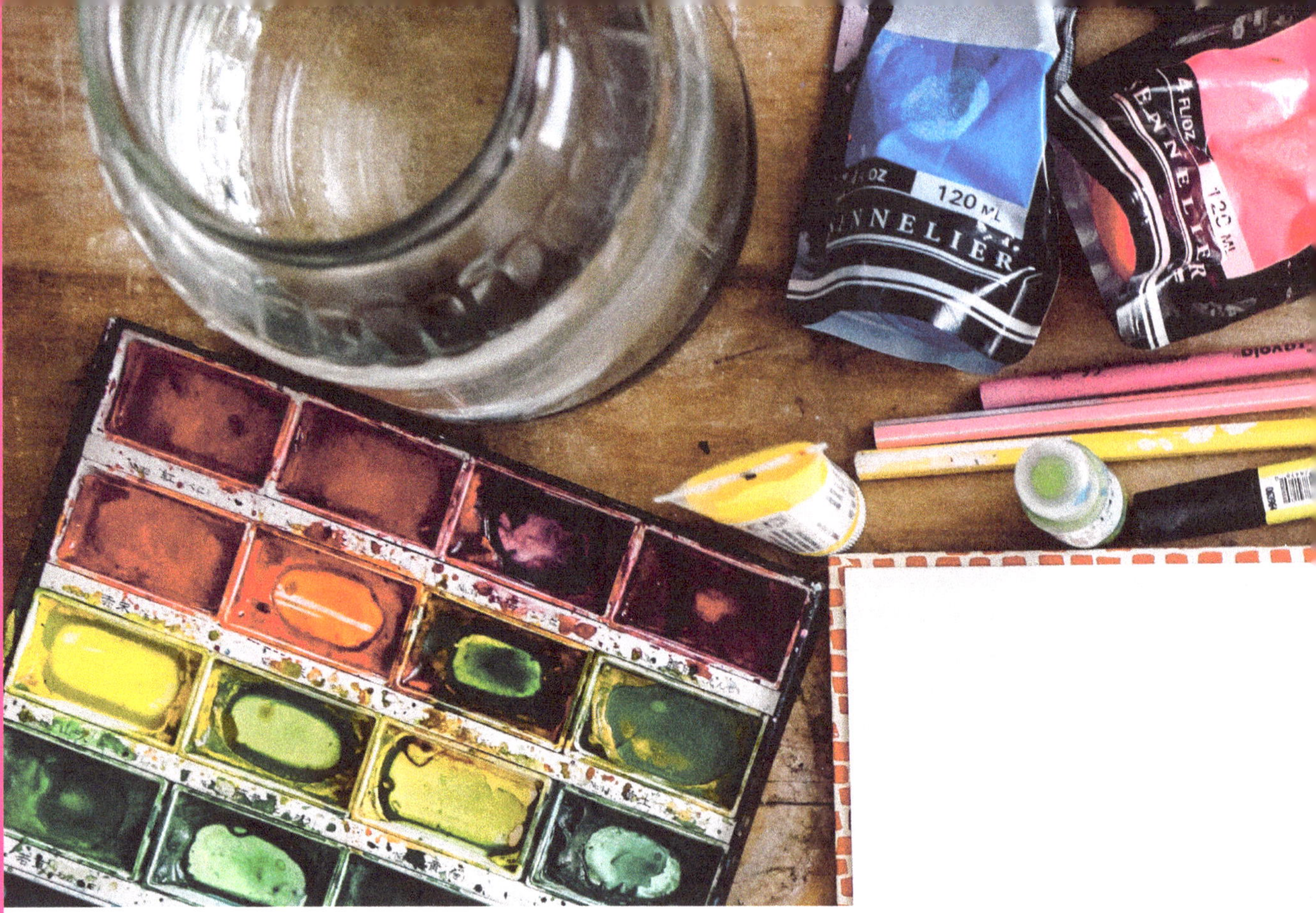

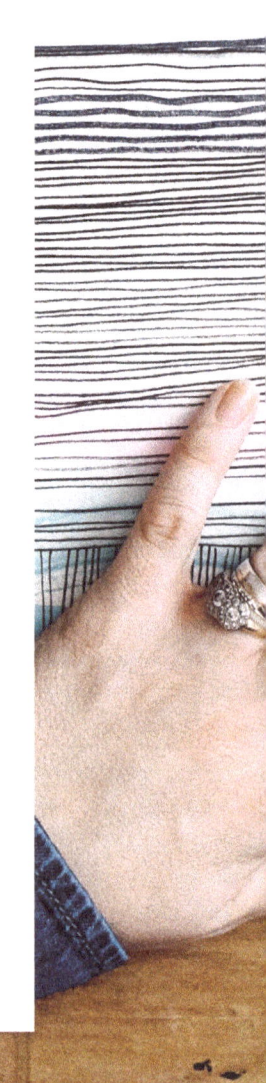

TECHNIQUES FOR EXPLORING AND EXPERIMENTING

This section contains a host of practical techniques that I use when making art. I explain different methods to explore and experiment, and share ways in which you can be inventive with mixing art materials. My hope is that you apply, adapt, and alter these techniques to use the art supplies you have.

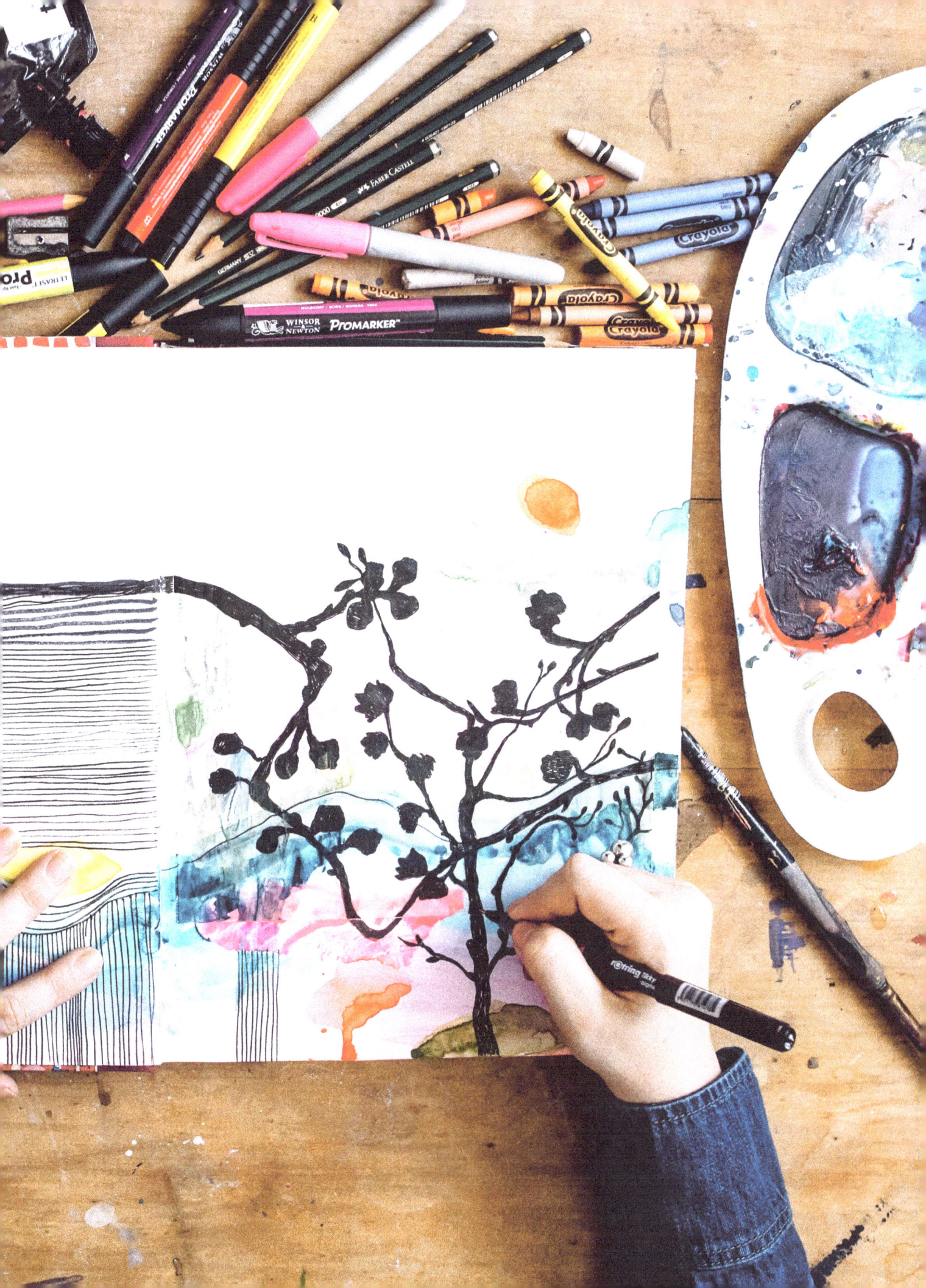

CONSTRAINTS

Infinite possibilities can sometimes be more paralyzing than liberating. It can feel daunting to know that you could do or create absolutely anything. Limitless options can lead to lack of action. You may find it useful to set some parameters and boundaries for yourself to help you overcome the issue of limitless choice.

Sometimes too much freedom can prevent us from knowing what to do so we respond by doing nothing. When this is the case, a few self-imposed parameters give our creativity something to push against. Read through the selection of constraints that follow and pick the one that most resonates with you. Consider developing your own list of constraints to use when your inspiration is lacking:

- Create a page in your sketchbook inspired by something you can see from where you are now.
- Select a book you love, open it at random, and create something inspired by that page.
- Open your fridge and pick out something to draw.
- Pick a color and then wander around your home seeking an item or collection of items to draw that are that color.
- Create pages that only use blue and orange.
- Create three pages in 30 minutes, set a timer, and move to the next page after 10 minutes.
- Repeat or revisit a subject you have already drawn or painted; we often gain new insight through repetition.

Pick one of these ten words as a starting point to create a page or series of pages in your sketchbook. For example, create a quick ideas map and list all the things that interest you about this word or concept. Think about how you could explore this theme in your sketchbook and then see where it takes you.

1. Weather
2. Maps
3. Home
4. Belonging
5. Science
6. Aging
7. Celebration
8. Injustice
9. Self
10. Seasons

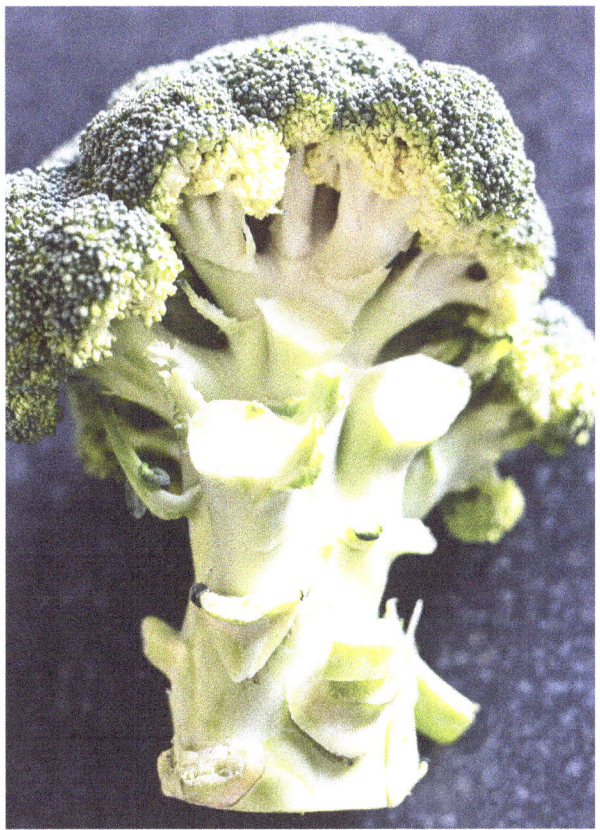

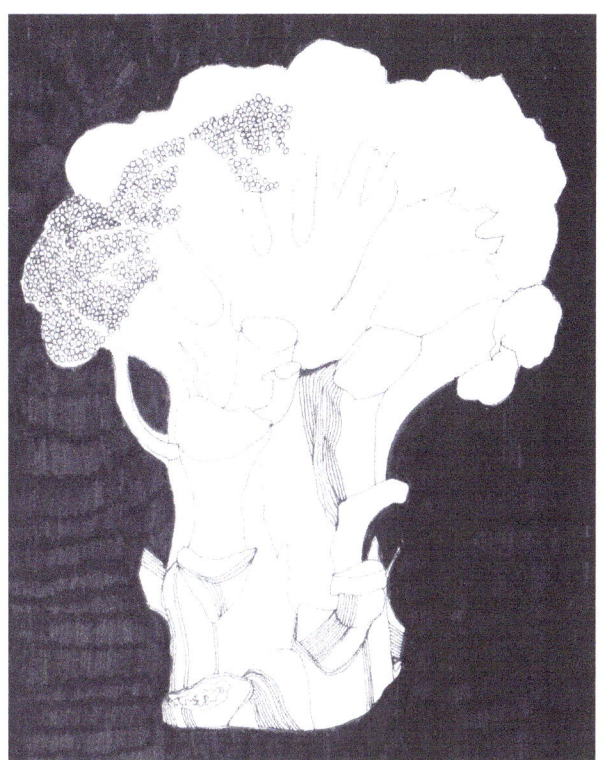

Constraints can help you overcome option paralysis. An example of a constraint could be limiting yourself to draw or paint a subject you find in your kitchen. I found this piece of broccoli in my fridge.

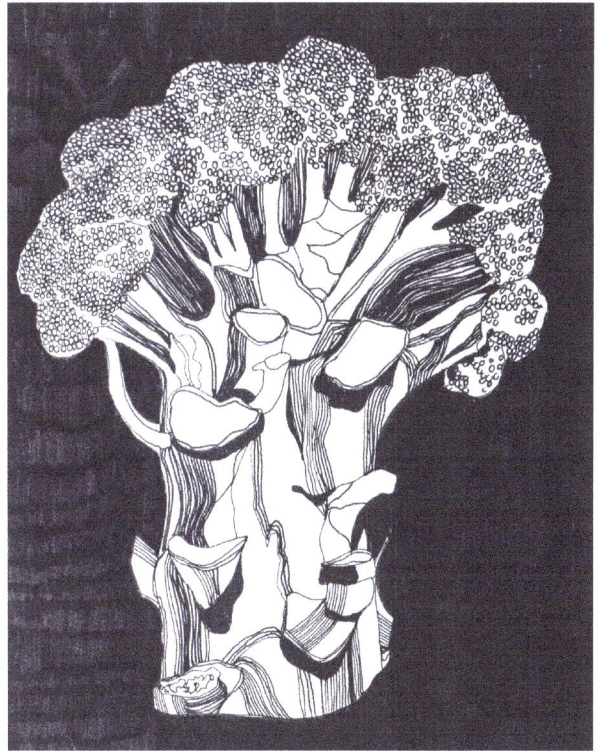

When you are drawing, consider the aspect of your subject that you want to emphasize or accentuate. As I started to draw the piece of broccoli, it reminded me of a majestic oak tree, so I emphasized its silhouette by coloring in the background with a thick black felt-tip pen.

SEEKING INSPIRATION OUTSIDE

I encourage you to actively seek the wonder and awe in the world. Slowing down and taking the time to look around you can be an effective way to find subjects to paint or draw in your sketchbook. By slowing down, paying attention, and being more present and aware of our surroundings, we gain insight and inspiration.

▼ ▶ The natural world is a wonderful source of reference material. Seek out aspects that interest you and that you want to explore further in your sketchbook. Try selecting one photo or prompt and use it as a starting point to create multiple pages, experimenting with different techniques, materials, or colors. Here are some photographs of my local park and the corresponding pages in my sketchbook.

Getting into Nature

Much of my artistic practice is informed by the colors and patterns in nature. I actively seek out visual references that appeal to me, looking for shapes, textures, patterns, silhouettes, colors, and layers. As with most things in life, the more mindful and curious I am, the more I see and discover. The more I look, the more I find.

Take your camera outside when you are looking for stimulus. Use the photographs you've taken as a springboard to create pages in your sketchbook. Use the color inspiration you have collected or the reference shapes or patterns as a starting point.

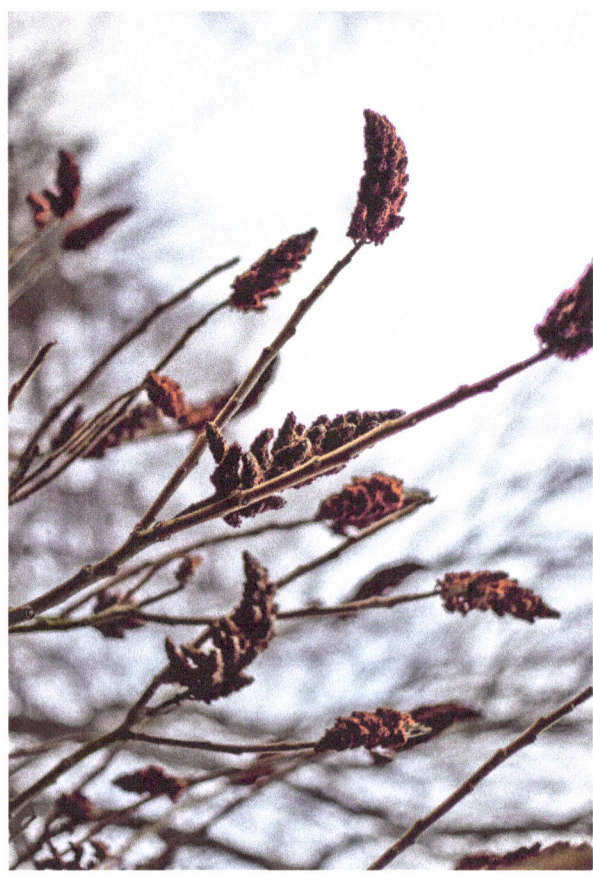
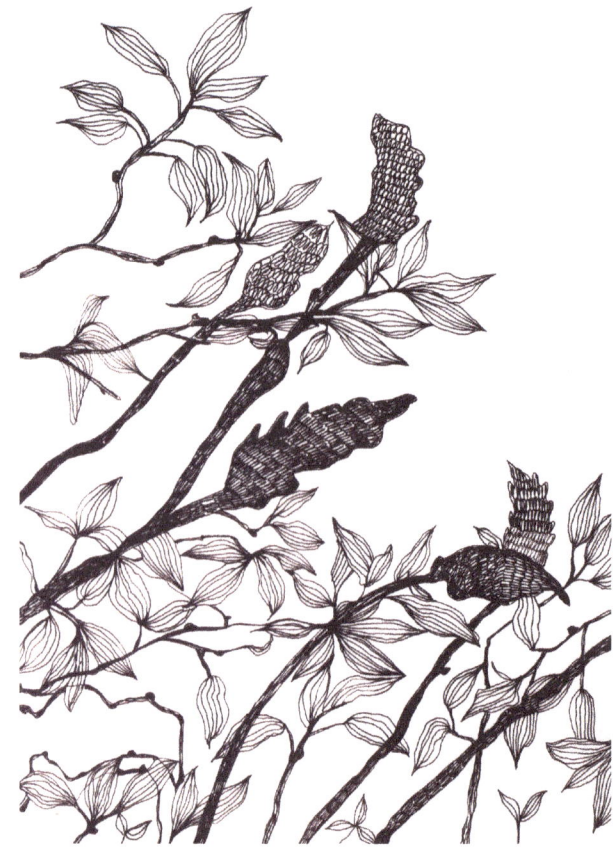

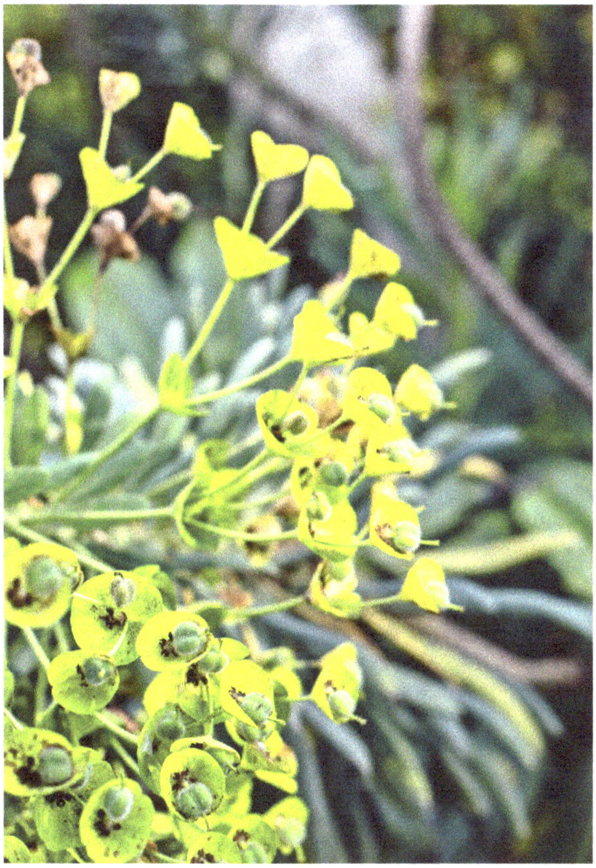

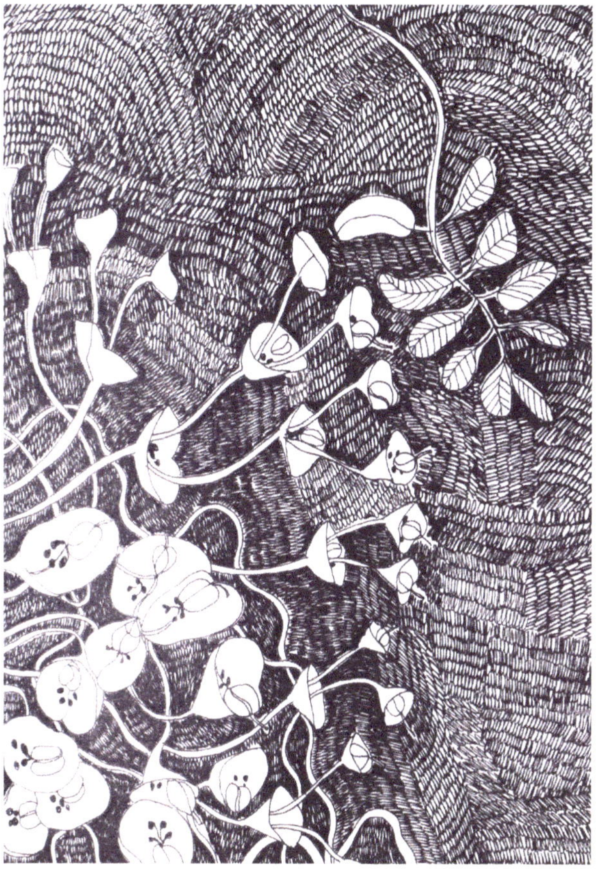

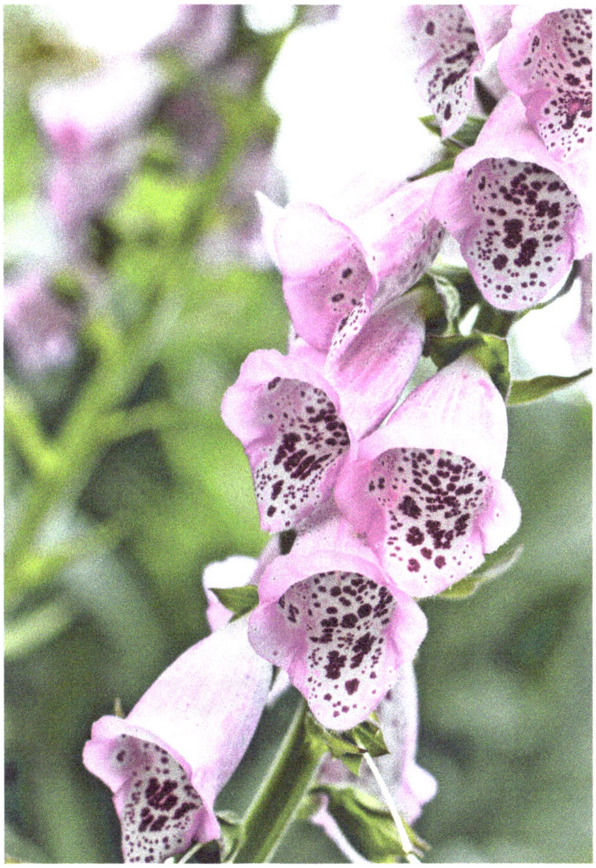

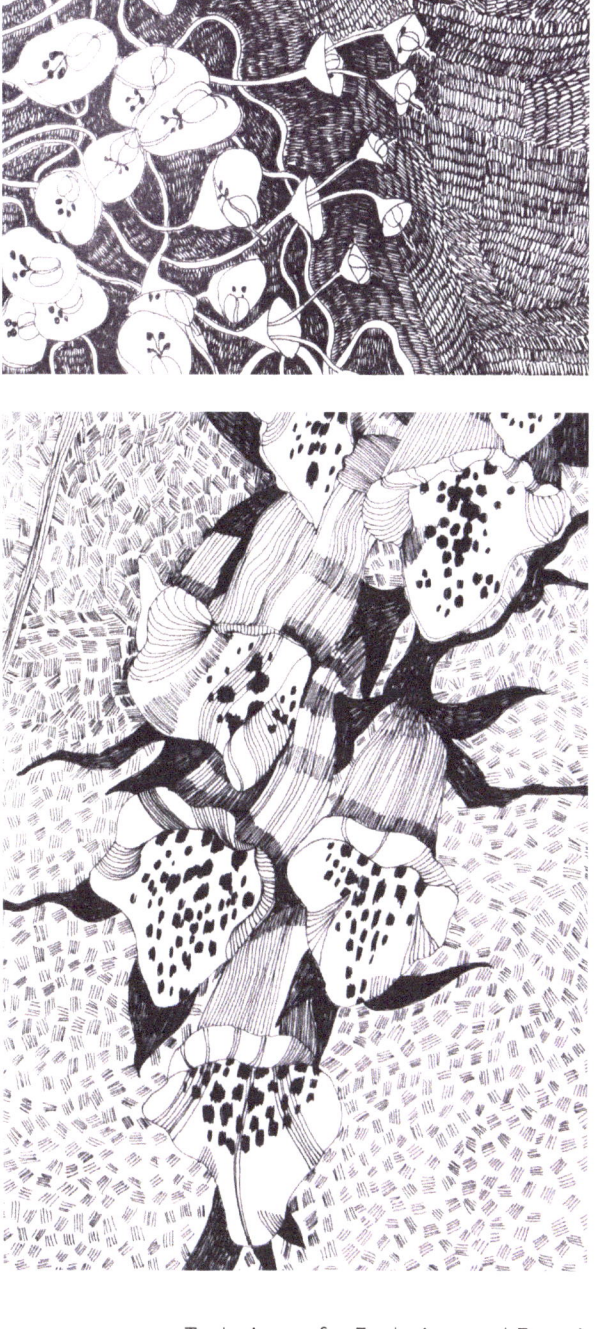

Collecting Reference Material

Go on your own inspiration safari to seek reference material and stimuli. Take photographs of the inspiring things you find in your neighborhood. It might be worth revisiting some of the items you put on your original inspiration map. You will be attracted to a completely different set of stimuli than me. Think about shapes, light, textures, colors, layers, juxtapositions, and creating a story. You might get excited about the built environment, straight lines, cityscapes, people, crowds, or graffiti.

Take lots of photographs of the things that interest you. Part of the joy of this exercise is getting to know what lights you up and fills you with a sense of creative potential. The magic in going outside and seeking inspiration is that you must question and then try to understand what makes you inspired, curious, or energized. The more you look for inspiration, the more you will find it and, importantly, the better you will understand your own creativity.

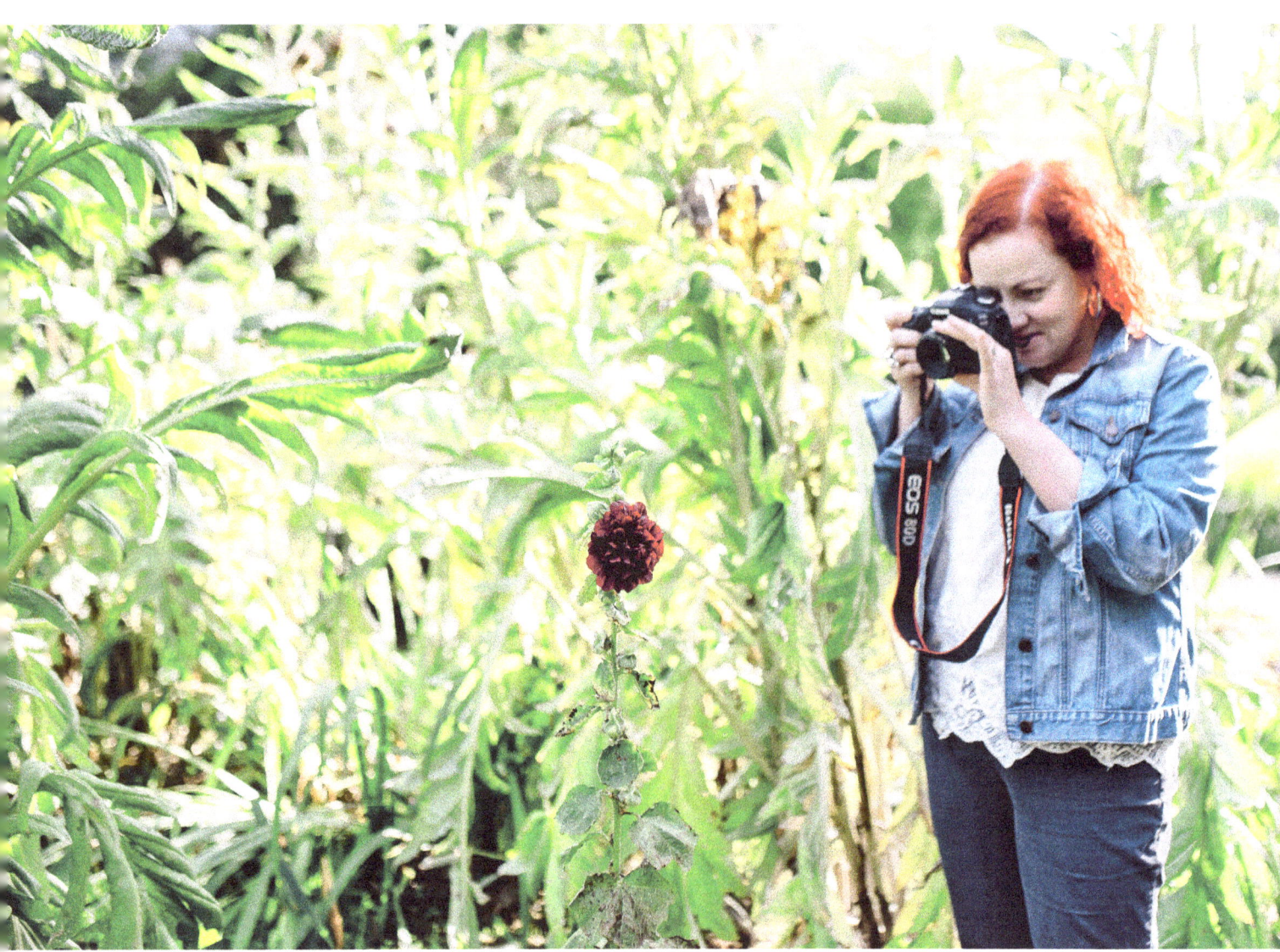

On a walk through my neighborhood park, I was attracted to this blossoming rhododendron bush. I then used this one photograph to paint three pages in my sketchbook.

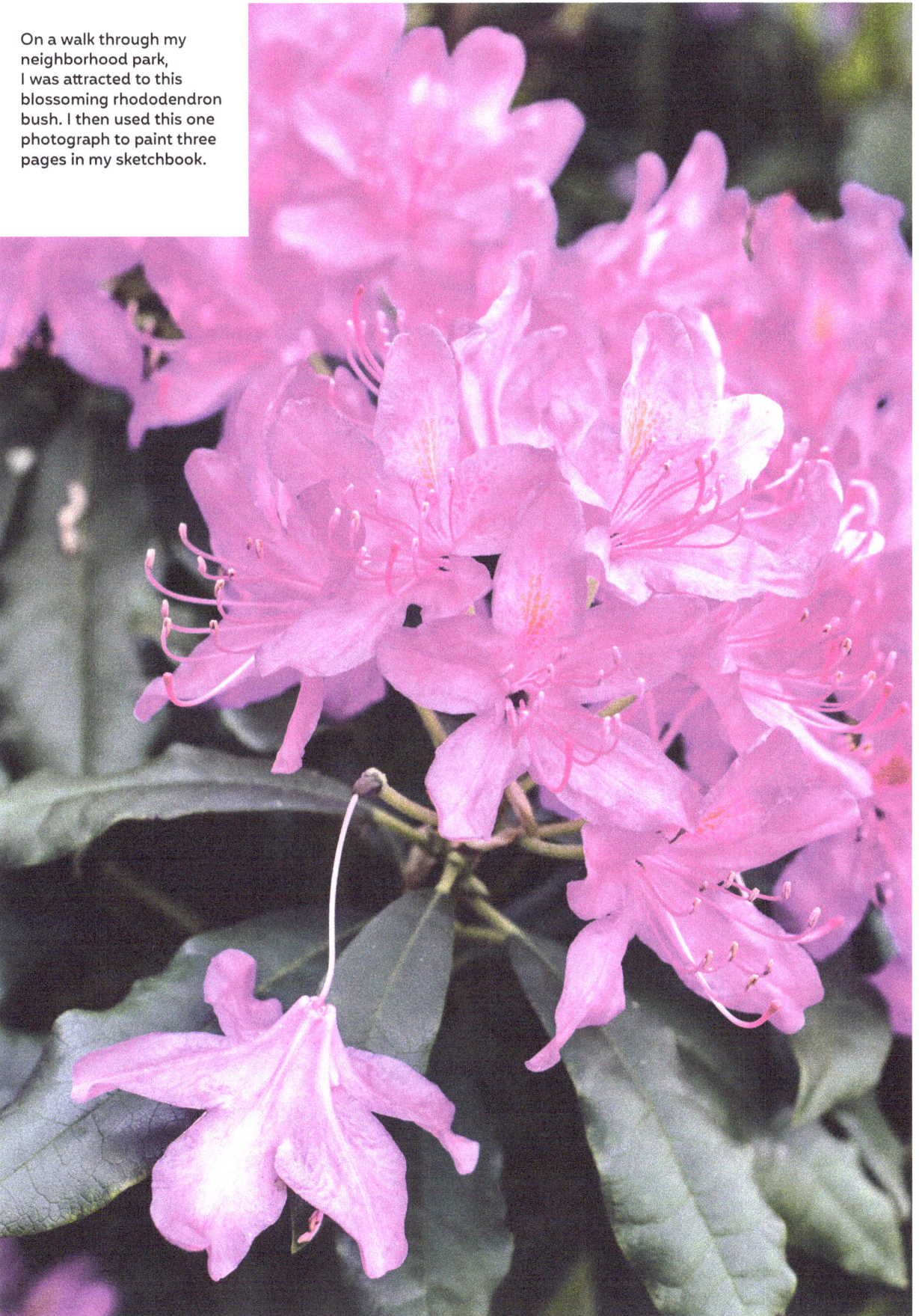

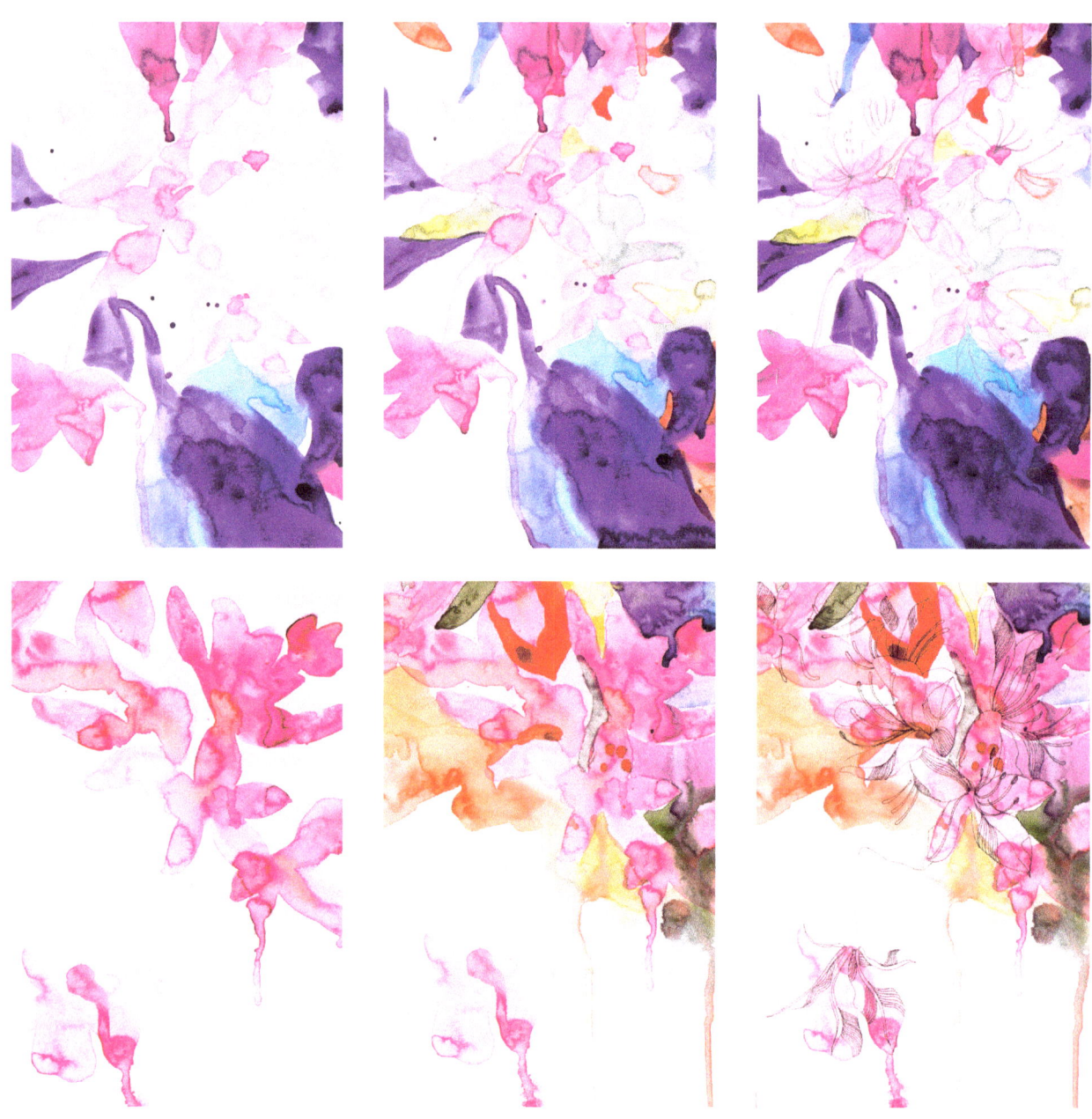

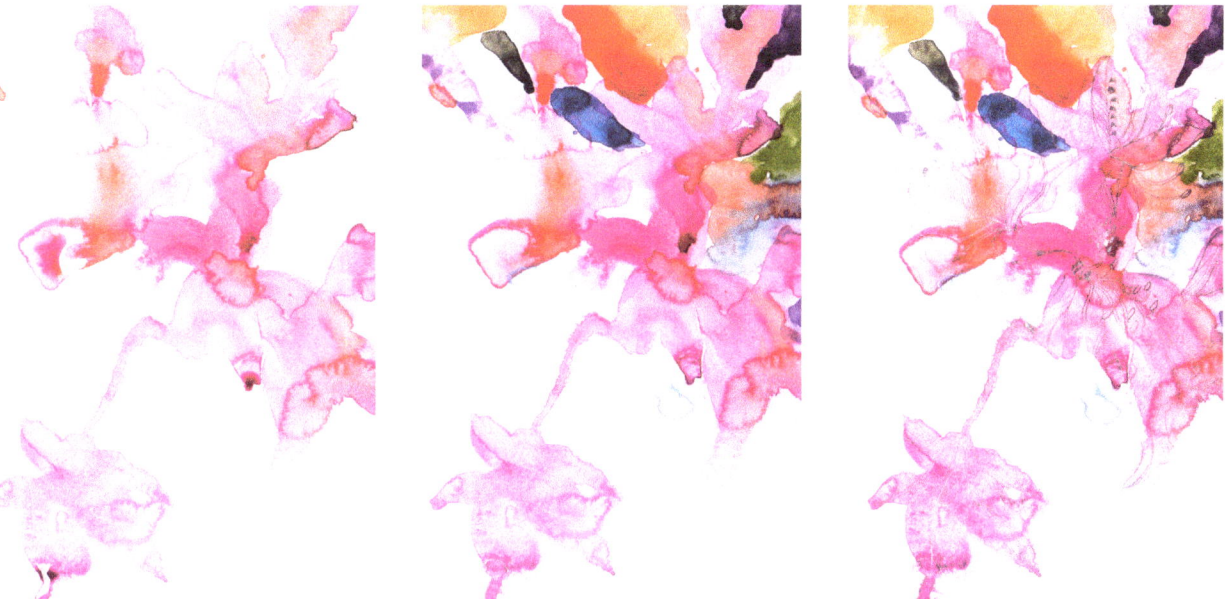

◀ ▲ Select a photograph that interests you. Begin with bold paint marks to represent the areas of the photo that fascinate you the most. I started with a loose and quick representation of the flowers in watercolor on all three pages.

Start with a big brush as it can make your first marks more expressive and courageous. It is always a good idea to start with bold, self-assured marks and then add more detail.

Leave these initial marks to dry. When you add your next layer, try to respond to the marks already on the page. My color choices bear little resemblance to the original photograph as I responded to what was already on the page and chose colors that I thought worked well with the original pink marks.

Finish the page by drawing in detail with a pen or pencil and emphasize the parts of the original photo that appeal to you.

Collecting Interesting Objects to Draw

When you are in nature or just walking around your neighborhood, be on the lookout for small natural objects or interesting items and artifacts such as leaves, twigs, a fallen flower, pinecones, or found objects. Seek out small and interesting items with detail that you would like to explore further and that you can take home and draw at your leisure. Select items you would like to understand better through drawing. In contrast to the speed-drawing exercises earlier in this book, taking your time with a drawing can also be rewarding.

When you spend a few hours drawing an object, you learn so much more about it, which allows you to fully appreciate its complexity and beauty. The extra detail and understanding you gain from looking at the real thing rather than a photograph can be quite amazing. By slowing down and observing, you can connect with your found object in a way that is quite special.

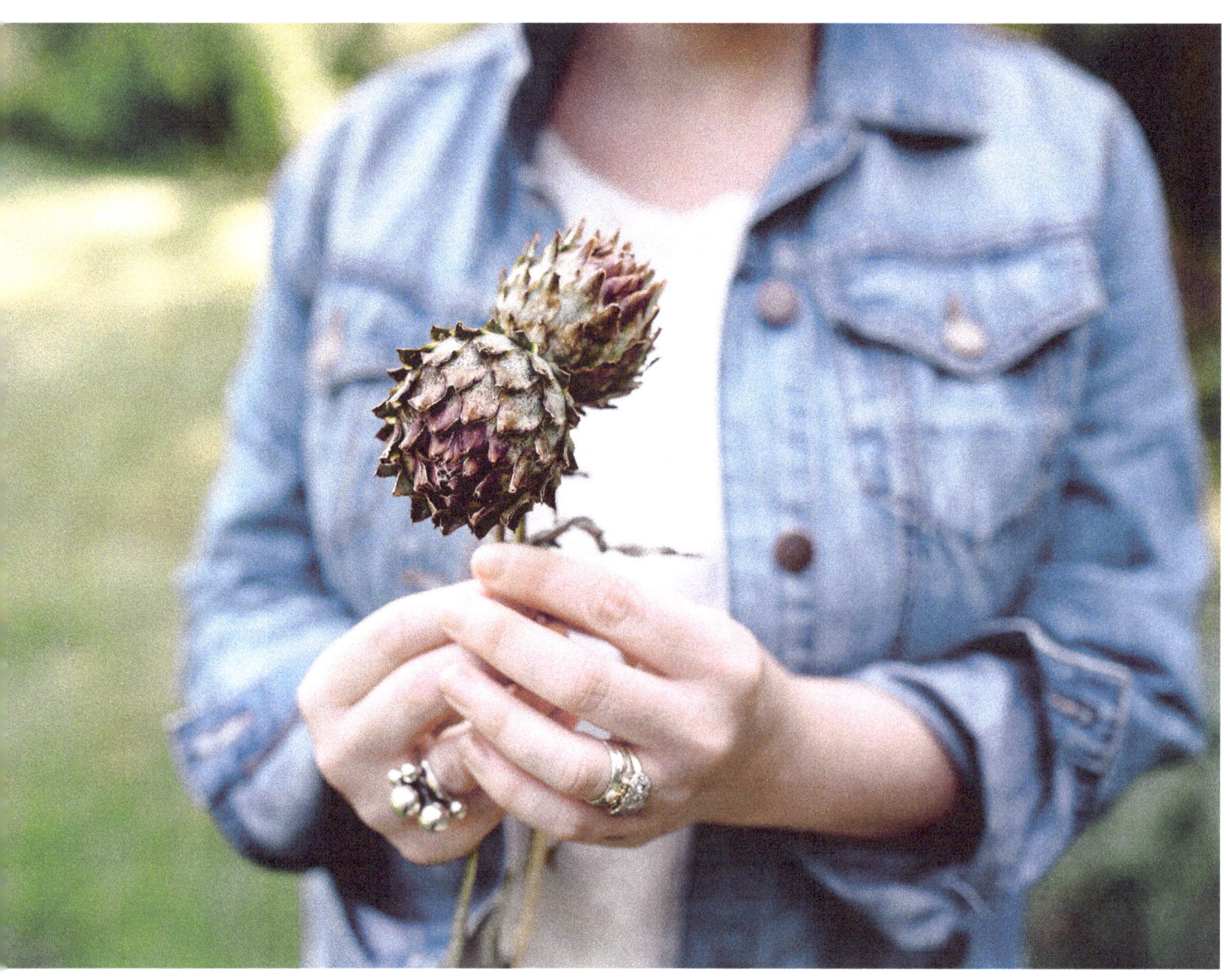

Slowing down and taking your time to draw
something can be revealing and rewarding.
You see and appreciate intricate details that
you may have never noticed before.

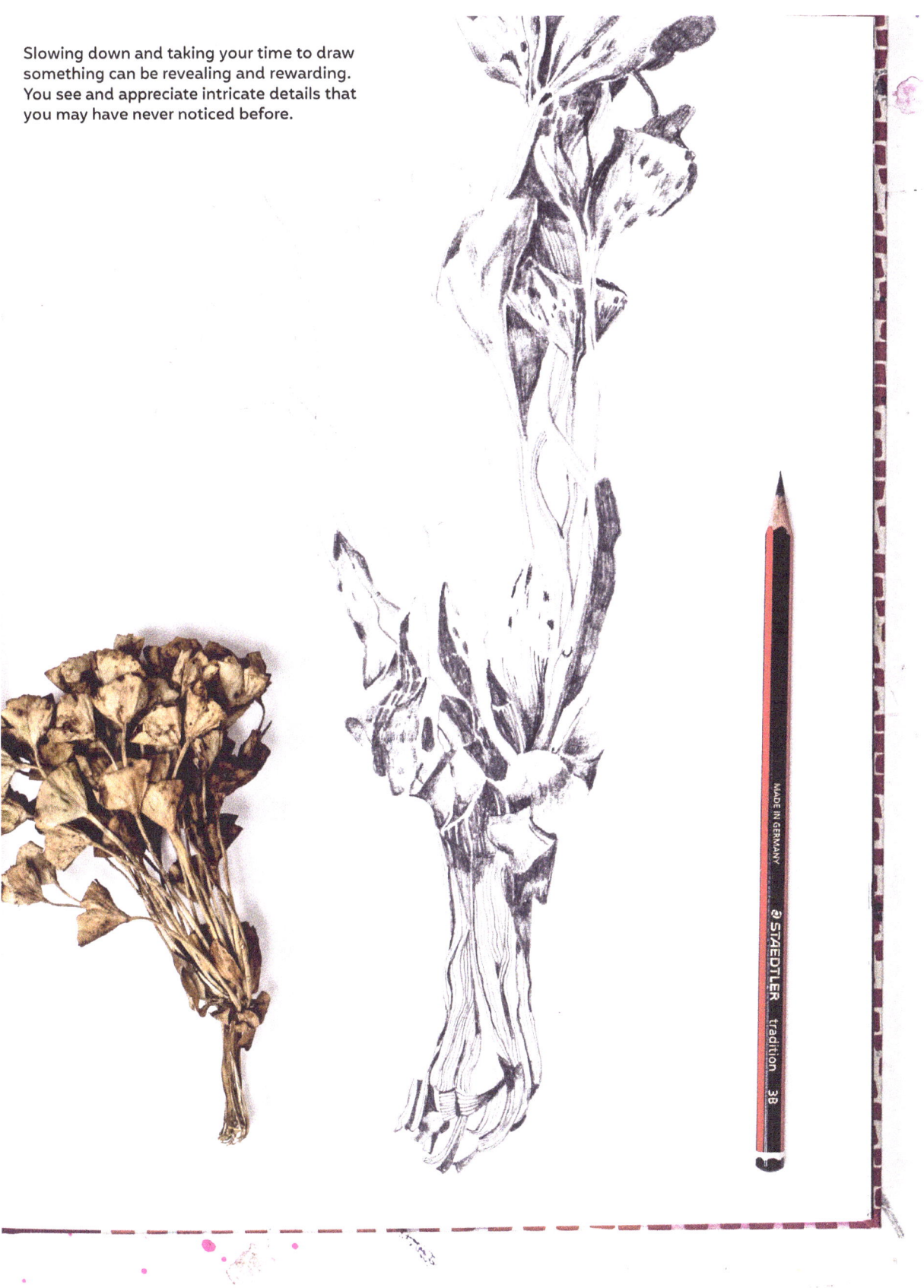

Taking Your Sketchbook Outside

In addition to seeking reference material that you can use when you get home, create and draw while outside. Getting into nature can be good for your art practice and your spirit. There is an increasing amount of scientific research that links being in nature with mental well-being, stress reduction, and increased creativity. For me, going to a park, to the coast, or to the countryside to draw or paint can be a beautiful and affecting experience.

You might find energy and interest in a city-scape, townscape, or the built environment. Choose the type of setting that resonates with you. Being in the location as you draw can lead to a real richness and vibrancy in your art.

Your eyes see so much more detail and nuance than you can ever discern from a photograph. I frequently draw from photographs but drawing what I see and experience outside brings a whole new dimension to my work. A photograph is flat. Being in the actual setting you are drawing allows you to understand the three-dimensional quality of the space. It also allows you to interpret and experience the place with all your senses. You are creating a sensory memory: hearing, feeling, smelling, and touching.

Drawing or painting outside means you are absorbing a whole array of sensory information that aids your understanding. It also takes a certain amount of confidence and lugging materials around, but the rewards are worth it.

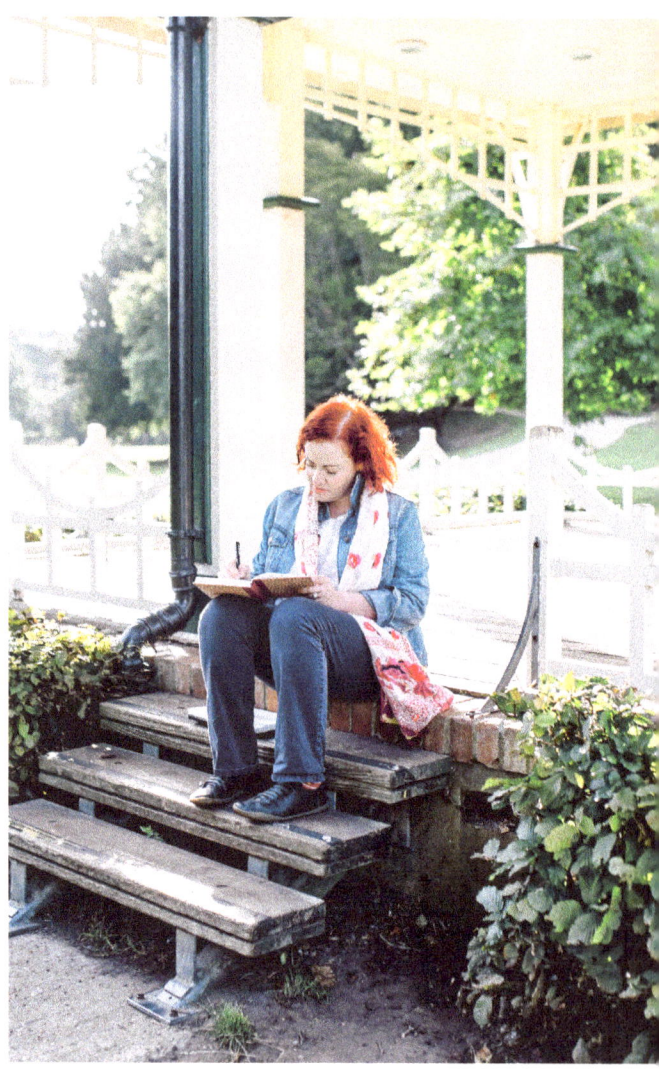

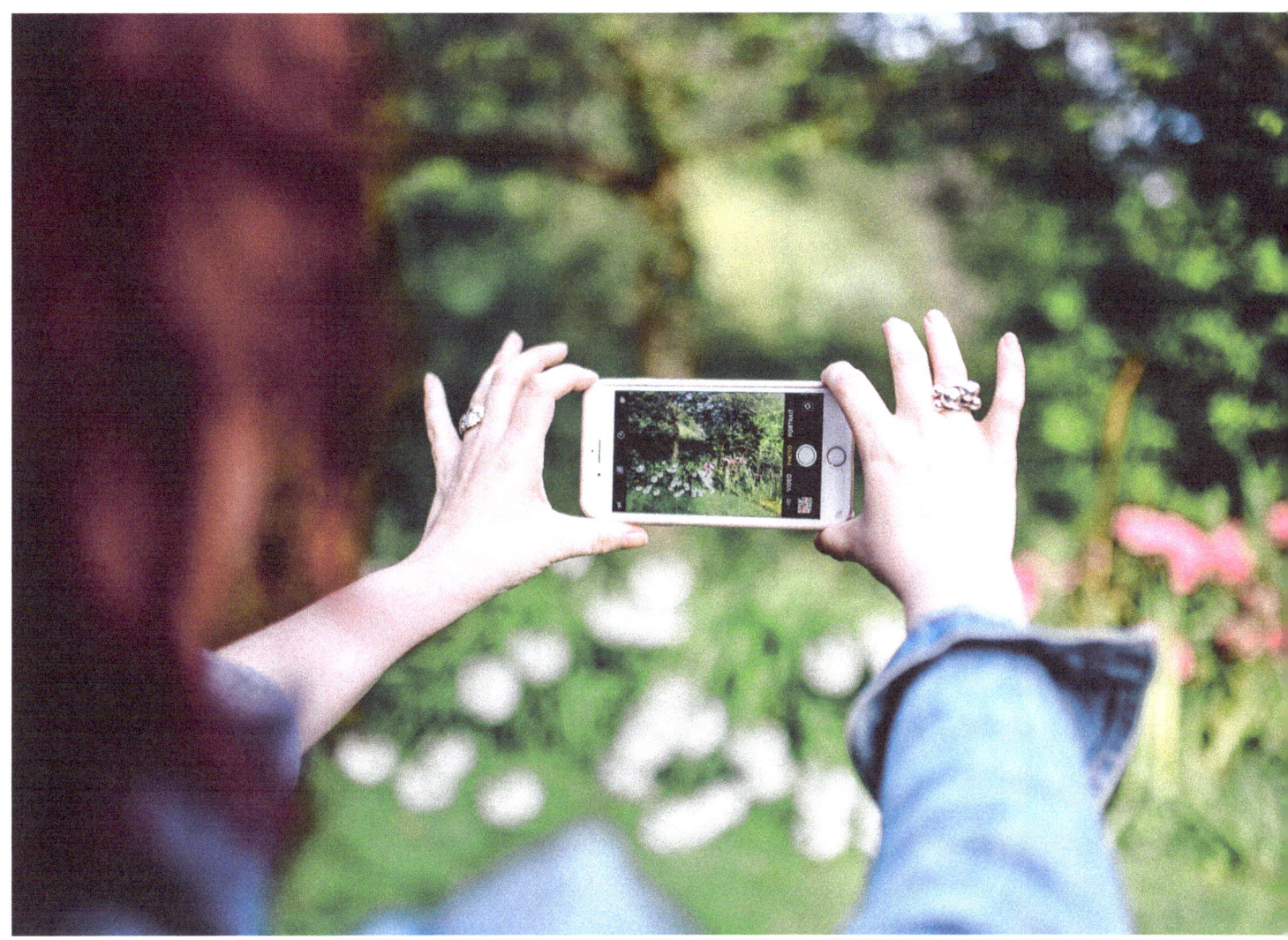

Here are a few techniques to help you create art when outside:

SELECT A VIEW

Consider using a viewfinder when selecting a scene to help you think about composition and the elements you want to concentrate on. You can create a simple, expandable, cheap, and cheerful viewfinder with two L-shaped pieces of card that you move around to create a rectangular frame. Or you can use your camera or phone to help select the area on which you'd like to concentrate. These techniques frame or crop the landscape so you can think about what attracts your attention and what you want to leave out. They can help you design the composition on your page as you frame the landscape to reflect the shape of your paper. You then put away the viewfinder and draw what you see in the area you have selected.

RULE OF THIRDS

The rule of thirds is a composition guideline that can be an effective aid when selecting a landscape to draw. Imagine your page with a virtual grid over it which splits the page into three sections horizontally and three sections vertically. The theory behind the rule is that significant aspects of your composition will be more visually pleasing if they are placed along or at the intersection of these lines. Think about the rule of thirds when selecting a horizon line or when positioning a tree or building. The basic premise is that a focal point is more interesting and a composition more dynamic if the key elements are off to the side and not right in the center of the page.

▶ Use the rule of thirds in landscape painting and drawing: mentally draw lines across your view, splitting it horizontally and vertically into thirds or nine virtual boxes. Place important aspects of your composition on the lines or at the line intersections. Off-center compositions tend to be more interesting and reflect the way our eyes travel around a page. Any rule is, of course, made to be broken, so experiment with where you place key elements of your drawing or painting and consider the effect it has.

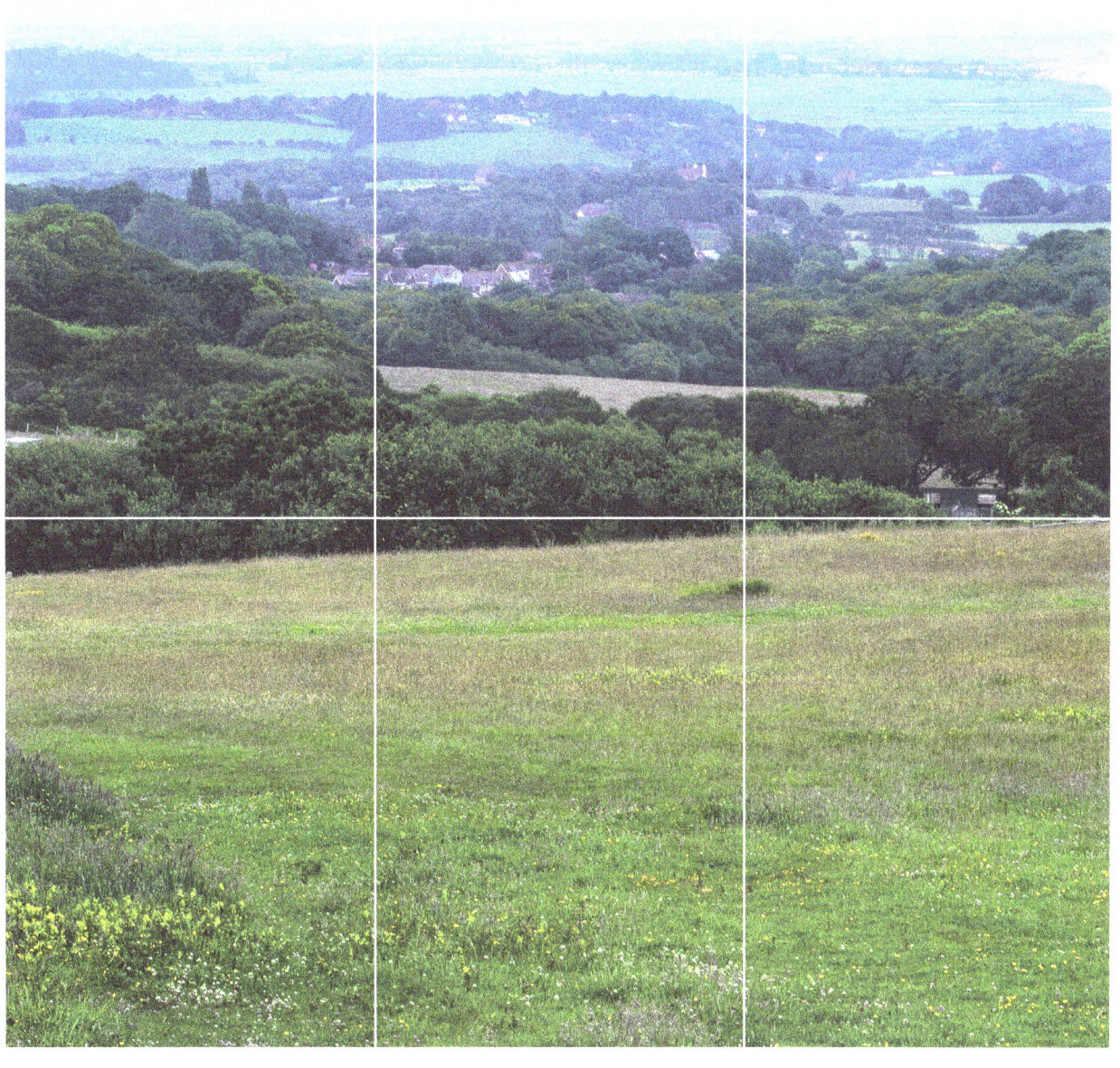

SIMPLIFY

Decide on the essential aspect of the view you have selected and simplify your art to reflect this. Distill the view into its most crucial aspects. Experiment by drawing or painting only the most important part of what you see. Mentally break down your view into bold shapes and eliminate the details. Squinting or scrunching up your eyes while you look at your view can help you to focus on the dominant shapes and silhouettes.

▼ ▶ Experiment by making quick studies and slower ones and see which you prefer. If you prefer to paint quickly and intuitively, you may want to take a stack of small pieces of thick watercolor paper and make quick studies on these prior to painting in your sketchbook.

The following ten studies were painted in watercolor on pieces of paper only 2 × 3 inches (5 cm × 7.5 cm) in diameter. The landscape has been simplified to little more than three stripes of color and painted with a big, fat brush. Painting many quick, small studies is a technique to help simplify your approach and get into the flow of painting without being too self-conscious about the outcome.

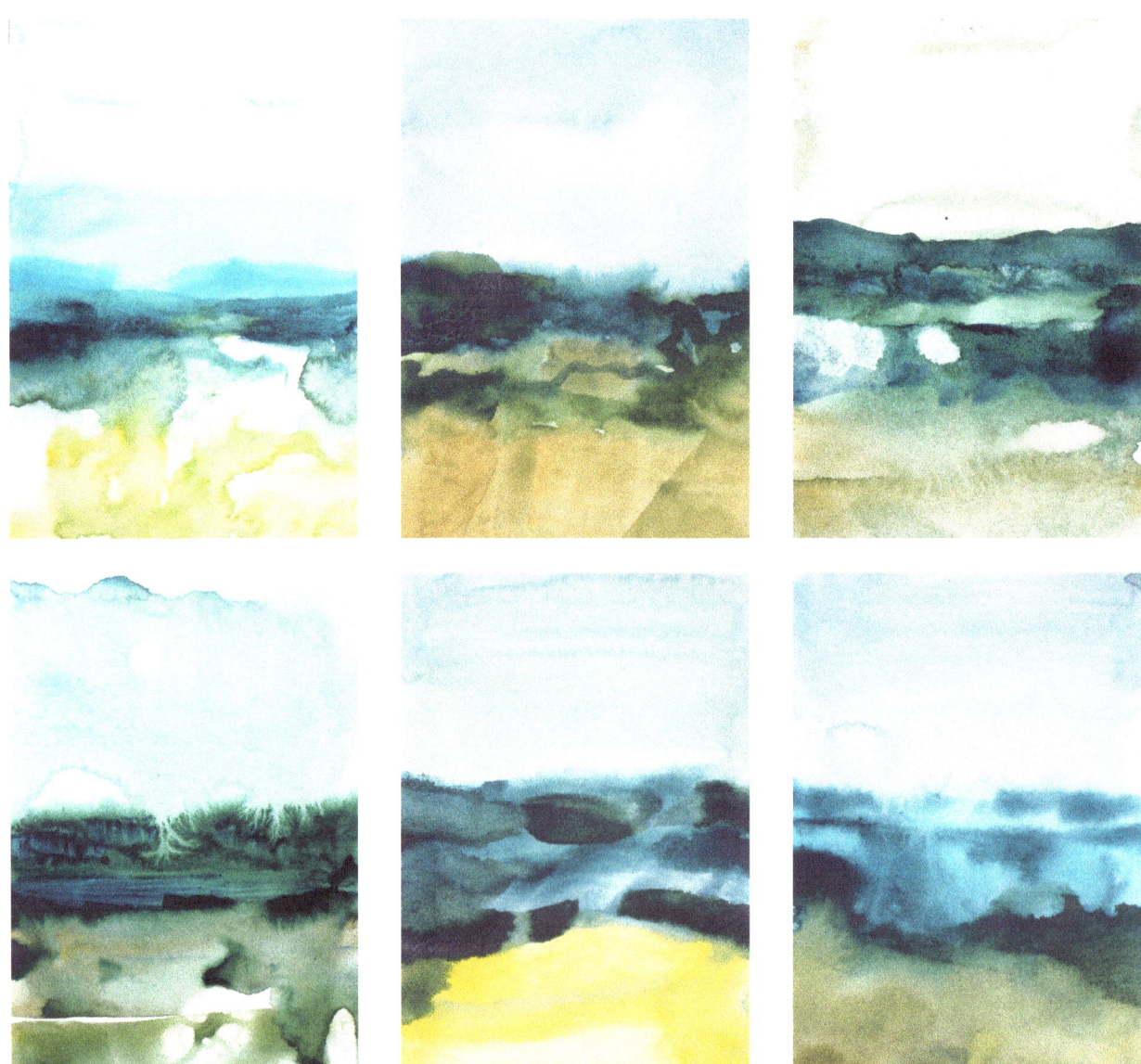

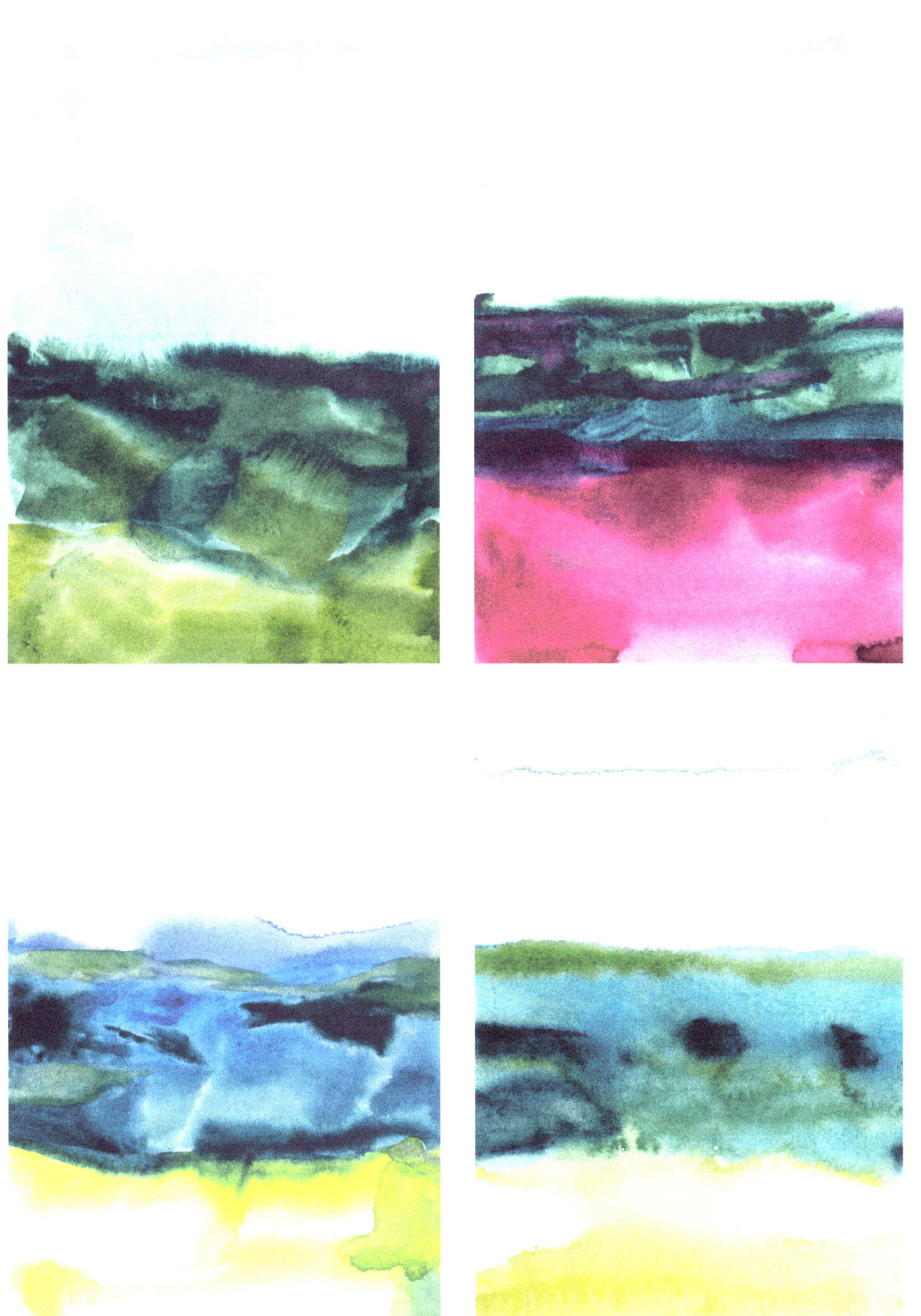

ELIMINATE OR ILLUMINATE

I encourage you to interpret the landscape you are viewing in your own unique way. Paint and draw the elements that interest you. We all see things differently and are moved by different elements. Before you start drawing or painting, ask yourself about what you see and why it appeals to you. Which aspect is most important?

Your sketchbook page doesn't have to be a superrealistic copy; you can choose to completely ignore parts, move trees around, and eliminate areas while illuminating others. Seek out the aspects that most intrigue you and think about how the landscape makes you feel, so you can capture a moment in time. Your drawing or painting is your interpretation. Your response is as much about you within the space as it is about the space itself.

NEAR AND FAR

When painting a landscape, know that the farther away something is from us, the bluer, duller, and fainter it looks. When something is closer to us, it looks darker, brighter, and more detailed. Use this knowledge to create the effect of space when painting a landscape that stretches into the distance.

PATHWAYS THROUGH

Consider the metaphorical pathway through your artwork and how you can direct the eye to your focal point. In a landscape, think about a path to your focal point, i.e., how you can lead the eye to the element that you want to emphasize. Our eyes often follow lines in paintings, so experiment with how you use directional lines to point to the area of most interest. This can be an actual path or the removal of dark or heavy shapes that appear to block the way.

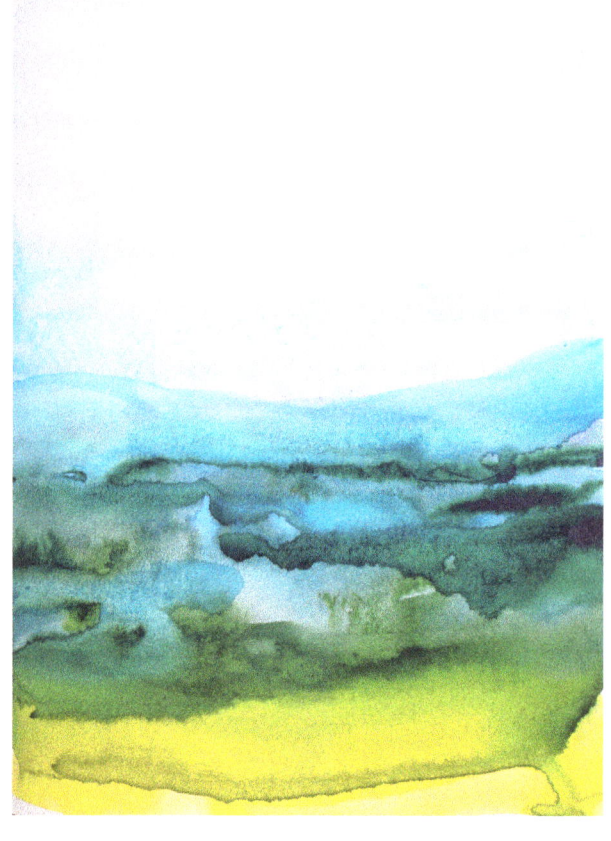

Distill the view to its simplest shapes and aspects.

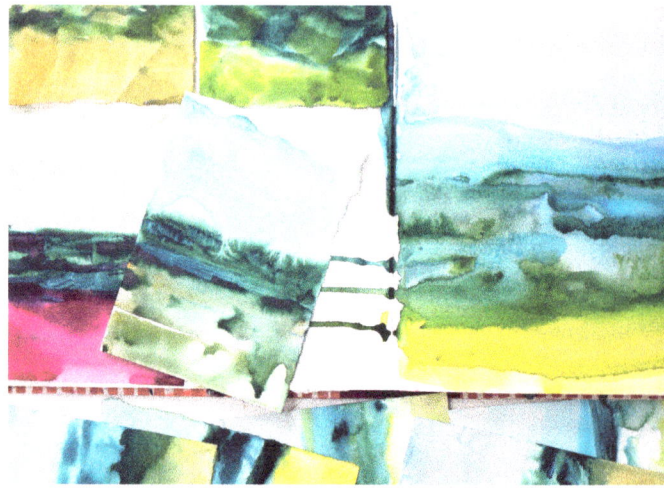

Small watercolor paintings tend to wrinkle and warp. An easy way to straighten them out is to let them dry completely, fold them inside an old tea towel, and iron them. Then paste them into your sketchbook.

SEEKING INSPIRATION INSIDE

Inspiration is everywhere. I invite you to walk around your home, thinking about the objects you surround yourself with, the things you have chosen to live with—the items, clothes, juxtapositions, patterns, books, and furniture that you have invited into your living space.

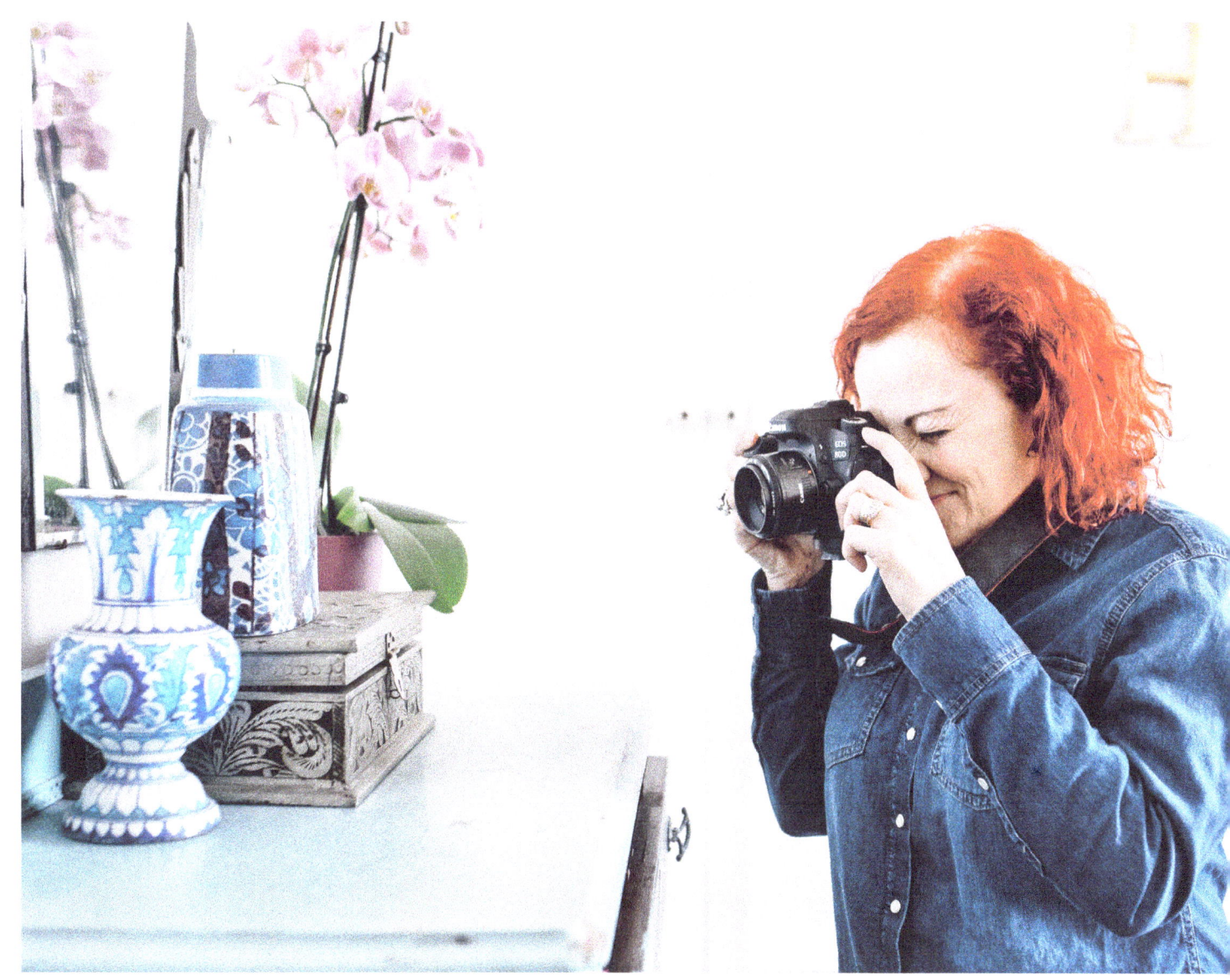

Beauty in the Mundane

The act of seeking and finding more beauty in our day-to-day lives can have a cumulative effect. The more beauty and interest we appreciate, the more beautiful and interesting our lives become. Sometimes the ordinary can be extraordinary. Try to see things with different, fresh eyes to uncover and discover what interests you as you go about your normal everyday routines.

Walk around your home with your camera or camera phone. Take photos of anything you find visually appealing—a small corner, an interesteing juxtaposition, or a shadow. Think about how you frame your photograph and whether it captures the area or element that interests you the most.

Gather three or four objects that have some meaning to you and use them together in a still life arrangement. It may be that you don't actually draw or paint the objects themselves in a representational way, but instead explore something of their essence in your sketchbook.

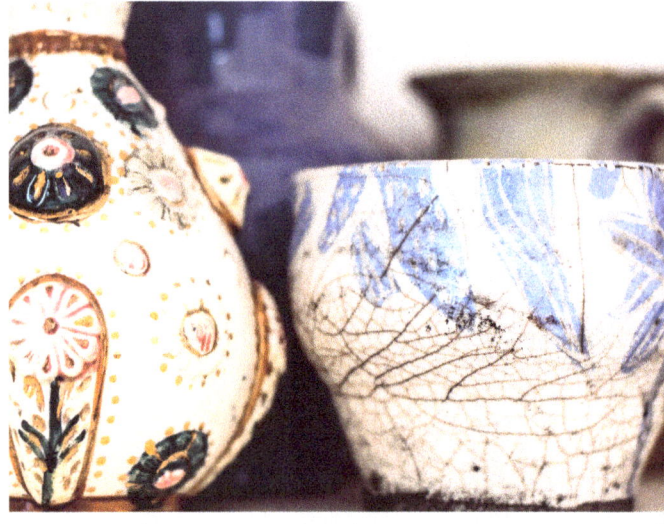

When selecting a subject to draw or paint in your sketchbook, consider both its aesthetics and its meaning and importance to you. This small pot was made at a pottery class with dear friends and reminds me of the special time we had. As well as its sentimental meaning, I am also drawn to the interesting patterns, cracks, and fissures in its glaze.

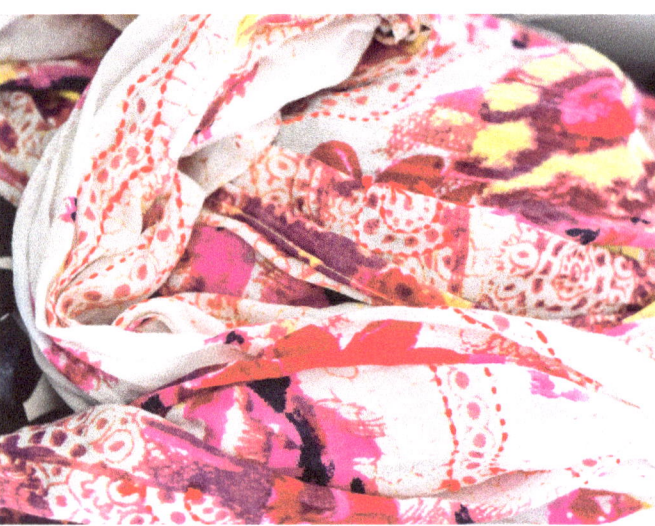

Try to find inspiration in your daily life. This scarf was scrunched up in my laundry pile. I appreciated the shapes it created and the colors as they folded together. I used it as a starting point for some abstract pages in my sketchbook.

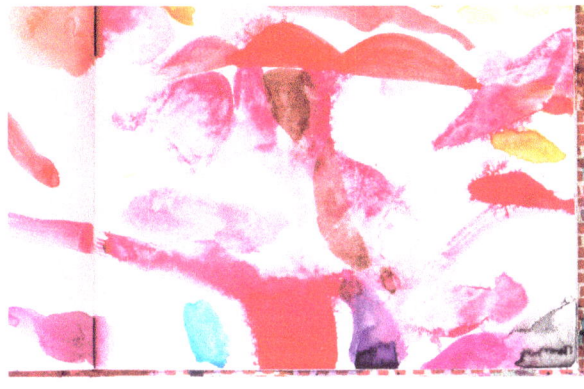

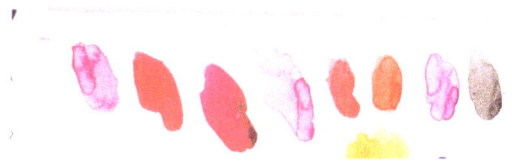

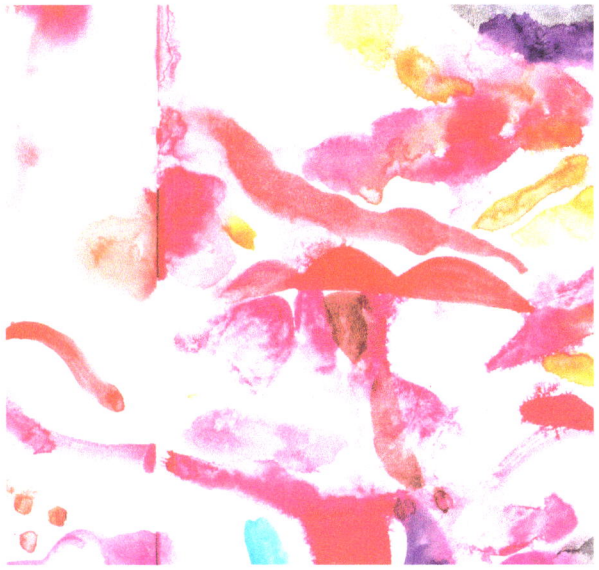

Select something of interest to draw or paint in your home. Consider the color palette you would like to use if you're using paint. Perhaps test out a limited color palette on a scrap of paper to see how your chosen colors work together.

Think about how you could distill your subject's essence into some basic shapes or abstracted patterns. Here I made a few quick watercolor brushstrokes in response to the photograph of the scarf. I immediately sprayed water on it to make the painted lines flow, dance, drip, and merge into each other.

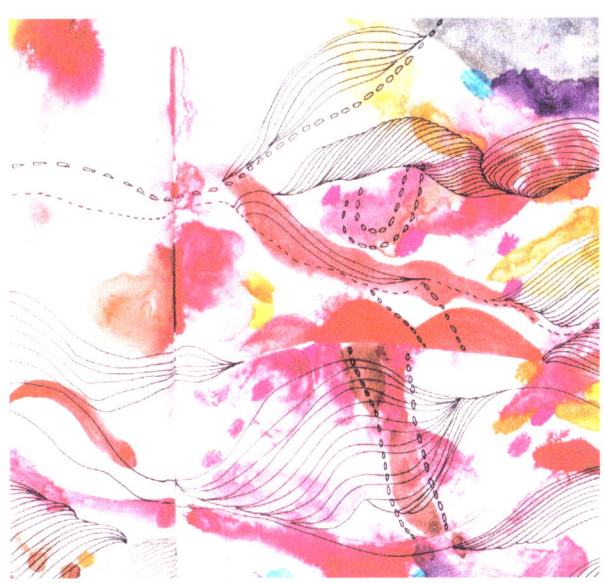

Let your initial marks dry and then respond to them, adding more detail with your chosen materials. I added hand-drawn detail using pencil, a fine-line black pen, and wax crayons.

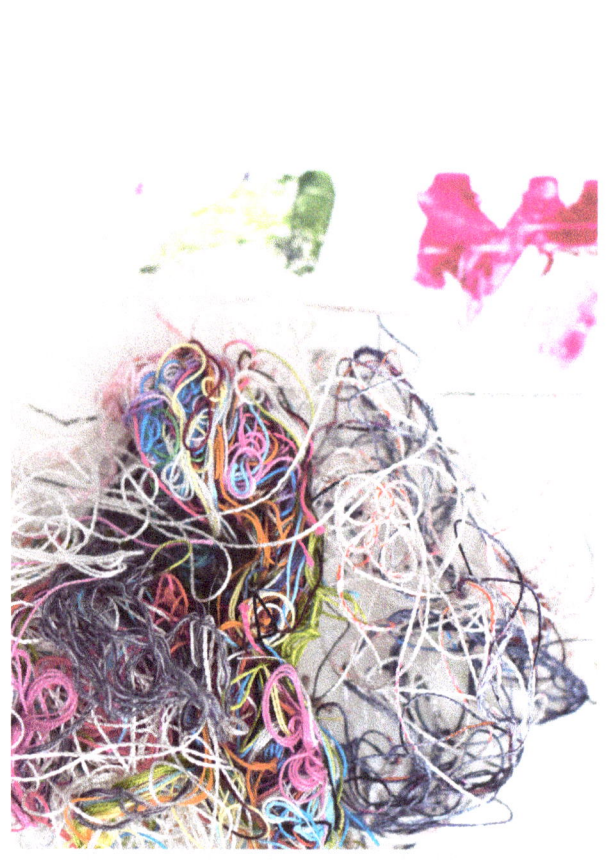

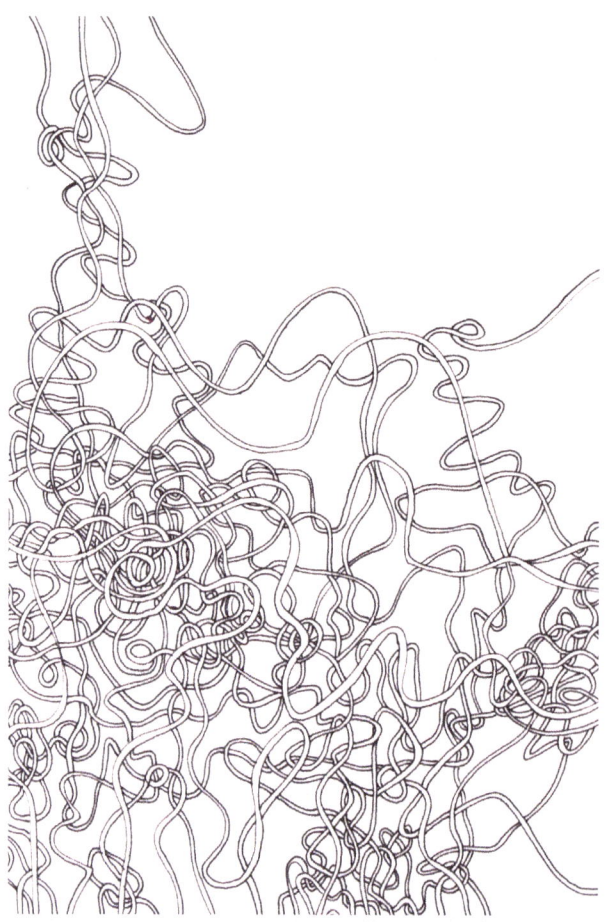

Find subjects in your home to explore in your sketchbook. This is a tangle of embroidery thread that was in an old bag of sewing accessories.

This page in my sketchbook was inspired by the interwoven lines of the embroidery thread. When you select something to draw from your home, always consider what it is about your subject that appeals to you. Be curious about your own interests to better understand them.

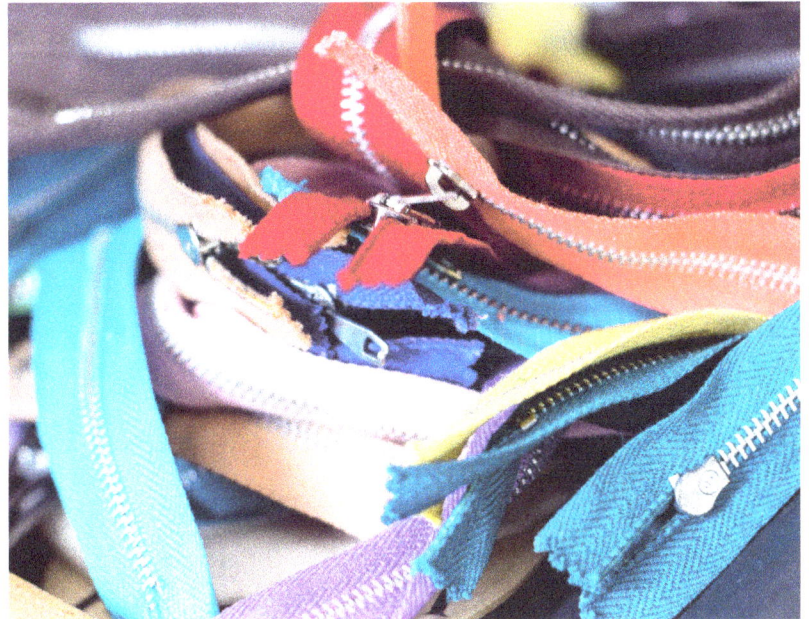

◄ This bag of zippers caught my eye. I was attracted to the shapes, the zig-zag texture of the fabric, and the patterns created by the metal teeth.

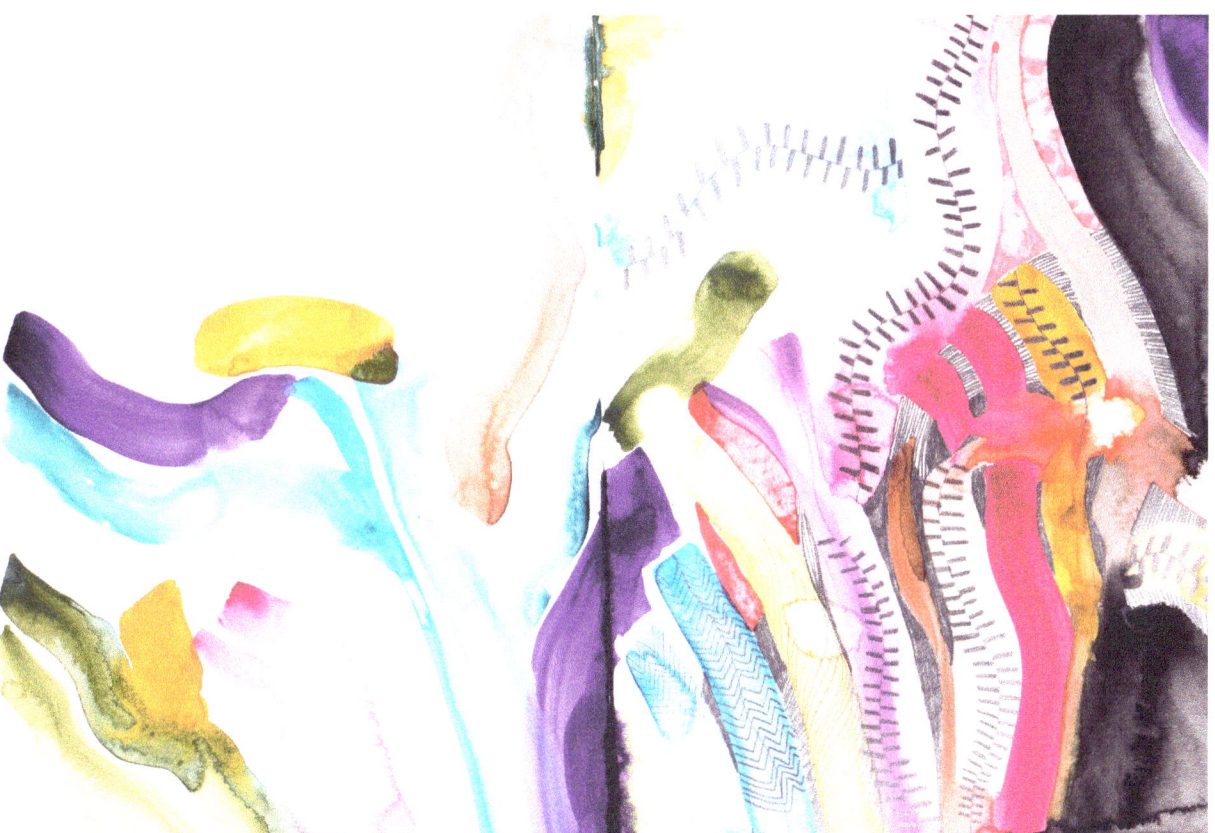

The zippers inspired these pages in my sketchbook. Take your own photographs and seek tiny inspirations in your home to kickstart some exploratory pages in your sketchbook. It only takes a small flicker of enthusiasm to get going. Once you have a small starting point or something to respond to, you can push off from the harbor and set sail.

MIXED MEDIA

Experiment by using your favorite art materials and supplies on the same page. Go wild with different combinations to discover the alchemy that can come from mixing things up. Sometimes combinations work beautifully and sometimes they don't. The element of surprise is part of the process of discovery.

The "anything goes" mentality can help you enjoy the process without being too concerned or judgmental about the outcome. When we give ourselves the freedom to explore and experiment, we learn more about ourselves as artists and creative people.

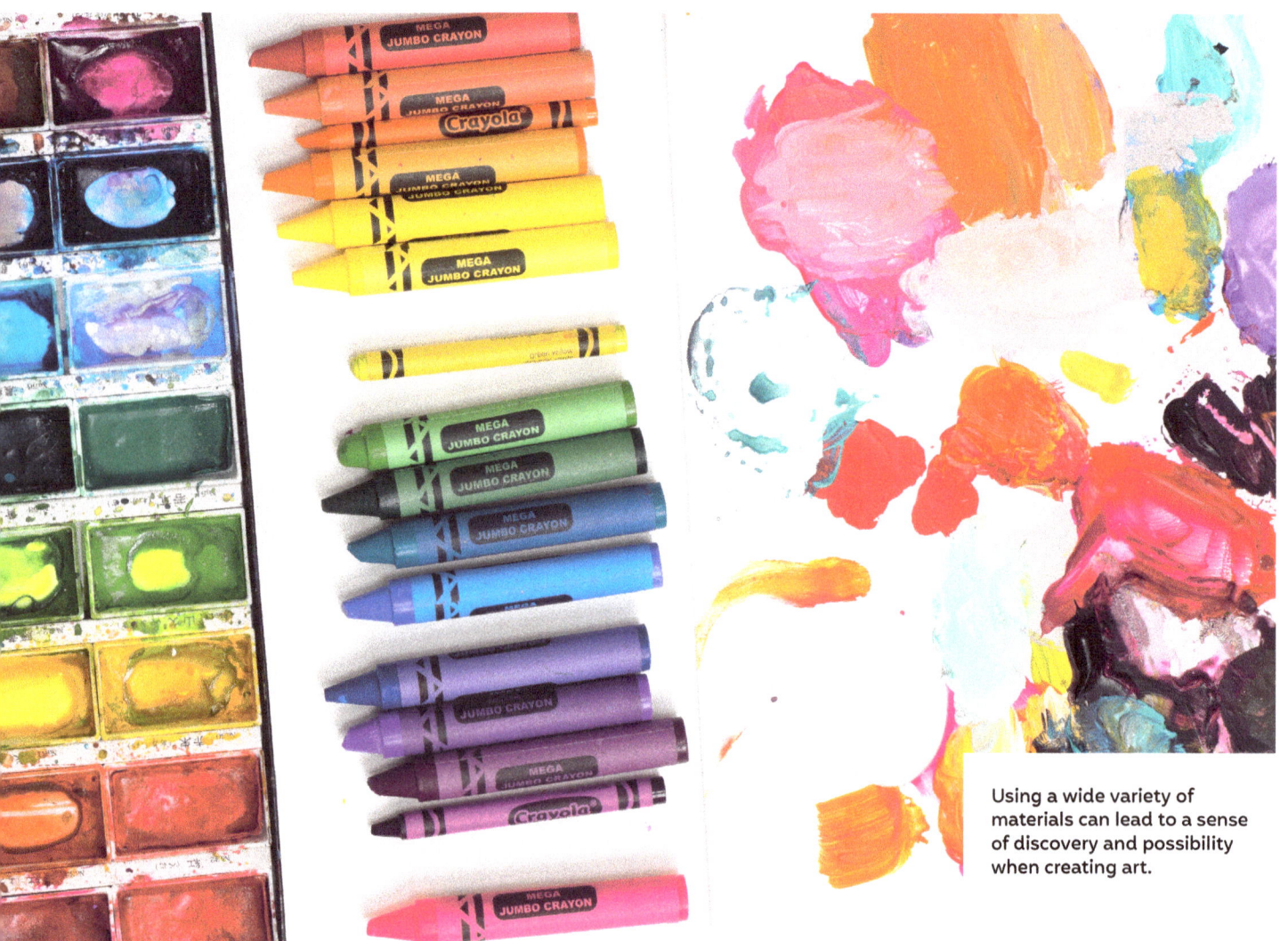

Using a wide variety of materials can lead to a sense of discovery and possibility when creating art.

Playing with our materials allows us to better understand their properties and unique qualities. This open inquiry about our art materials allows us to relish and enjoy the sensory and tactile nature of making art. In touching the materials, we create a physical connection to our tools and our creations. Be bold. Foster a sense of adventure and revelation by using the materials you have in various combinations. Here are some of my go-to mixed-media combinations:

Paint and Pen

Create a colorful background or foundation layer using watercolor or another type of paint, then draw over it with a black fine-line pen. Do this intuitively, with no plan or external stimuli; just let your imagination be your guide. Then try it again, this time responding to an external reference such as a photo or object. Consider which process you prefer and why. The more you understand the way in which you like to work, the more you can create a process that feels personal and meaningful.

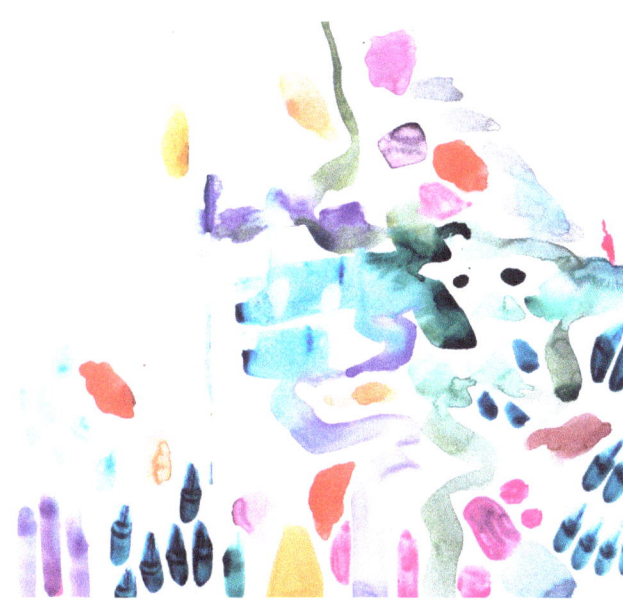

On these pages, I made marks using paint with no plan or purpose. Instead I just enjoyed exploring the paint and witnessing how the colors worked in relation to each other, responding to the last mark on the page when I placed my new mark, and letting what I had already created inform my next step. Try this yourself. Create an initial painting with no set plan; just follow your instincts and listen to your inner wisdom.

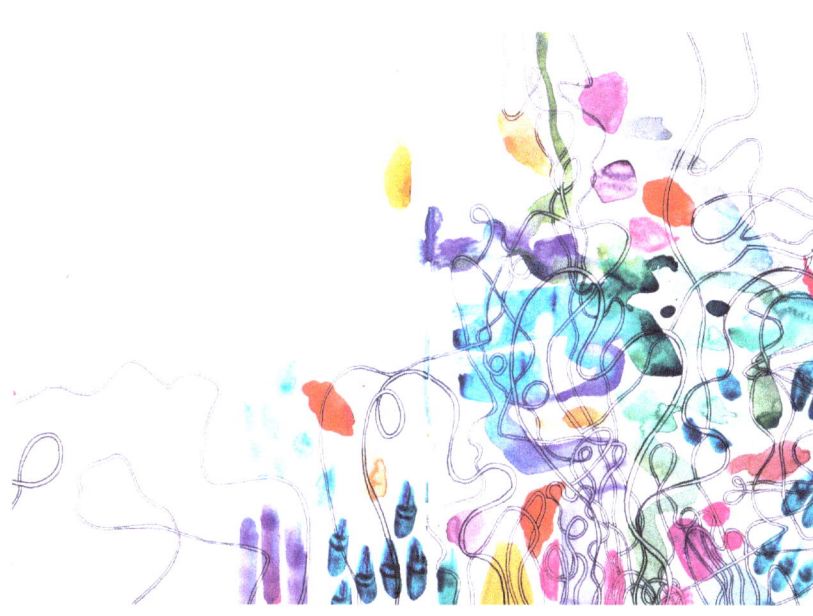

Once the initial layer has dried, add details in pencil or pen. You may emphasize certain aspects of your original painting. Think about your own vocabulary of expressive marks and how you can incorporate them.

Resist Technique

Wax crayons or candles under watercolor paint act as a resist to the paint, creating an interesting effect. Use children's wax crayons to draw an image and then paint over it with watercolors. The wax resists the paint that has been brushed over the top, and the paint pools into small dots on the original crayon drawing.

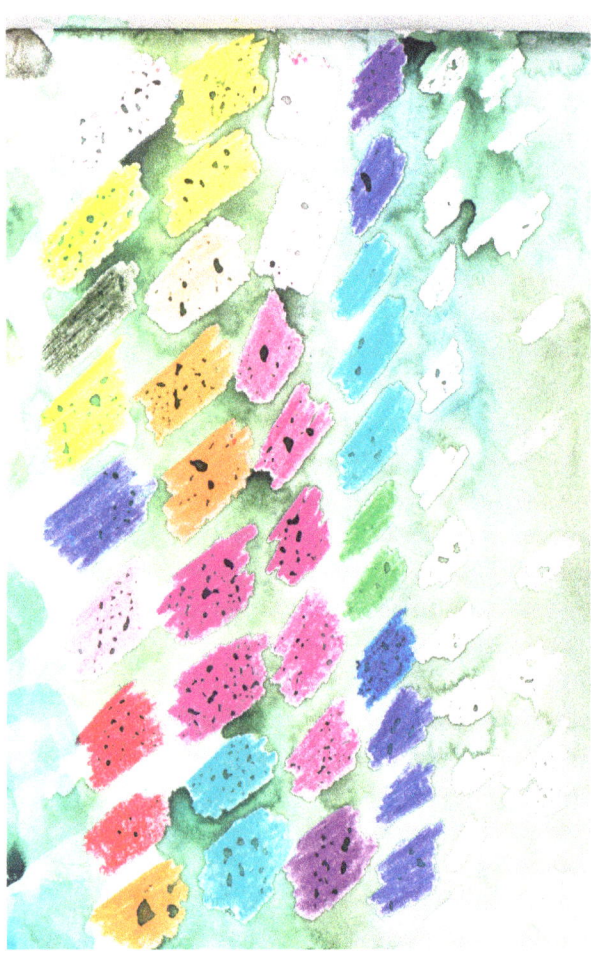

▲ ▶ Wax crayons under watercolor paint create a pleasing contrast as the wax acts as a resist to the paint. Experiment with different color combinations to create different effects.

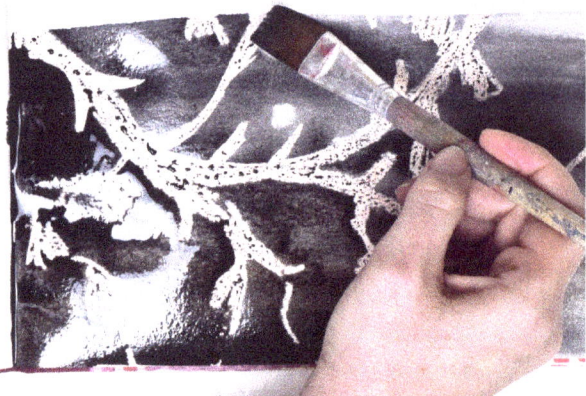

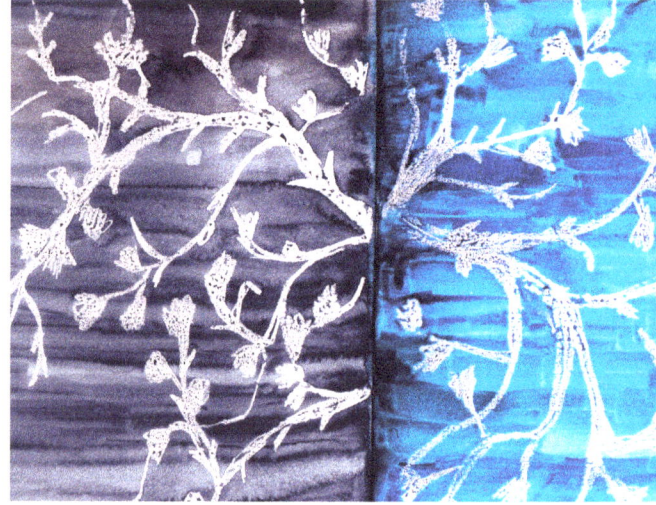

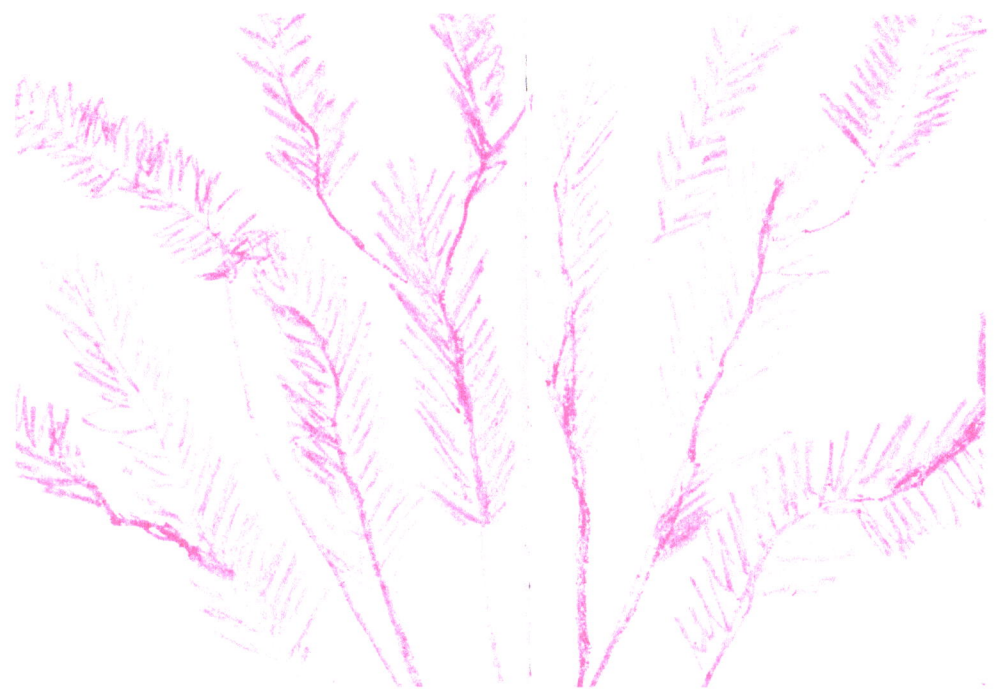

Complete a drawing in wax crayon.

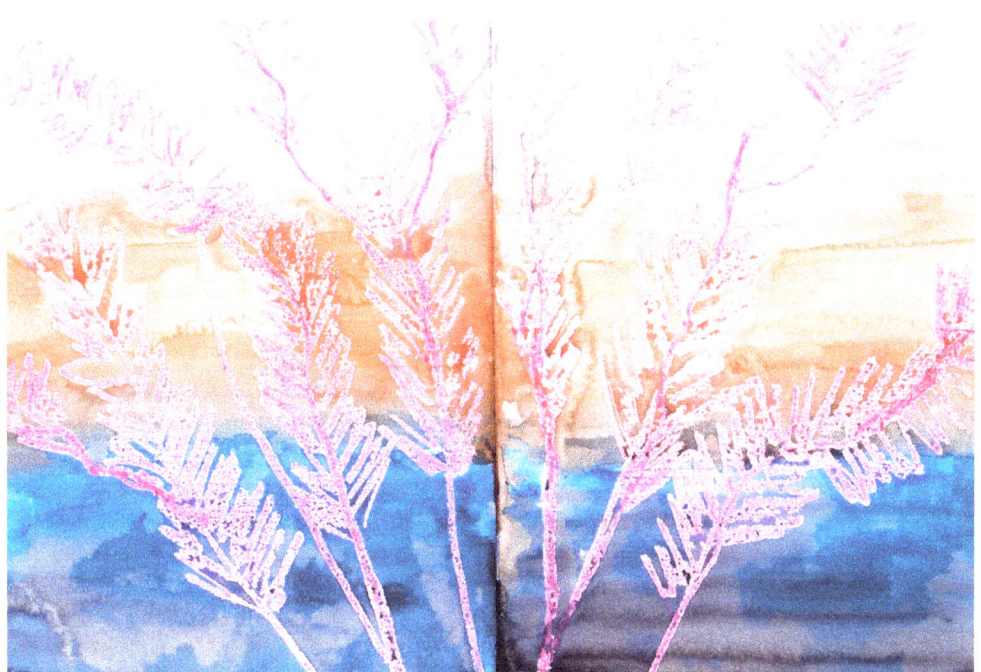

Draw with wax crayons and then paint over them with watercolors. Here I used three stripes of different watercolors to create the illusion of a landscape.

Underpainting

Underpainting is when you paint an initial layer of paint and this serves as a base for subsequent layers of art. Experiment with creating a wild and wonderful underpainting using a variety of tools, colors, and techniques. Do absolutely anything you want on this first layer, knowing that you will later paint over it. Once the underpainting has dried, create a more planned composition over it. A ghost or elements of your original underpainting will show through, giving your sketchbook page a more complex and distinctive look.

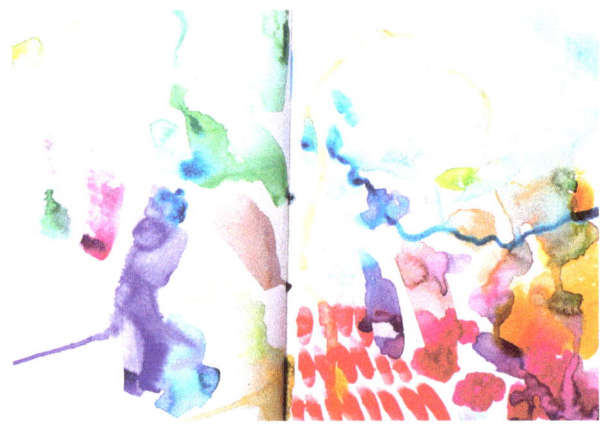

Create an initial layer. You can be bold and expressive on this layer as you know you will be painting over it. This gives you the freedom to create anything—magical things often happen in this freedom. I used watercolor paint and created many colorful blobs and splotches and then misted water over the marks to encourage the paint to mix on the page. Once you complete this first layer, leave it to dry.

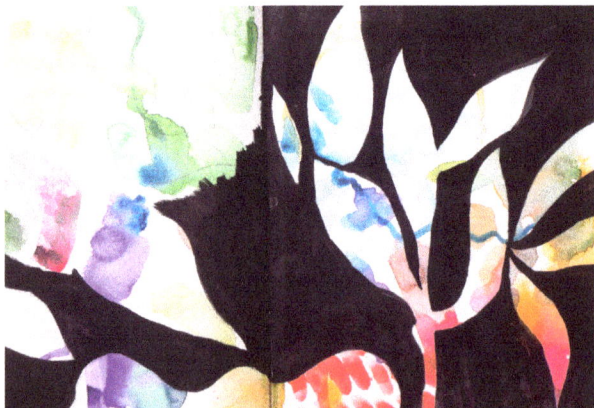

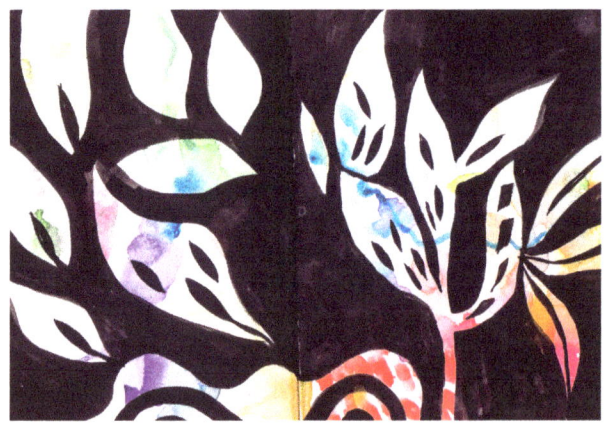

▲ This second layer was created with black ink, but you can experiment with acrylic paint or another material. I drew a quick outline of the leaves in pencil and then filled the negative space with black ink. When deciding where to place the leaves, I selected the aspects of the underpainting I liked the most and wanted to remain visible. Choose the areas you want to highlight and those you are happy to eliminate. Your choices will dictate what you paint over and how you position your composition. You may see something in your underpainting that sparks an idea for the next layer.

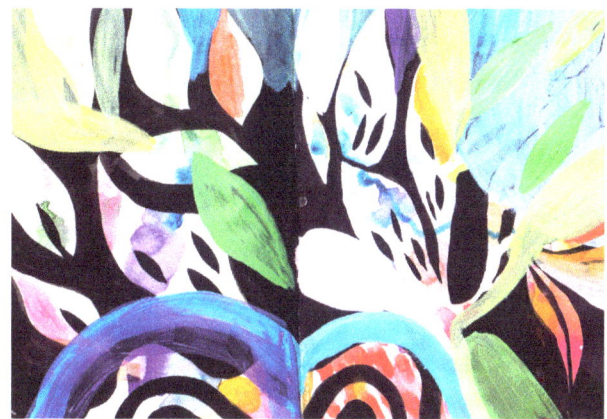

Keep building up layers and experimenting with different materials and color combinations. The third layer on this page used acrylic paint.

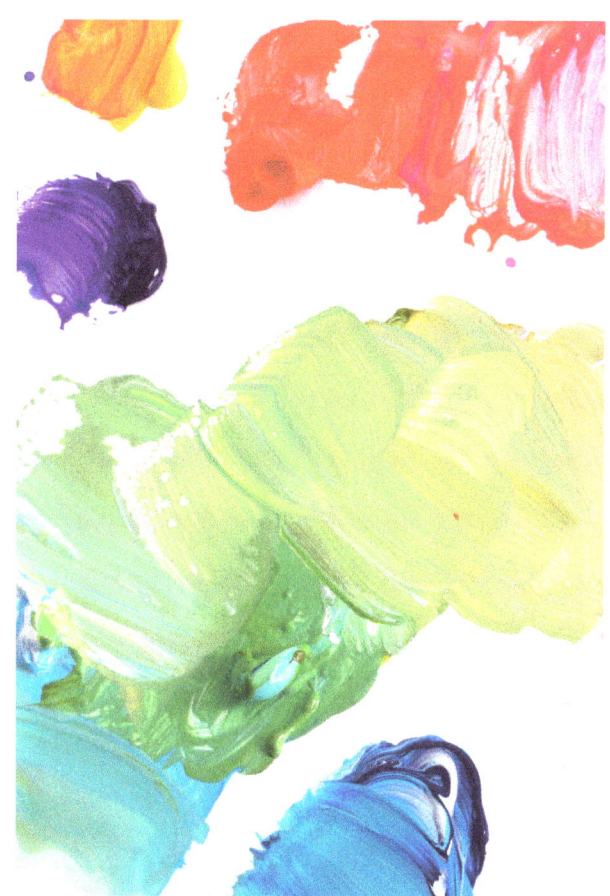

You may see something in your underpainting that sparks an idea for the next layer.

I selected a few colors of acrylic paint to put on my palette. Experiment with the way you set up your palette when you use paint from a tube. Consider how the layout affects how you feel as you create and the art you produce. A limited palette of three or four colors encourages you to mix them and be intentional about what you use. You may prefer an organized palette or to be messy and intuitive.

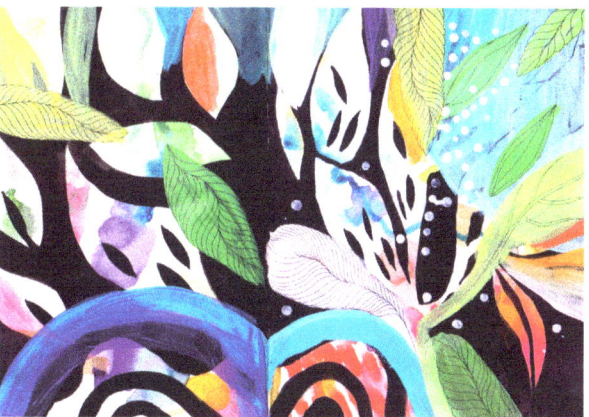

Start bold and progress to more detailed and nuanced applications with each subsequent layer. Add finer and final detail to your last layer.

Mixing It All Up with Multiple Layers

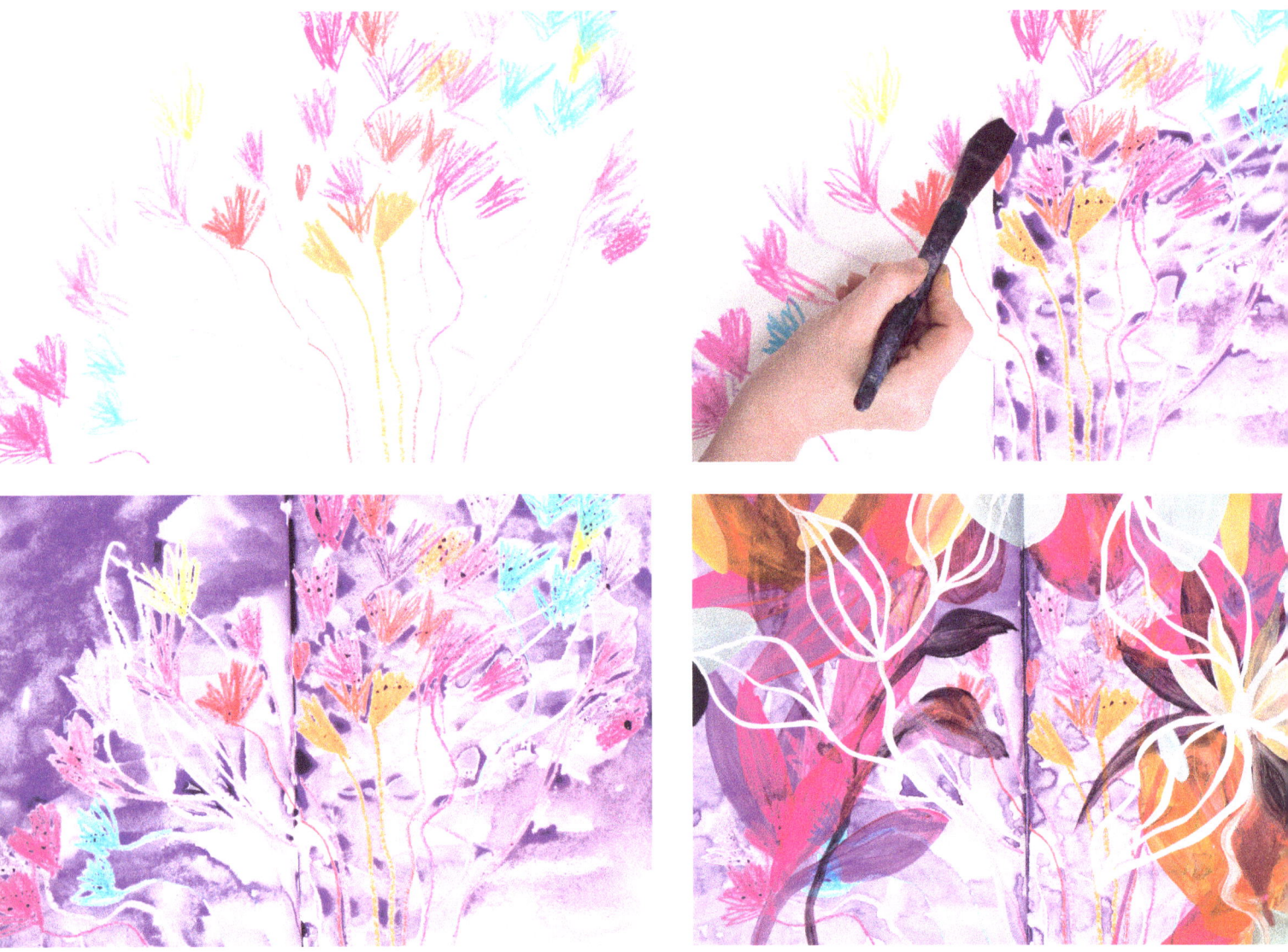

▲ I created this double-page painting from my imagination but was influenced by flora and foliage. I drew the first layer in wax crayon. The second layer is watercolor paint that resists the wax crayon. The third layer is acrylic paint. This trio of materials, in this order, is one I particularly like and come back to often. The wax crayon creates high-intensity points of interest and the watercolor provides a subtle background that helps the top layer of acrylic paint stand out.

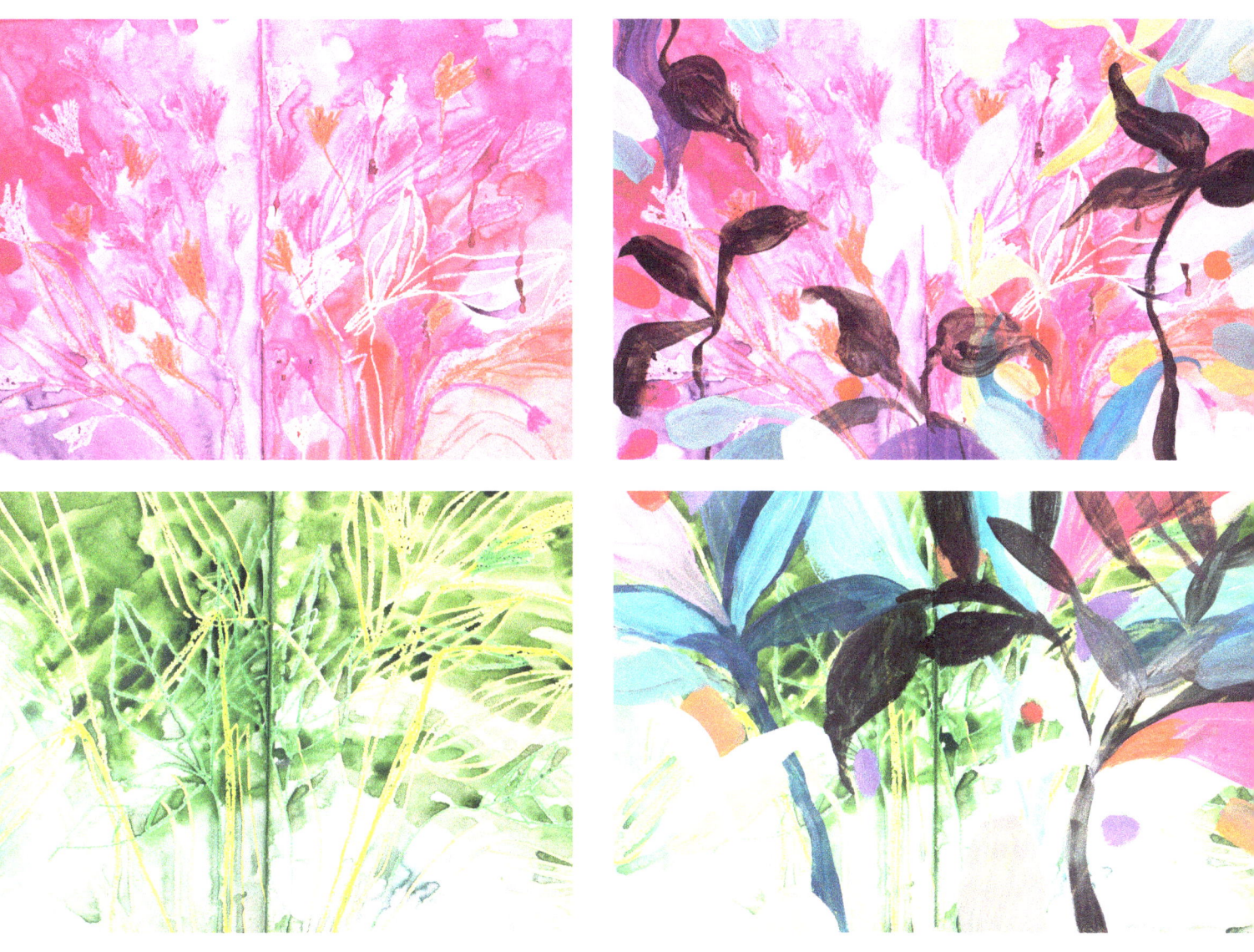

▲ I created these two spreads using the same combination of three layers—first wax crayon, then watercolor paint, and finally acrylic paint. Mixing materials in unique and interesting ways will make your art and sketchbook feel personal to you. Experiment to find a combination of art materials that reflects you and the art you want to create.

Making Your Own Tools

Experiment and create your own mark-making tools from discarded, foraged, and found bits and pieces. Search your home or neighborhood for items you could dip into ink to make interesting and unusual marks. Consider the items you throw away or use discarded natural pieces such as:

- String
- Nails and screws
- Old credit cards
- Bits of cardboard
- Old packaging materials
- Twigs
- Leaves
- Feathers
- Pinecones

If you need to make your objects easier to work with or dip into the ink, tape them to an old pencil or stick to effectively turn them into brushes and tools. Pour ink on an old plate or container and dip your tools into it. Discover the marks they make on your page. Be free and easy: play and see whether you can create a series of marks that you may want to permanently incorporate into your sketchbook pages or artistic practice. I often use this technique to make my own patterned papers on cheap copier paper that I then use as collage material for my sketchbook.

Making your own tools and experimenting with marks in this way is a good reminder to remain playful, curious, and inventive in your art making. Creating with random objects leads to elements of surprise. It encourages you to not be too attached to the outcome, takes the pressure off, and allows you to approach your art making with a sense of discovery.

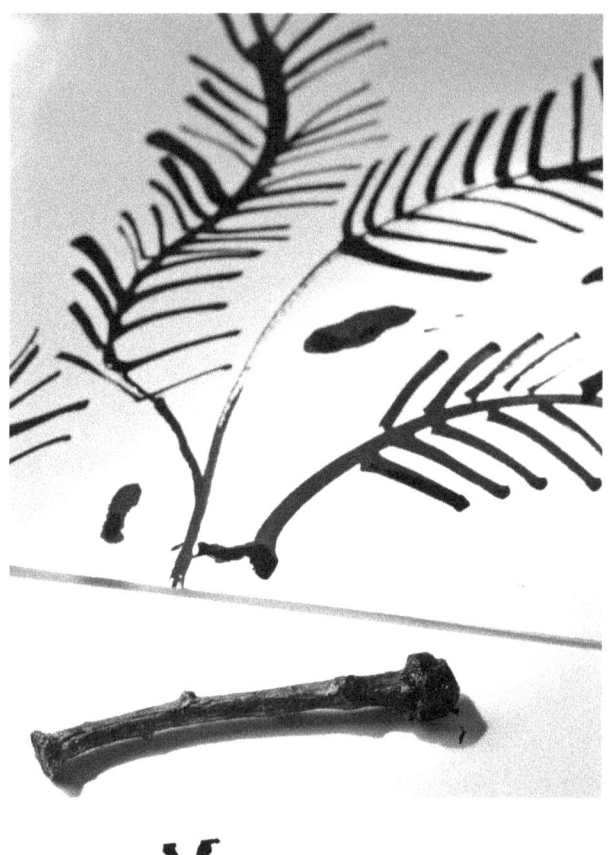

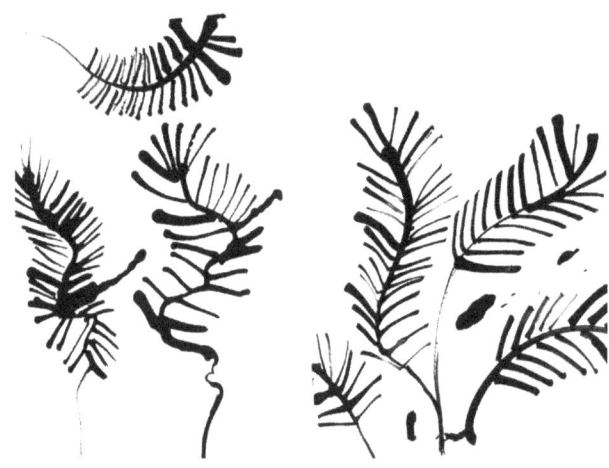

▲ Creating art with unusual objects, such as twigs, can help you to foster an attitude of discovery and inquisitiveness.

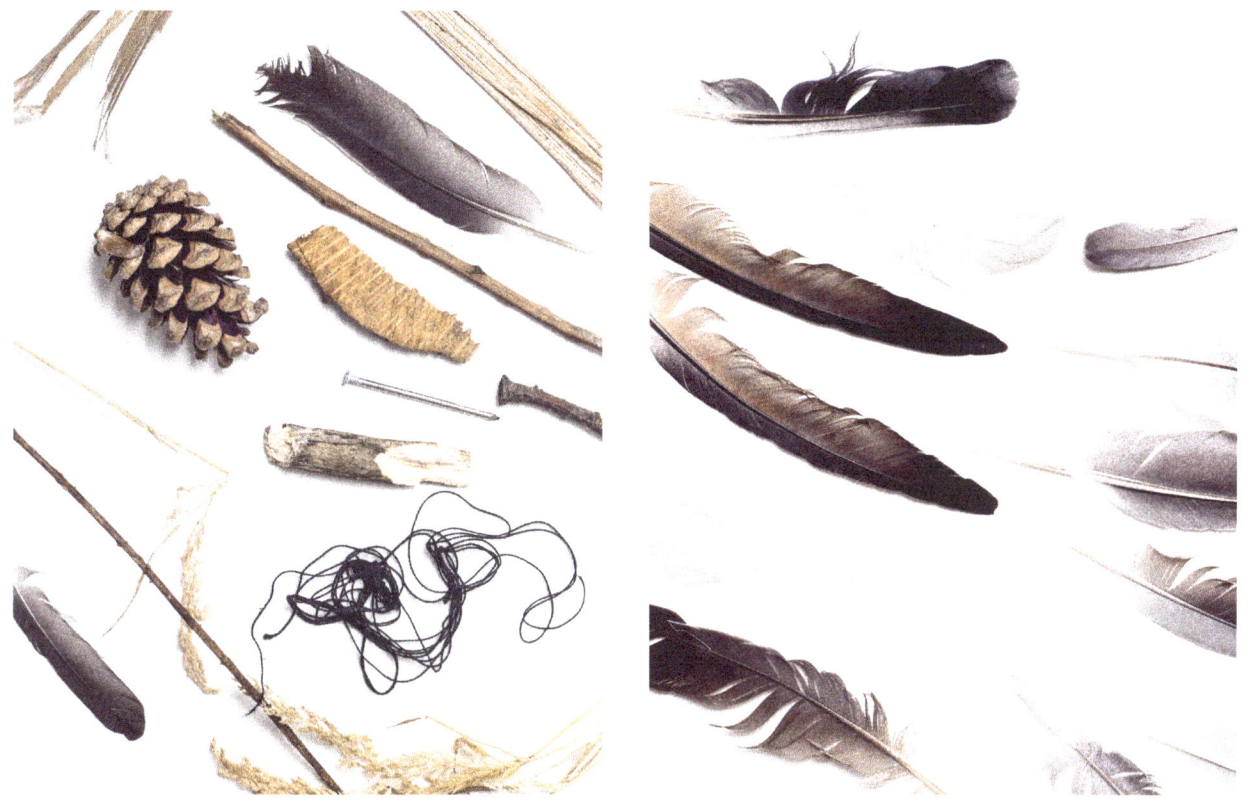

▲ Gather together an array of small, low-value objects that you are happy to dip into ink and turn into art implements.

Once you acquire your own lexicon of marks, whether it be through homemade tools or experimentation with your art supplies, incorporate these marks into your art. Your personal palette of expressive marks can make your art come alive and be a unique expression of you. Your marks are the foundations of your art and part of your signature style. Play with pressure and speed and see what you can make from very little. Use many pages, don't limit yourself, and be expansive.

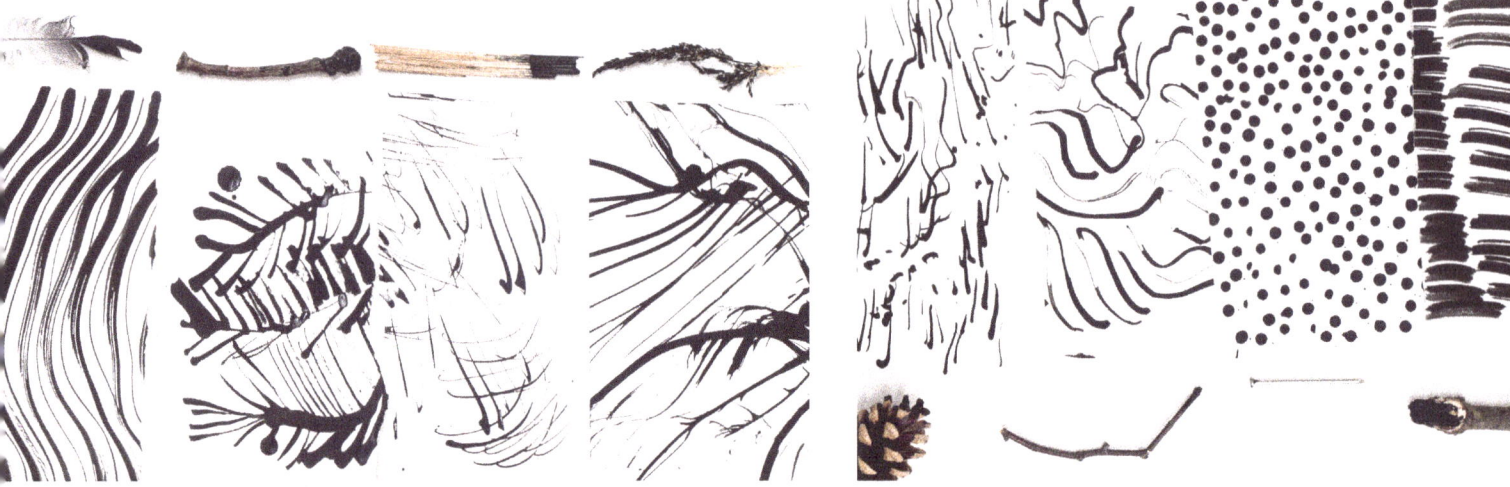

Discover the mark-making possibilities of each item and which ones resonate with you.

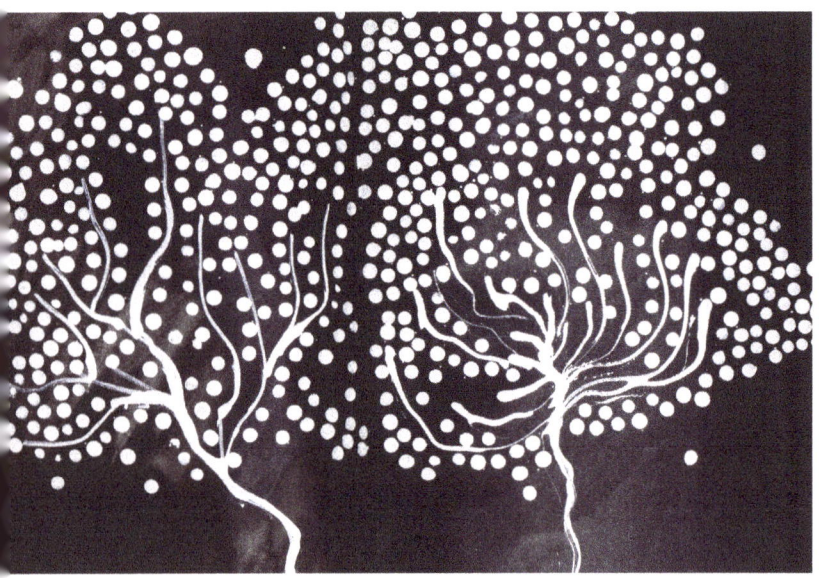

▲ ▶ Consider how you can incorporate the marks you have made into your sketchbook practice. Perhaps you would like to create papers for collage use or draw and paint with these tools. Here I used nails and twigs to create leaf shapes. I used black ink on white paper and white ink on a page I prepared with a base coat of black ink.

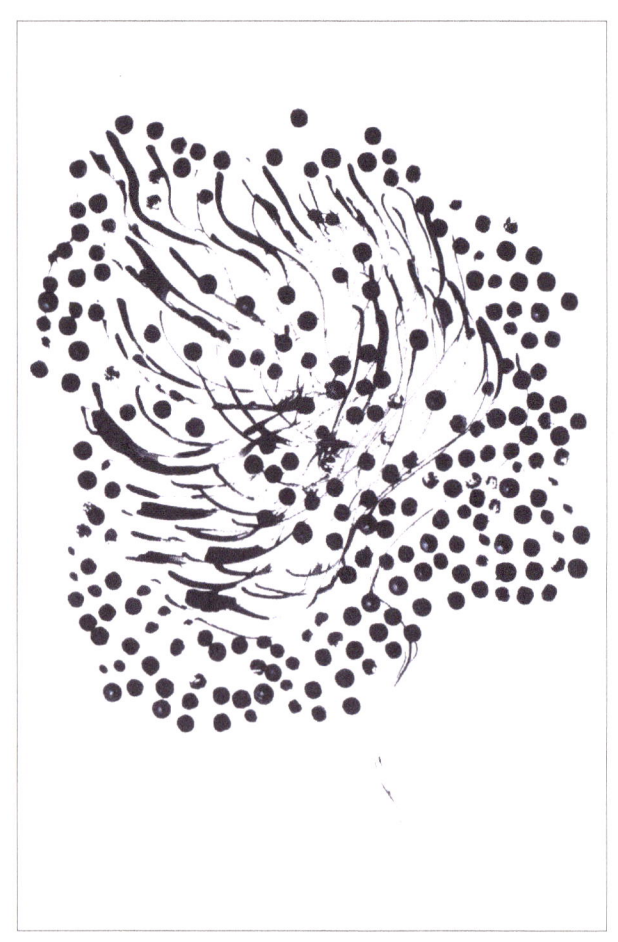

Collecting and Making Papers for Collage

Keep a collection of interesting, diverse papers to use for collaging in your sketchbook. Use them to create a background or cut them up to incorporate into an artwork. Just sorting and sifting through a pile of hand-chosen papers can prompt ideas. Enjoy the tactile nature of sifting through a stack of lovingly collected papers.

▼ Looking through a selection of papers you have made or collected can prompt ideas and spark a starting point from which to create.

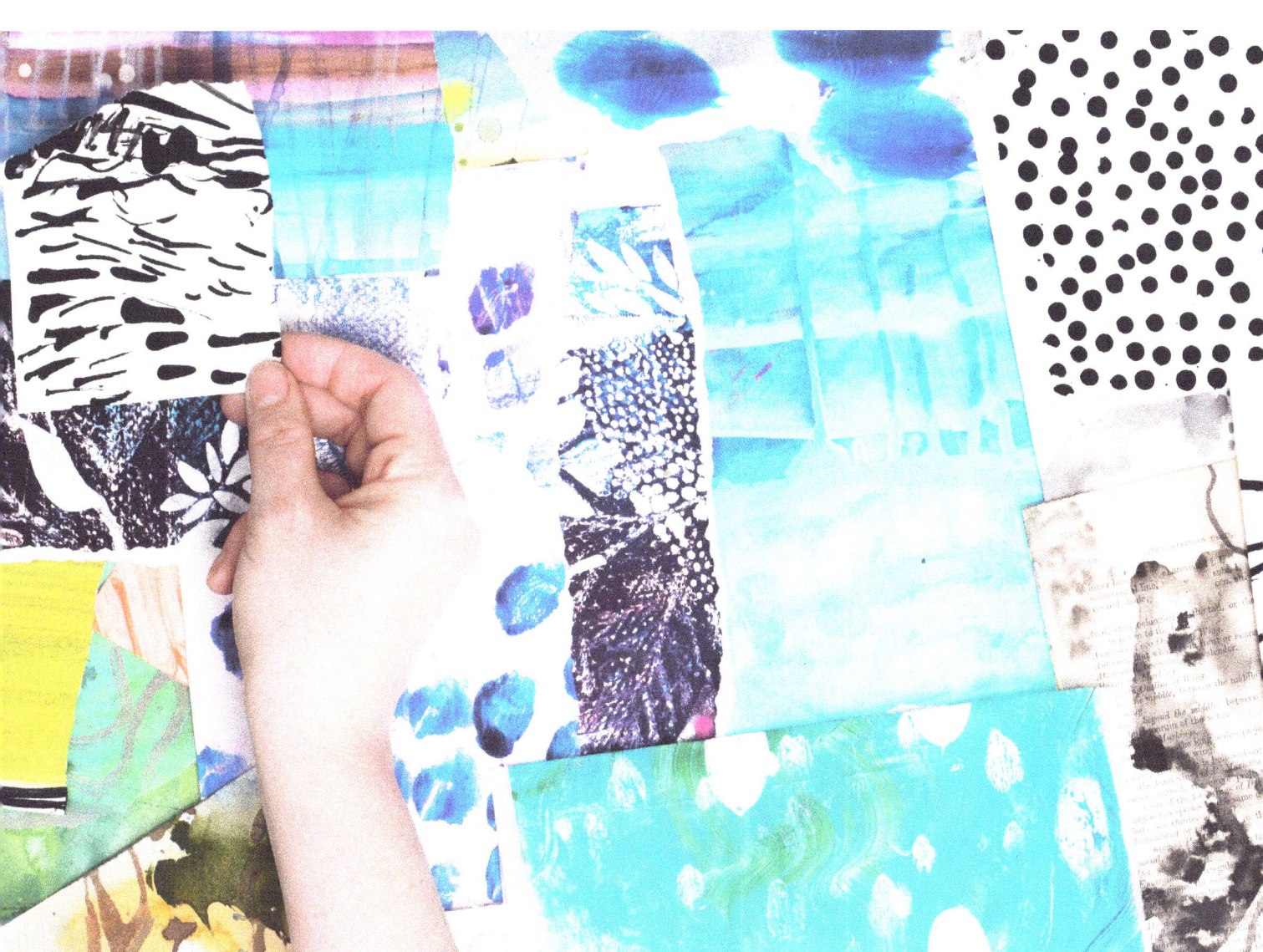

I invite you to collect your own papers for collage. Consider exploring the following ideas:

- Go through old magazines and cut out sections of pattern or color that appeal to you.
- Repurpose found papers, maps, old envelopes, old letters, and various tickets or receipts.
- Consider using the pages of old and worn books.
- Photocopy sections from your sketchbook to play around with, cut up, and alter into something new. I especially like to do this if there is a drawing or page I really like and want to preserve. Photocopying it and experimenting with the copy is a low-risk strategy that keeps the original intact.
- Keep interesting pieces of packaging or wrapping paper, shiny candy wrappers, or foil wrapping.
- Gather bits and pieces from past artistic experiments or pages on which you've cleaned your brushes or tested color choices.
- If you have leftover paint, use it to paint blank sheets of paper to incorporate later into collage pieces. Try using bold and exaggerated brush marks to create interesting textures. Also, use the mark-making tools exercise (page 104) to create pages for collaging.

▶ **When collecting or making papers for use in your sketchbook, consider those that hold aesthetic appeal or some meaning to you.**

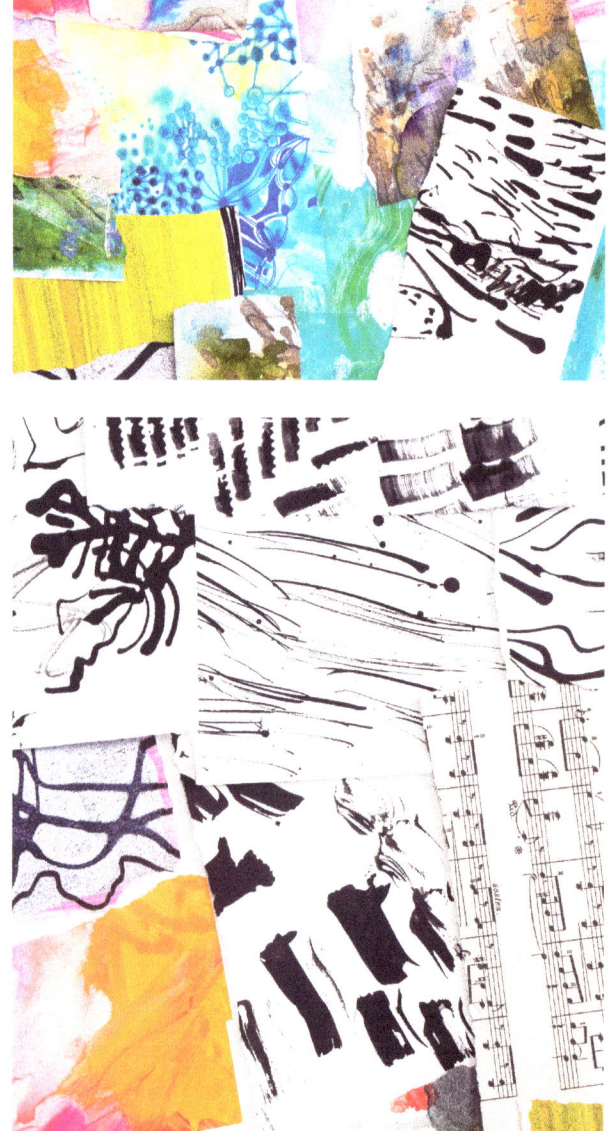

Using Collage Papers

The following are collage techniques that I use in my sketchbook. Use them as a starting point for developing your own practices.

▼ **Choose a photograph as a reference or starting point. I selected a photograph I had taken of leaves on a wet day.**

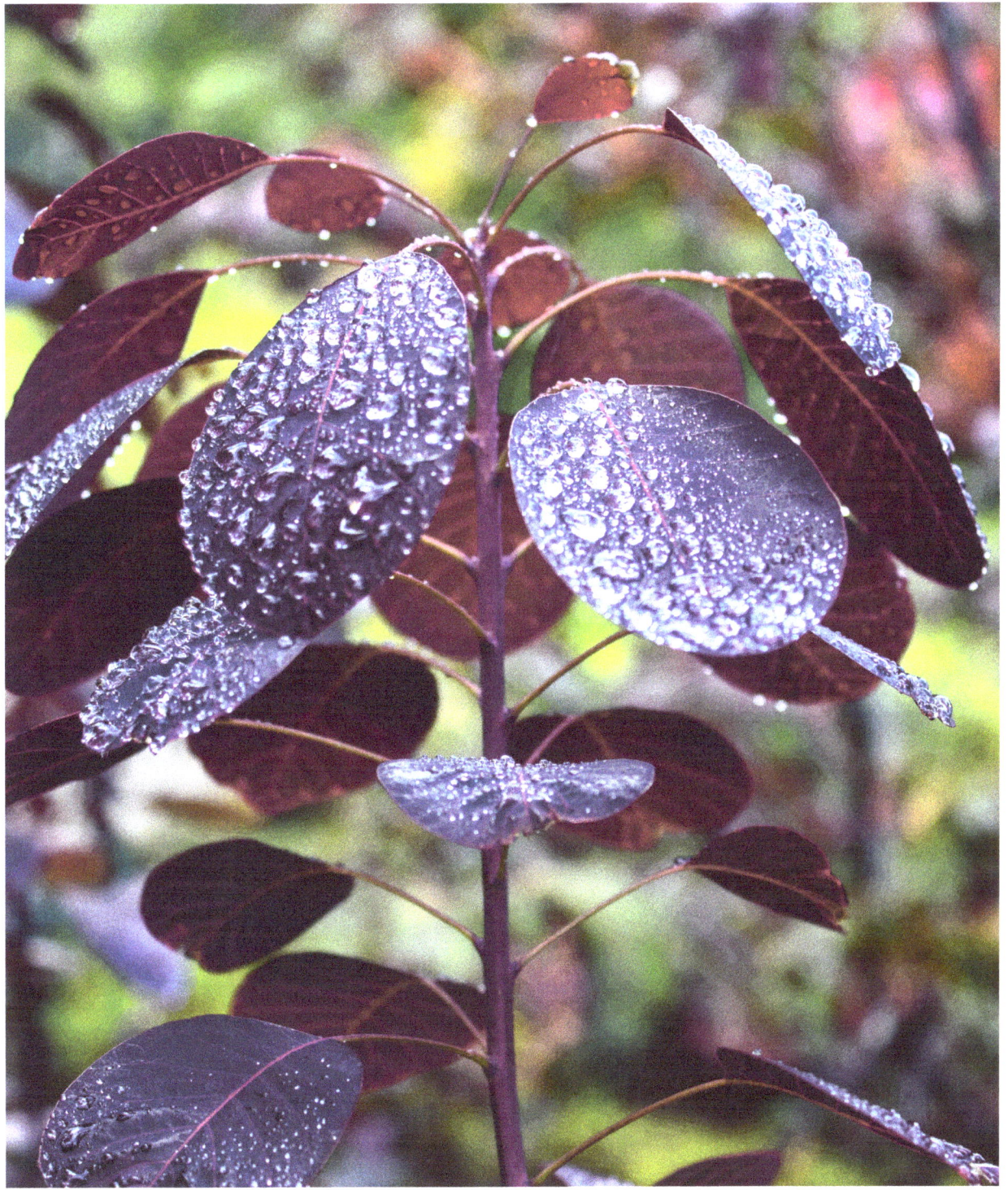

COLLAGE USING A REFERENCE PHOTOGRAPH

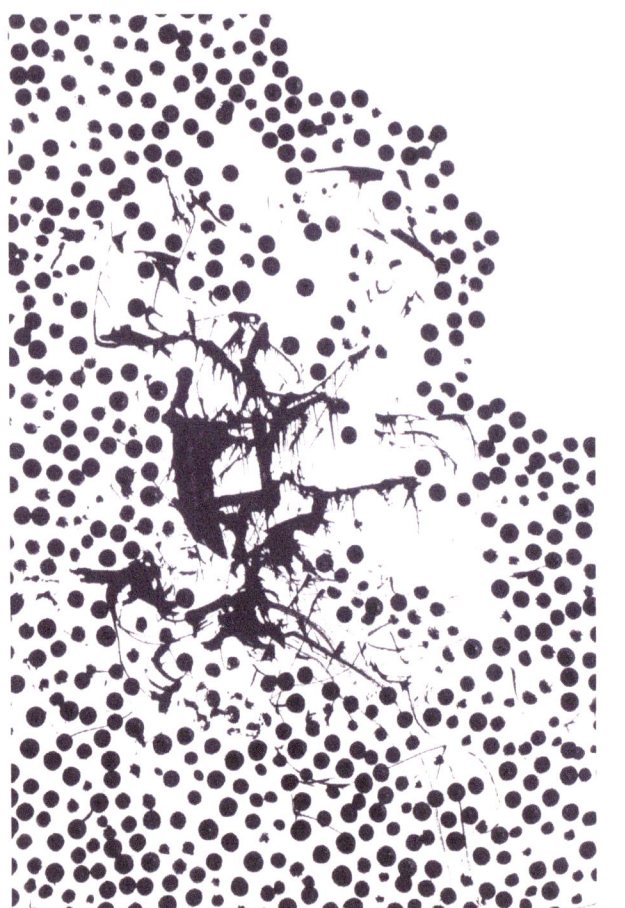

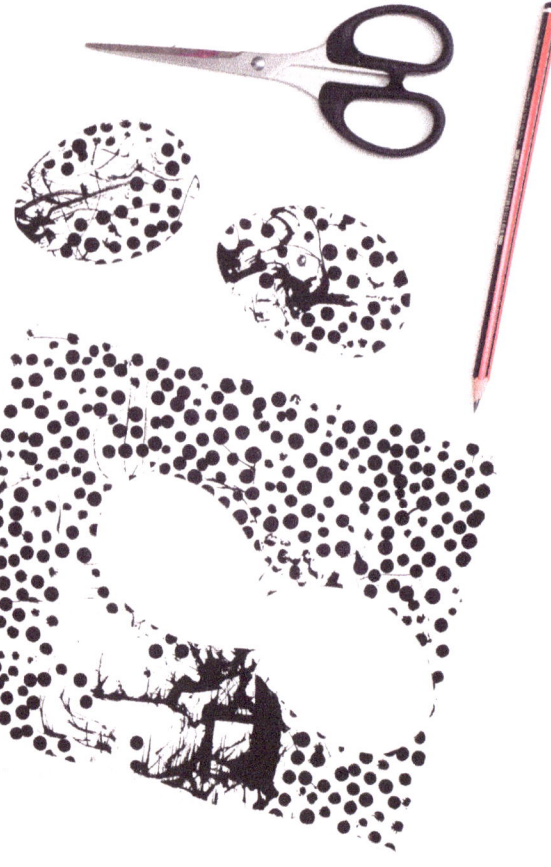

Look through the papers you have collected. Select those that you want to incorporate into this collage. They may mirror an aspect of your reference photograph in some way. I selected a patterned page of dots I created with a nail and a twig dipped in ink.

Select the areas of the collage paper to incorporate into your sketchbook. You may find it helpful to draw the shapes you want with a pencil before you cut them out. Reference your photograph and use it as a guide to the shapes you draw and cut.

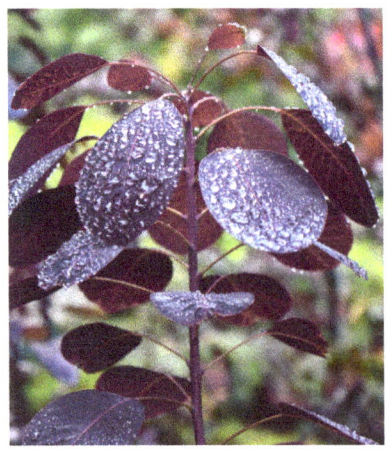

◄ Reference photograph.

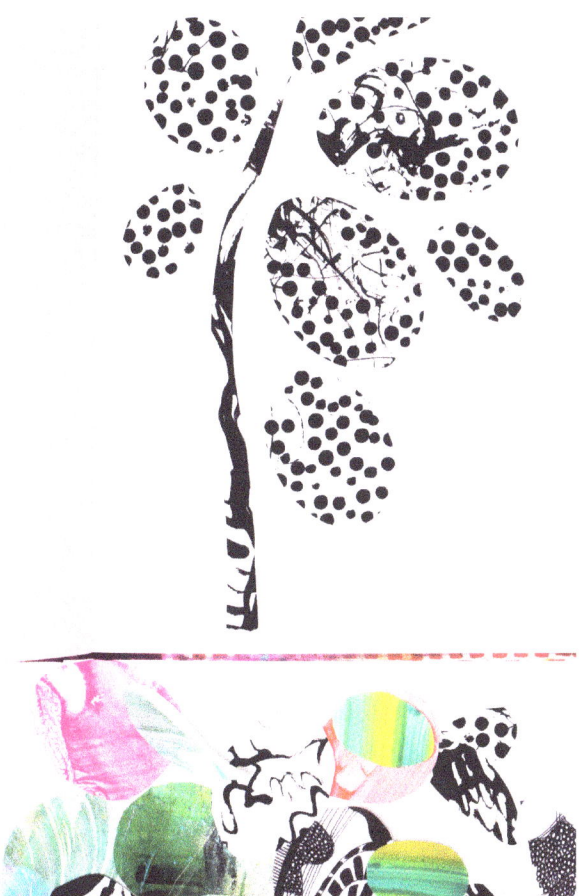

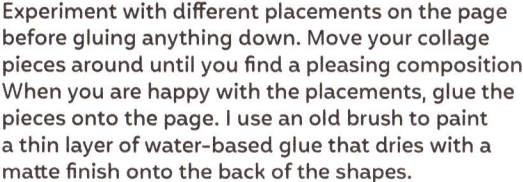

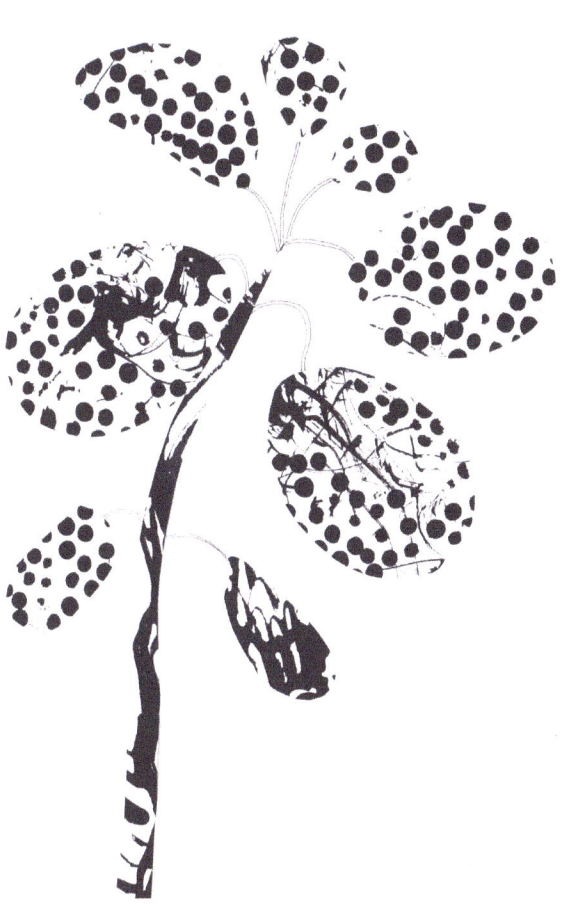

Experiment with different placements on the page before gluing anything down. Move your collage pieces around until you find a pleasing composition. When you are happy with the placements, glue the pieces onto the page. I use an old brush to paint a thin layer of water-based glue that dries with a matte finish onto the back of the shapes.

Let the glue dry and finish by adding drawn details, if needed. I used a black fine-line pen to connect the leaves to the stalk.

COLLAGE FROM IMAGINATION

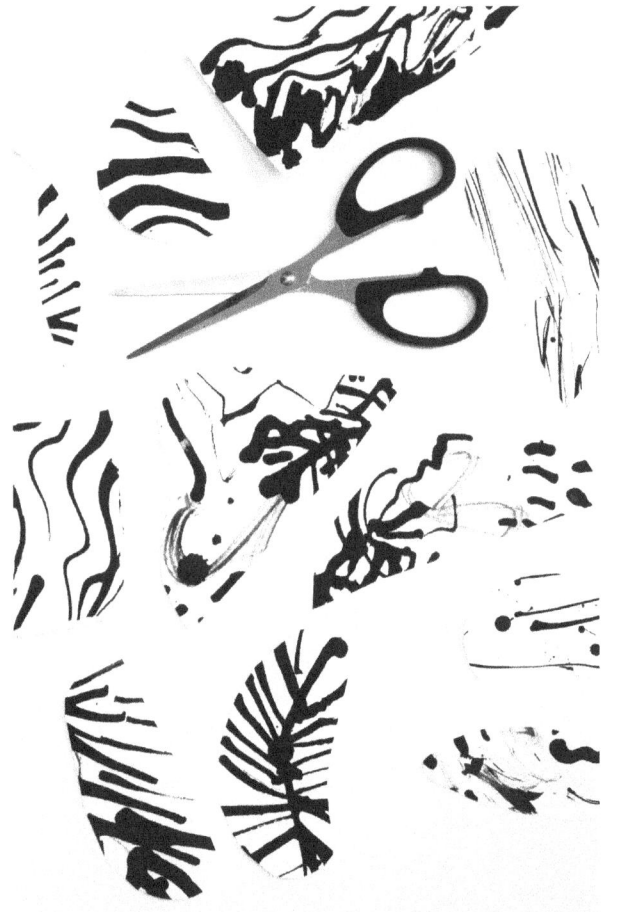

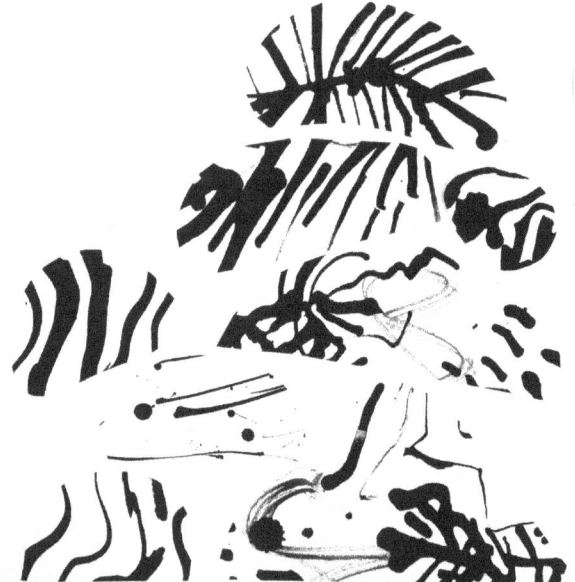

Consider how your collage elements relate to one another, arrange them on your sketchbook page in various ways, and choose a composition that appeals to you. Paint a thin layer of glue on the back of each collage piece and press them on your sketchbook page. Wait for the glue to dry.

Use your collection of papers to spark ideas. Create a collage from your imagination. Experiment by working instinctively with no plan and no intended outcome. Choose a few papers from your collection and let this selection alone be your starting point. Cut out shapes and elements intuitively.

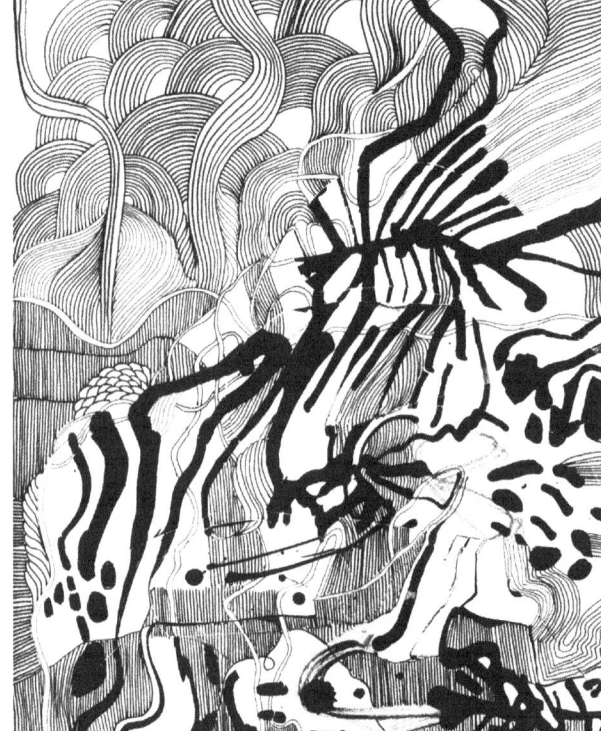

▶ Consider using your art materials to add drawn or painted elements to your composition. When I returned to this collage after the glue dried, I was reminded of rocks and a waterfall. I added drawn lines with a black felt-tip pen and a fine-line pen to emphasize this aspect.

COLLAGE AND PAINT

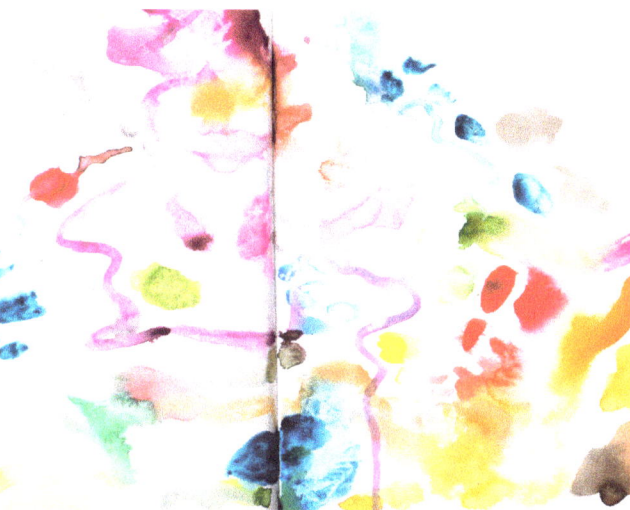

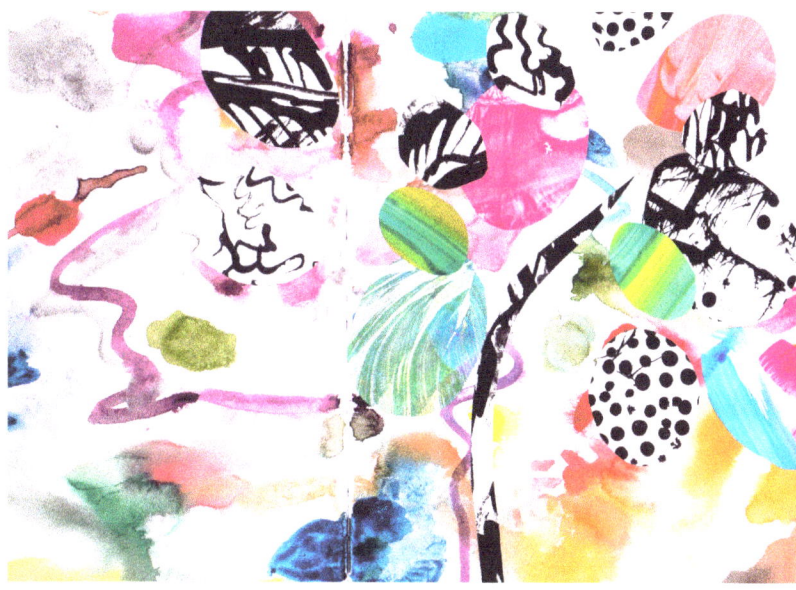

As described earlier in the mixed-media section (page 100), create an underpainting in your sketchbook, a wild and wonderful creation where anything goes. This is just the foundation layer for your collage; it helps cover the white page and give your collage a background. I painted this one with watercolors. If you are using a reference source or photograph to inspire you, use it to inform the colors and types of marks in the underpainting.

Once the underpainting is dry, make a few selections from your collage paper collection. Cut out the shapes and elements you want to include and arrange them on the page before gluing. This allows you to experiment and move them around to find the most pleasing composition. Glue them when you are happy with their placement.

▶ Once the collage elements are glued in place and this layer has dried, consider whether you would like to incorporate additional drawn or painted elements. I drew additional lines to emphasize the leaves.

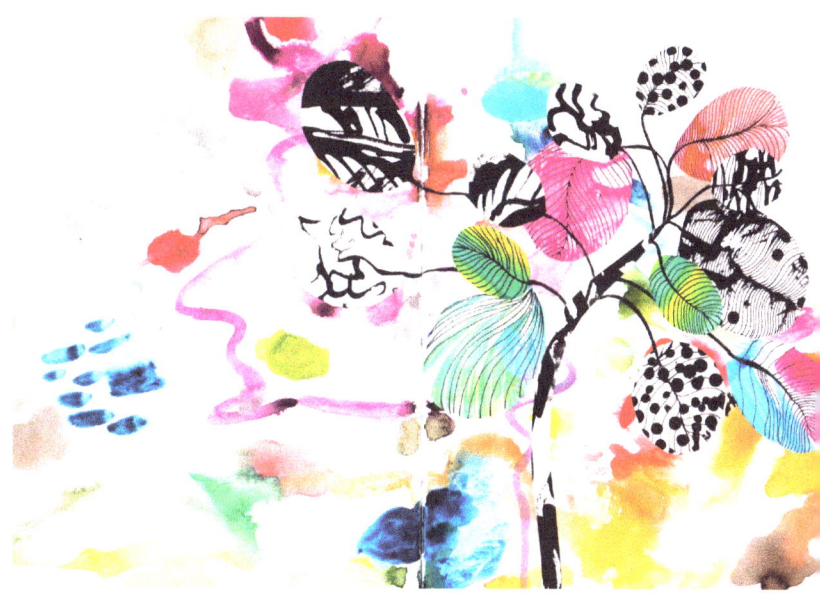

Black and White Versus Color

Experiment with both monochrome and colorful applications. You may want to re-create the same image over and over again, using different colors and techniques each time. This sort of repetition can be enlightening. It can become an iterative process where you learn about your subject, hone your preferred color palette, and discover the techniques that best serve your art.

Experiment by mixing black and white components with colorful elements on the same sketchbook page. You may find the high contrast between the achromatic and the multicolored elements to be pleasing. The following are ways to explore monochrome and color:

- In most camera phones it is easy to turn a color photo into a black and white one, or you can do this by printing an image in black and white instead of color. This exercise allows you to better see and understand the light and dark areas of the subject or painting.

- Think about the meanings you associate with certain hues. Some colors can carry powerful symbolism and associations that you can explore or exploit in your work. Write down the words or associations you have with certain colors. For example, blue can represent winter, coldness, distance, feeling blue, spirituality, the sky, and so on.

- Create one image several times using a different dominant color each time. Then consider how the color affects your creation. Think of the story or emotions that various shades can convey and the meanings you give them. The same image may have a very different meaning if it is painted red than it would if it were painted black or yellow.

Re-creating the same image using various colors and techniques can be an effective way to learn about your artistic style and preferences.

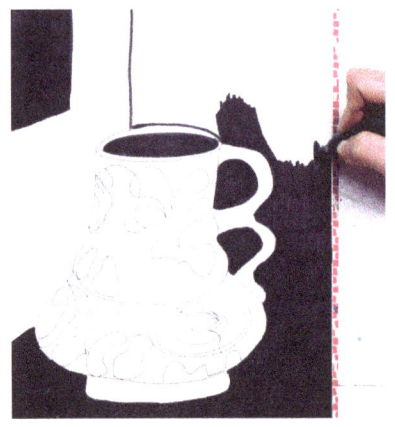 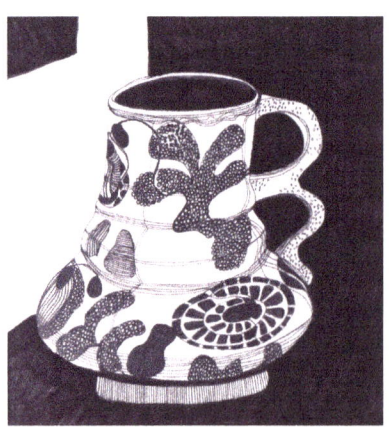 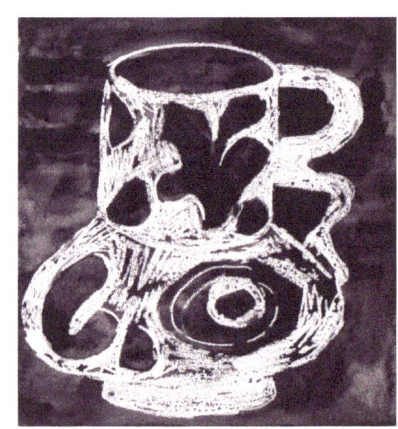

▲ Here I re-created the vase in numerous ways. I started with a black pen drawing and rendered the background with a black felt-tip pen to make the detail of the vase stand out.

▲ Experiment by re-creating the same subject with different art materials. I used the wax-resist method and drew the vase in white crayon, then painted over it with black watercolor paint.

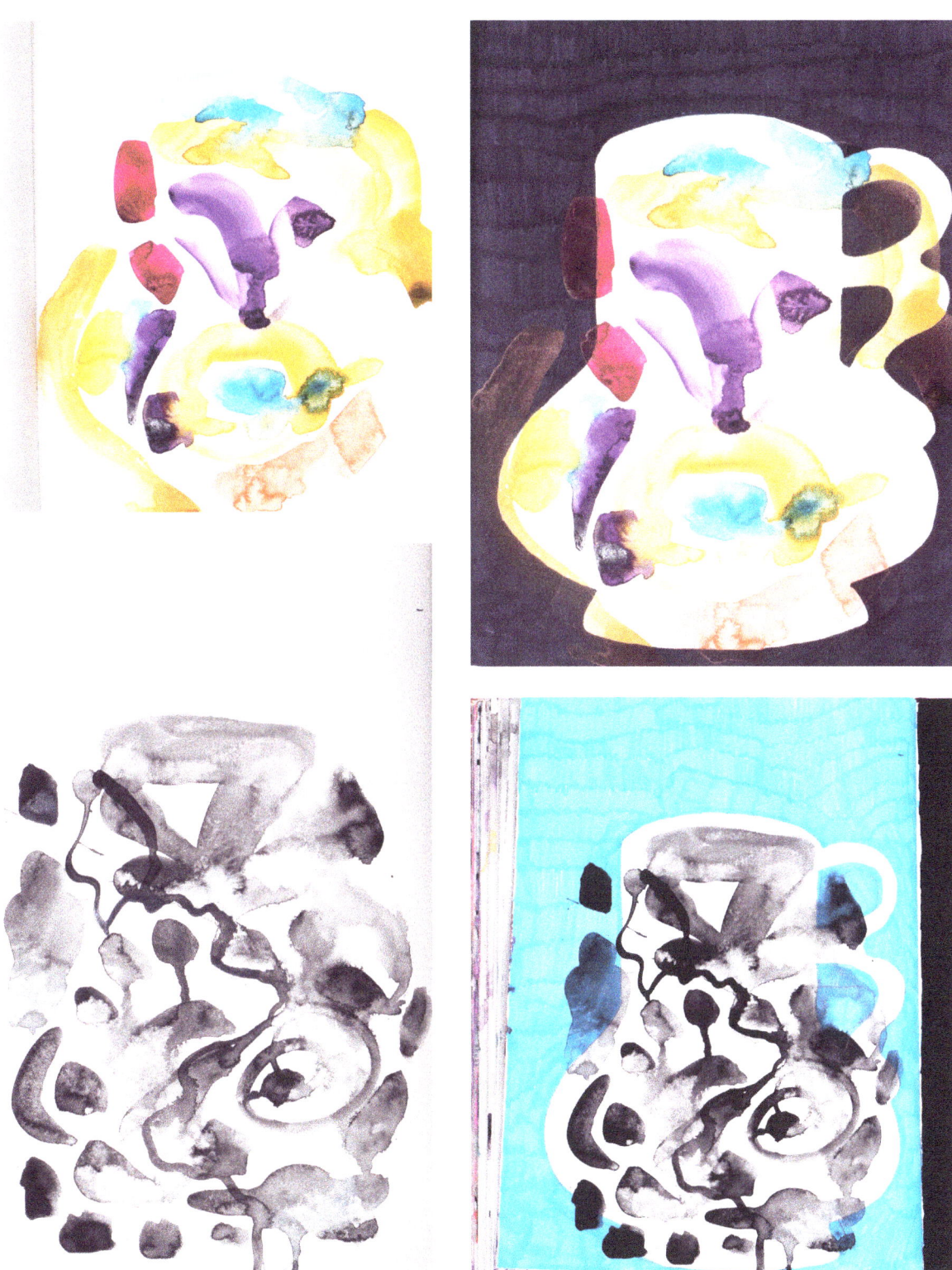

▲ Using monochromatic elements and color on the same page can add visual interest. Here I started with bold watercolor brushstrokes in the underpainting. Once the paint dried, I drew the silhouette of the vase and background using a thick felt-tip pen. I reversed the color and the monochromatic elements on each page.

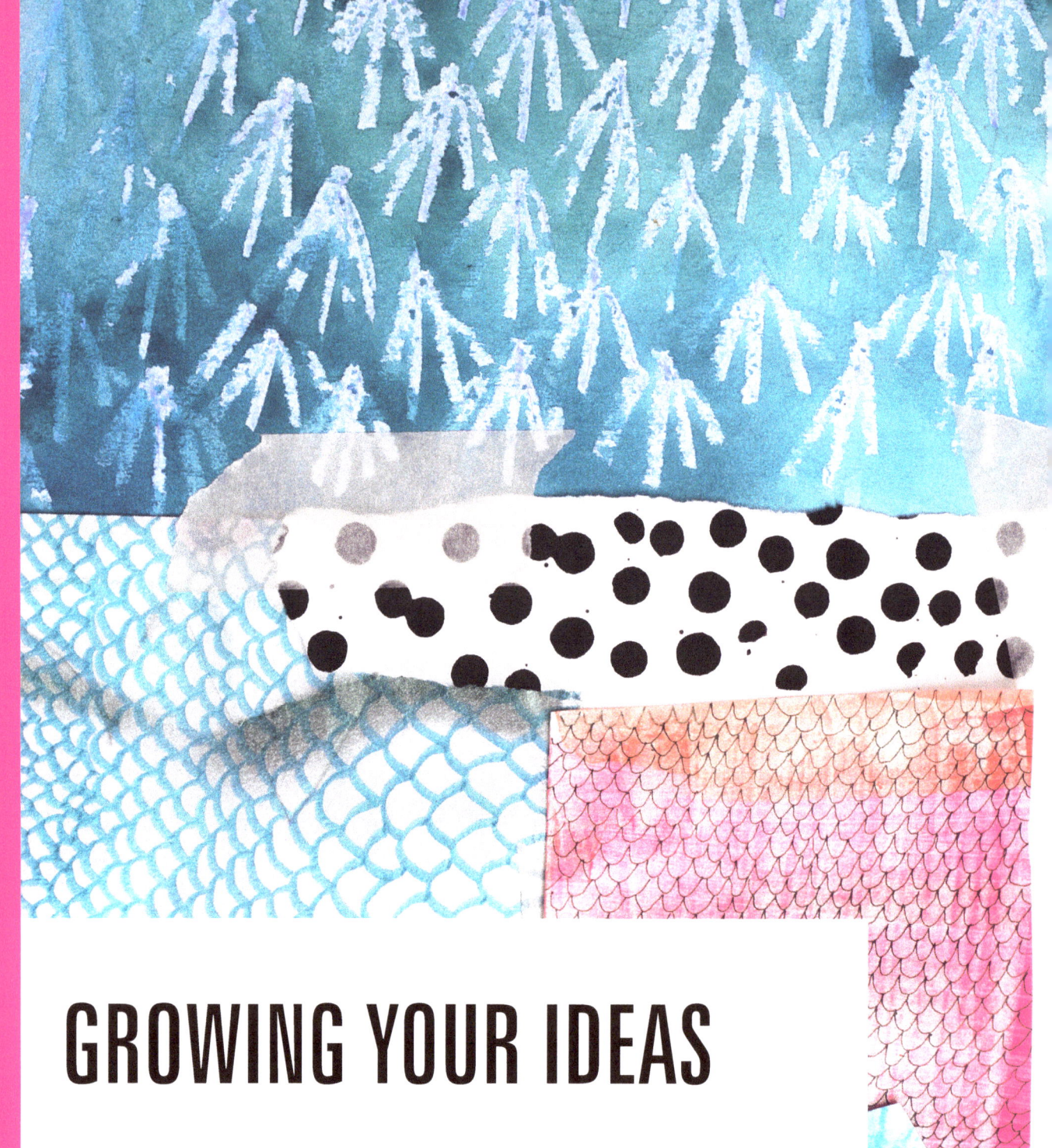

GROWING YOUR IDEAS

Now it's time to take the practical tools and techniques you've learned in previous chapters and expand upon them. Begin with a theme or topic that fascinates you and experiment!

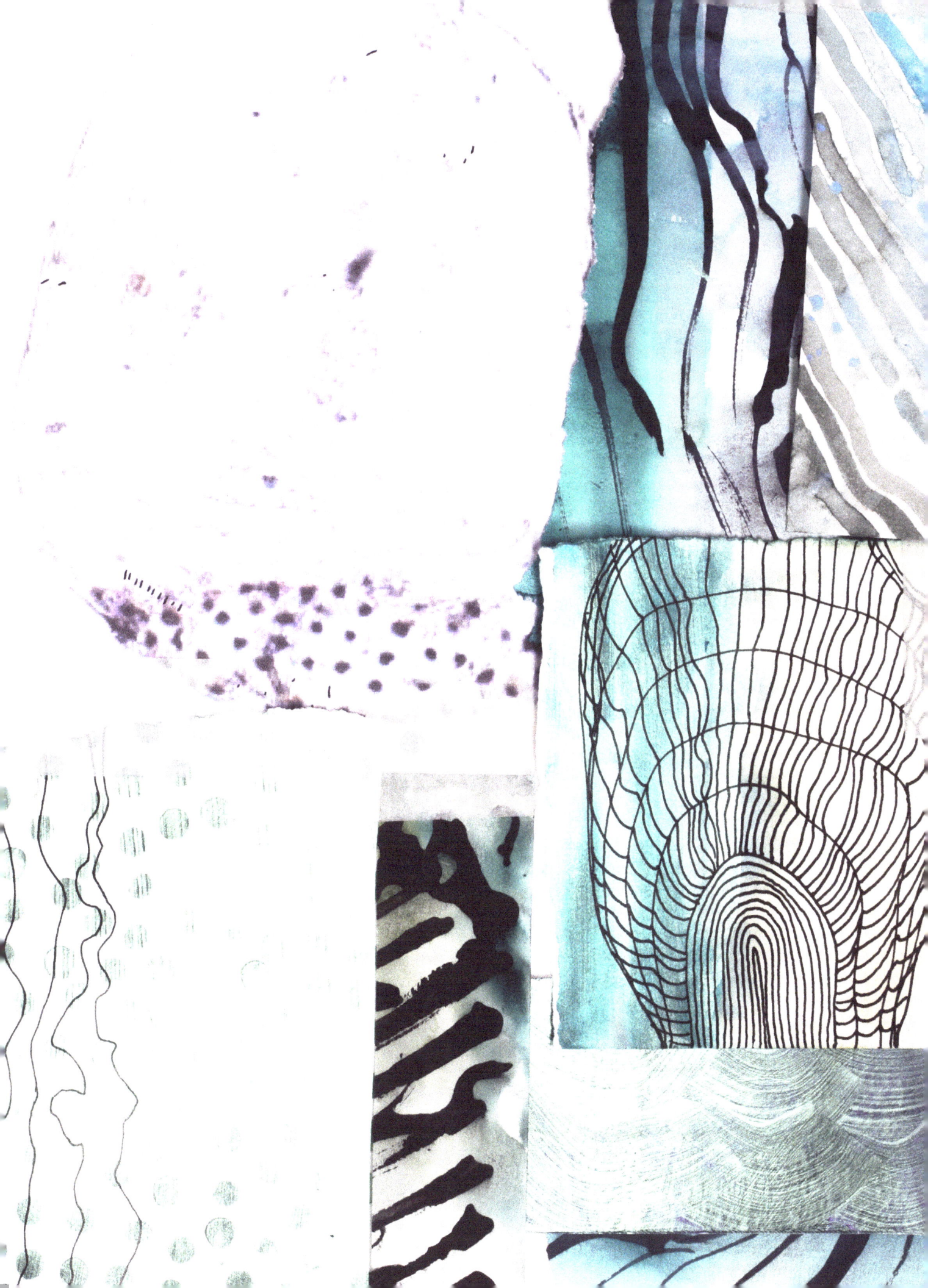

THEMES

Looking for a theme to jumpstart your sketch-book artwork? Take these starting points and build on them, play with them, and make them your own. Select the themes and topics that have the most meaning and significance to you.

Experiences

- Select a place where you have traveled and create art that responds to the visit using memories or photographs.
- Create pages that reflect a personal experience that is important to you, a journey, a hobby, or a life change.

- Select a cause that is close to your heart and consider how this could be the starting point for art in your sketchbook.
- Create pages that are reflective of your world view, beliefs, or things you know to be true.
- Draw the story of your life or key moments.
- Consider your personal values and use one as a starting point to create art pages, i.e., courage, truth, or equality.

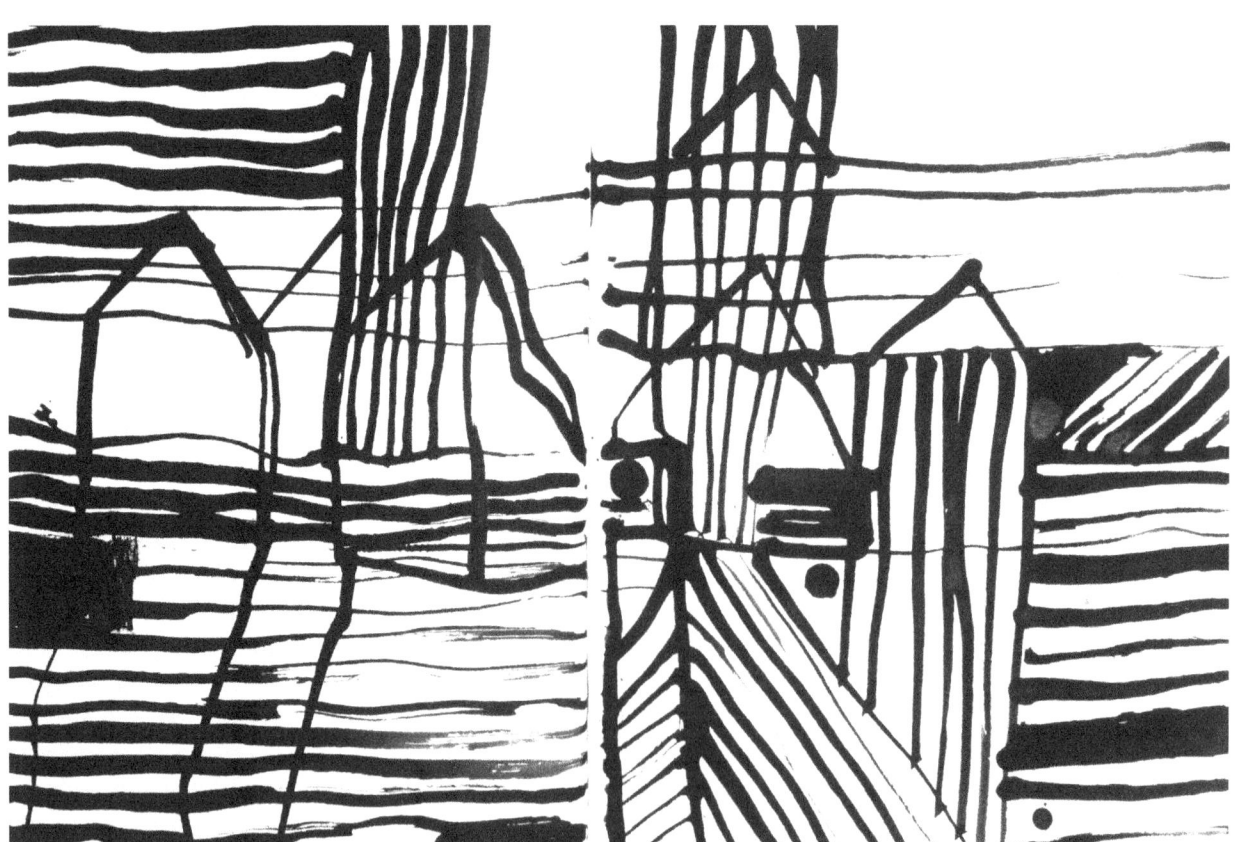

This example of an imaginary landscape was made with a twig dipped in ink.

People and Places

- Draw a series of self-portraits that highlight something important about you or include symbols or motifs that are personal to you.
- Create pages in your sketchbook that explore aspects of a place that has meaning to you.
- Use where you live as a starting point and create art in your sketchbook that is inspired by home.
- Create a page in your sketchbook dedicated to a person who is special to you.

Emotion and Imagination

- Select an emotion that resonates with you and try to depict it.
- Create art pages inspired by a childhood memory.
- Create an imaginary world, city, or landscape in your sketchbook.
- Dedicate a page of your sketchbook to a dream.
- Select a poem or song you love and use it to inspire a page in your sketchbook. For example, you could try the expressive mark-making exercise while listening to the song and see what it does to the quality and variety of your marks.

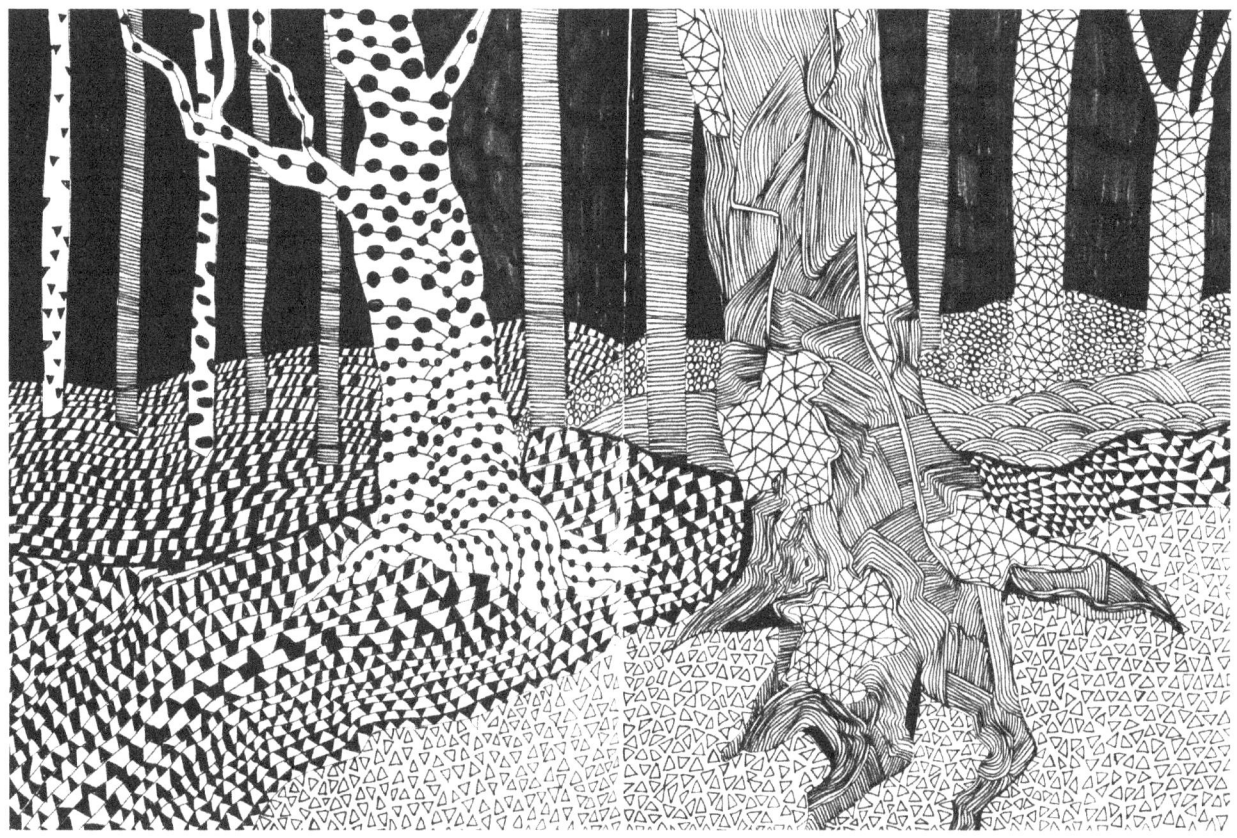

Try creating a landscape or cityscape from your imagination. This patchwork forest was drawn with a fine-liner pen and marker pen. Experiment with incorporating patterns and marks from the mark-making exercise.

Objects and Things

- The objects we surround ourselves with have meaning. Select a few items that have significance to you and use them as a starting point for a sketchbook page.
- Pick an object that you find beautiful and draw it repeatedly on the same page or with different materials.

- Dedicate a page to something you were going to throw out, such as a piece of overripe fruit, a vegetable, or a piece of packaging.
- Reserve a page for a found object. It could be something that someone else has discarded or something from nature, such as a pinecone or branch that you found on a walk.

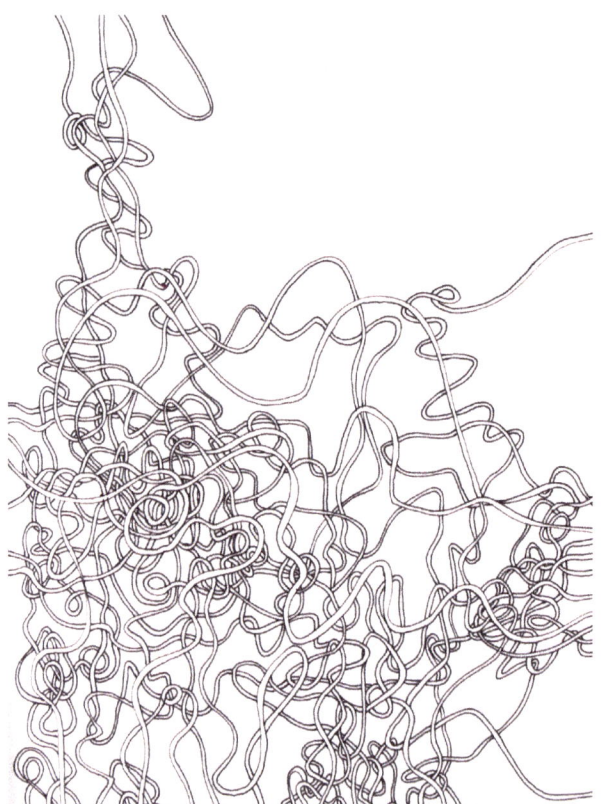

Beauty can be found in simple discarded items. This sketchbook page was inspired by some jumbled string.

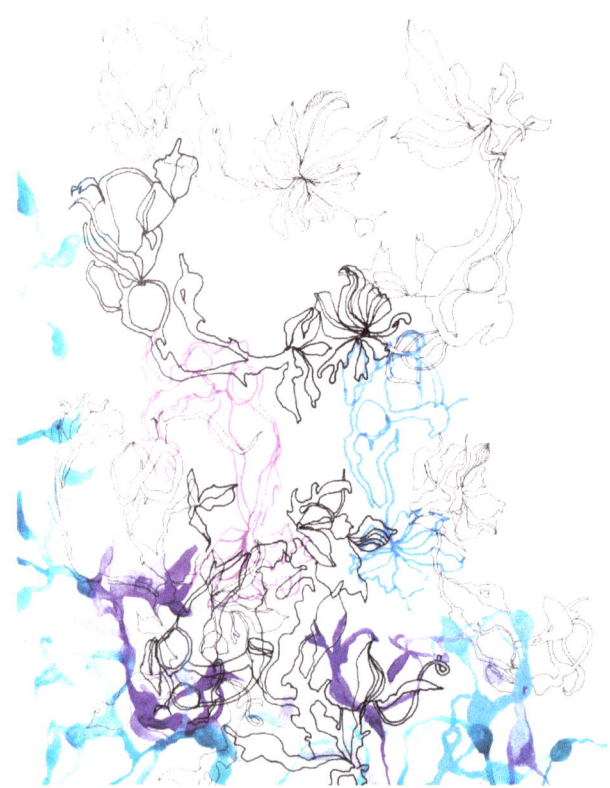

Experiment by drawing an object over and over again on the same page. This page contains lots of quick drawings of a small piece of seaweed I found on the beach.

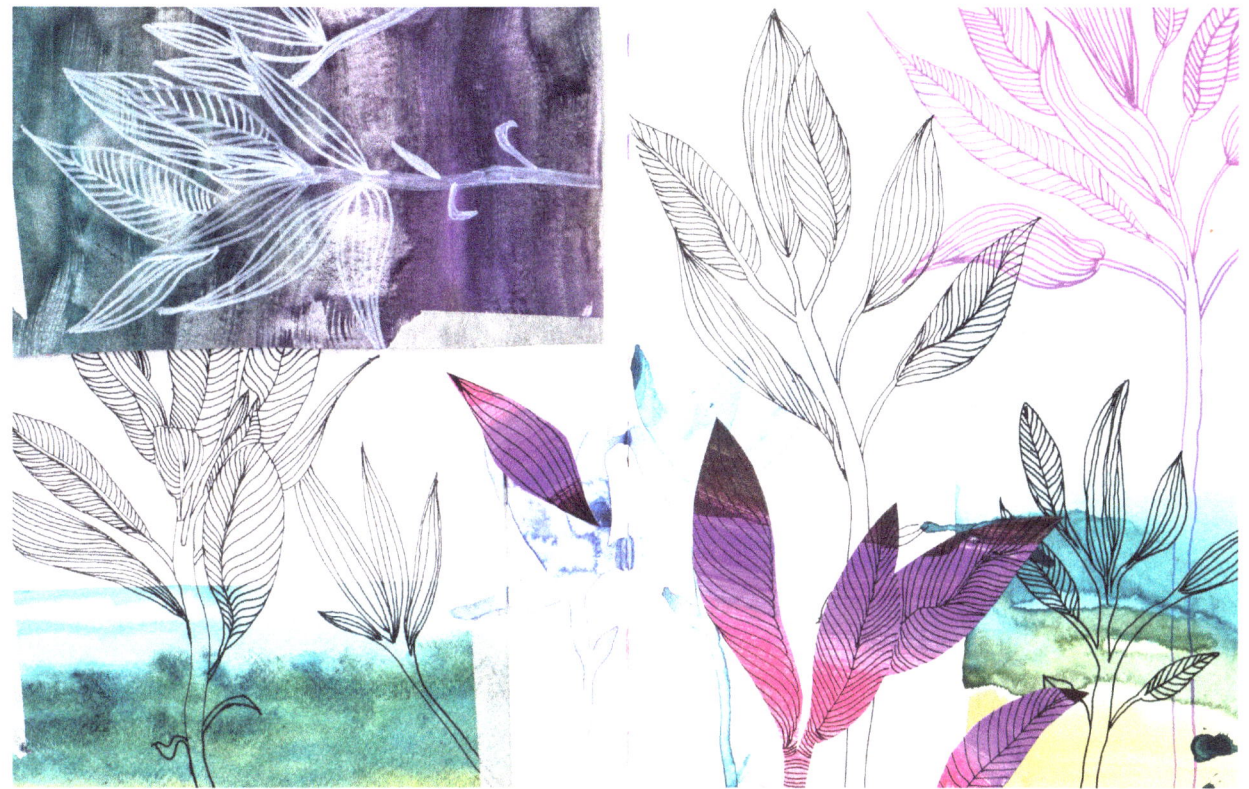

A single interesting starting point can take you in many different directions. Experiment by using repetition on the same page. I created these leaves using many different art materials, including collage, black fine-line pen, watercolor, and a permanent white marker pen.

Pick one of the following themes and look for examples of it in your home or neighborhood. Take photographs to use as reference material for your sketchbook pages:

- Looking through
- Balance/imbalance
- Juxtapositions
- Weathered/rusting
- Circles
- Lines and angles
- Skyline
- Relationships and connections

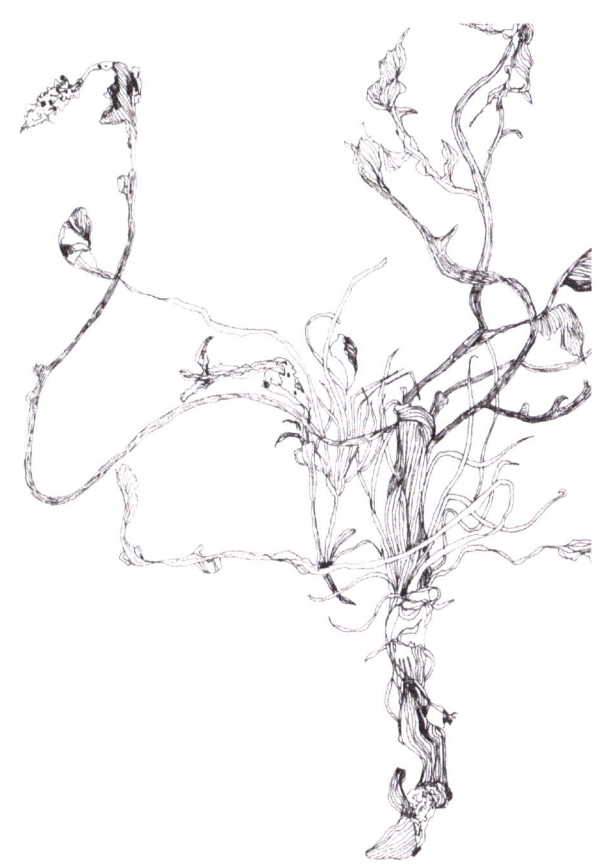

▶ A small, seemingly insignificant item can be fascinating to draw. Try drawing a found twig or a dried weed, for example.

EXPANDING AN IDEA

One way to grow your ideas is to revisit your inspiration map and pick one of its threads to expand upon. New ideas can come from expanding a single concept on your map.

Begin by taking the one idea and placing it at the center of a new map. Write down all the ways you may want to explore this theme—anything at all that comes to mind. Write down everything—don't edit yourself—and just let the ideas and associations flow. On my original ideas map, I wrote down "fish scales." I grew this idea by scribbling down ways in which I might employ the inspiration of fish scales in my sketchbook. Some of my ideas included using iridescent paint, looking at the shape of fish scales under a microscope, making fish scales from aluminum foil, investigating the purpose of fish scales, and researching different patterns.

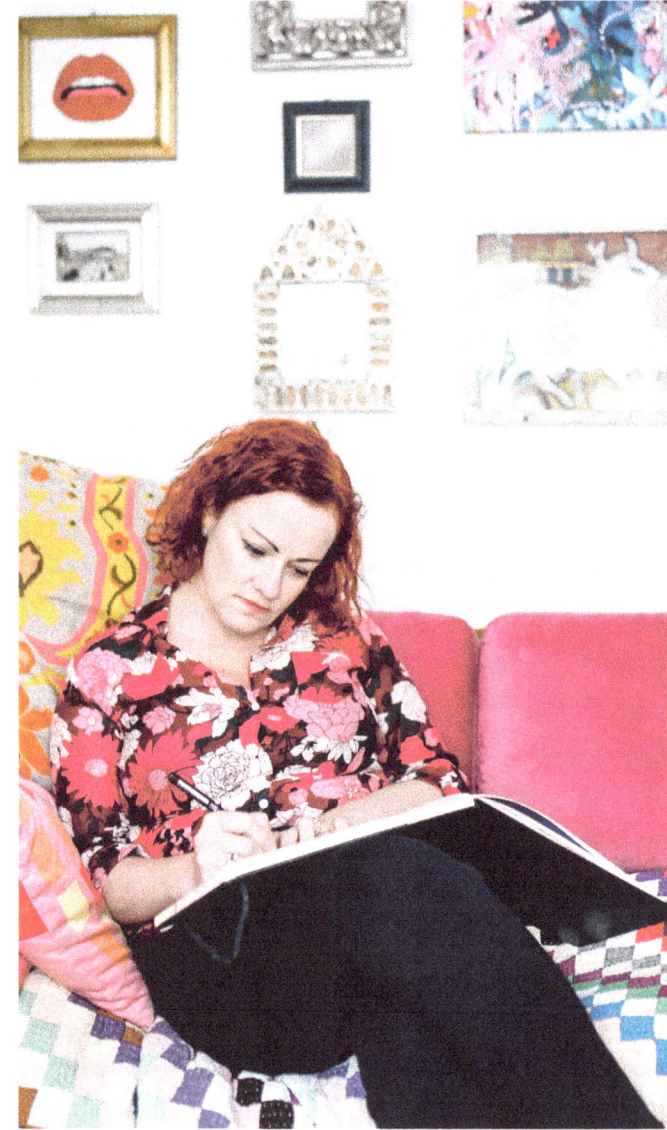

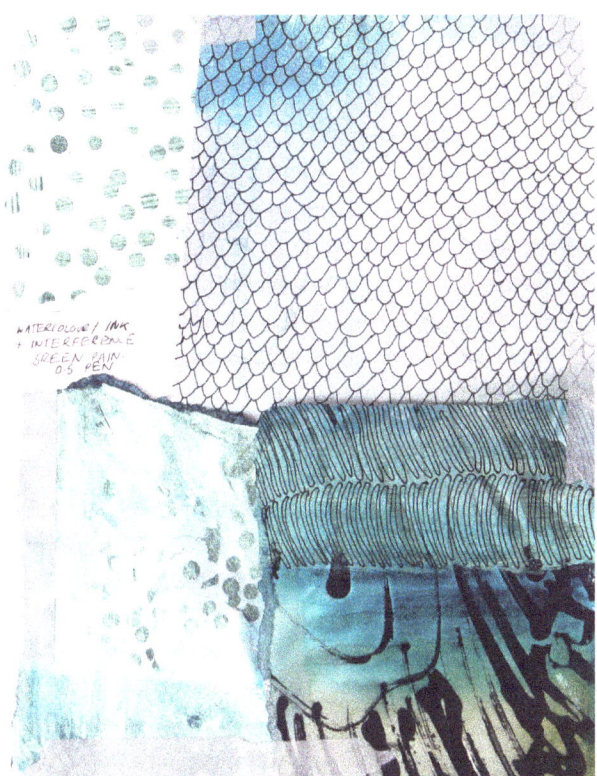

WATERCOLOUR / INK
+ INTERFERENCE
GREEN PAIN·
0.5 PEN·

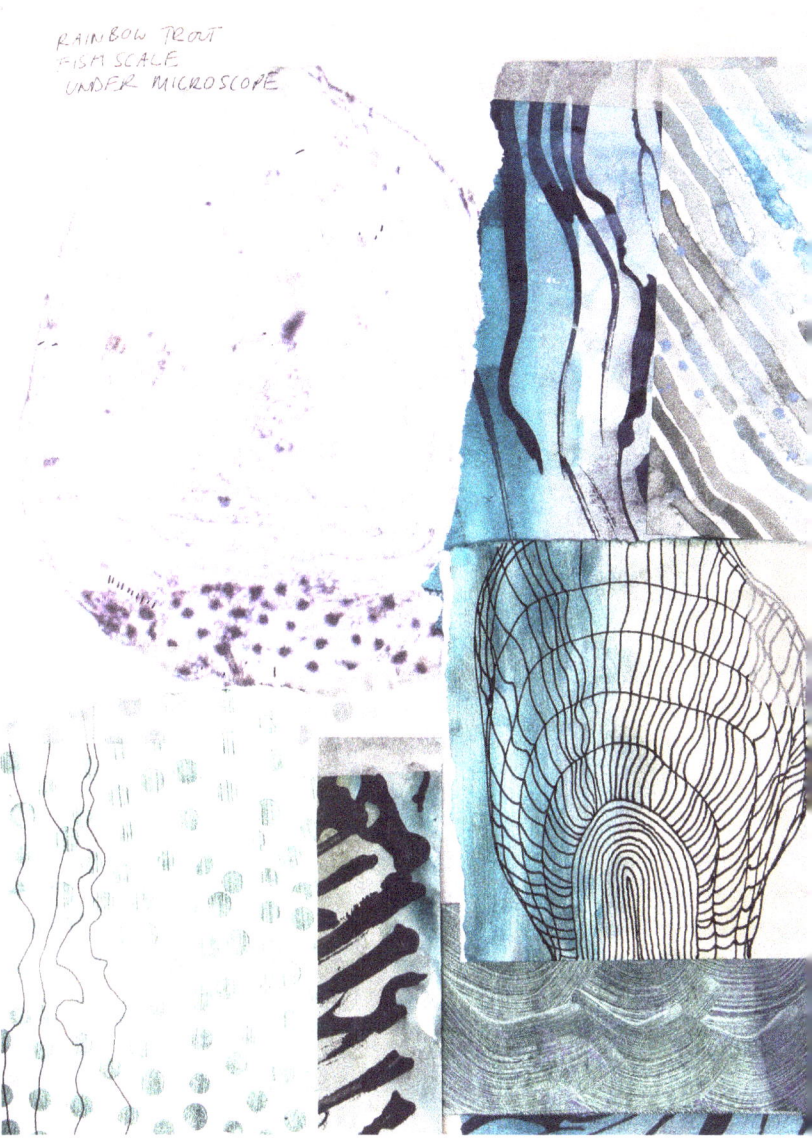

RAINBOW TROUT
FISH SCALE
UNDER MICROSCOPE

▲ ▶ Use your sketchbook to capture ideas. Your sketchbook doesn't need to be full of completed artworks; instead use it as a repository for fledgling ideas, the beginnings of something, or the seeds of a thought you may want to revisit later to grow and nurture.

Combining Ideas

Make interesting and personal art works by not only layering art supplies, but by mixing layers of meaning and combining ideas.

Your sketchbook can be a place to integrate your interests and allow them to intersect and intertwine.

Taking two disparate ideas from your inspiration map and fusing them together on one sketchbook page can be a starting point for creating art that is personal and has a unique significance for you.

Select two ideas from your inspiration map and combine, contrast, or juxtapose them on one page. Weave these ideas together in a way that only you can. Make interesting combinations, associations, or surprising connections.

As you develop your artistic practice, you will become more confident in finding your own stimuli. Spending time considering and unpacking what it is you want to achieve through your art makes it easier to define your direction. Clarity of intention informs action.

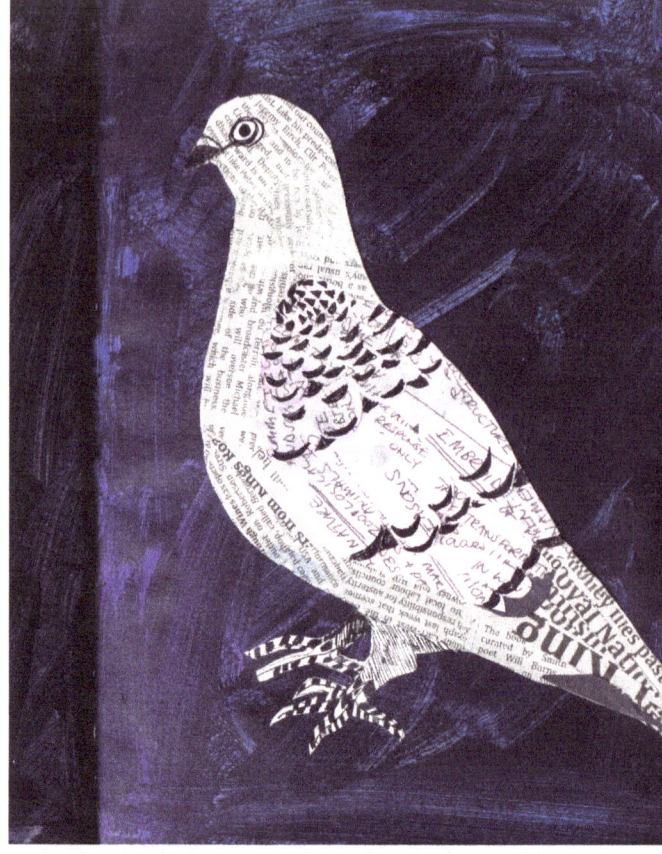

Combine two disparate ideas from your inspiration map and see what happens. Sometimes joining ideas can lead to a new concept that is bigger than its constituent parts. On my original inspiration map, I had written two separate ideas: 1) making sketchbook art from rubbish, and 2) pigeons. I combined these two and made a pigeon from rubbish.

Researching and Investigating

Once you come up with an idea, research can help you understand its context and help you to grow and strengthen it. Research can help you develop your own response to a theme and provide multiple doorways for you to step through. The following are a few ways to research your topic:

- Look for artists who have explored similar themes. Read about them online or in books. If you have the chance, visit galleries and look at their work. Taking notes, drawing, or engaging directly from an original artwork can be illuminating.
- Use other artists' work as a springboard. This can help you learn and develop your own approach and style.
- Look back at your own artwork and sketchbook and take notes about the subjects, processes, or elements that you enjoyed and would like to explore further. You may want to annotate your sketches or pages and write down ways in which to expand on them.

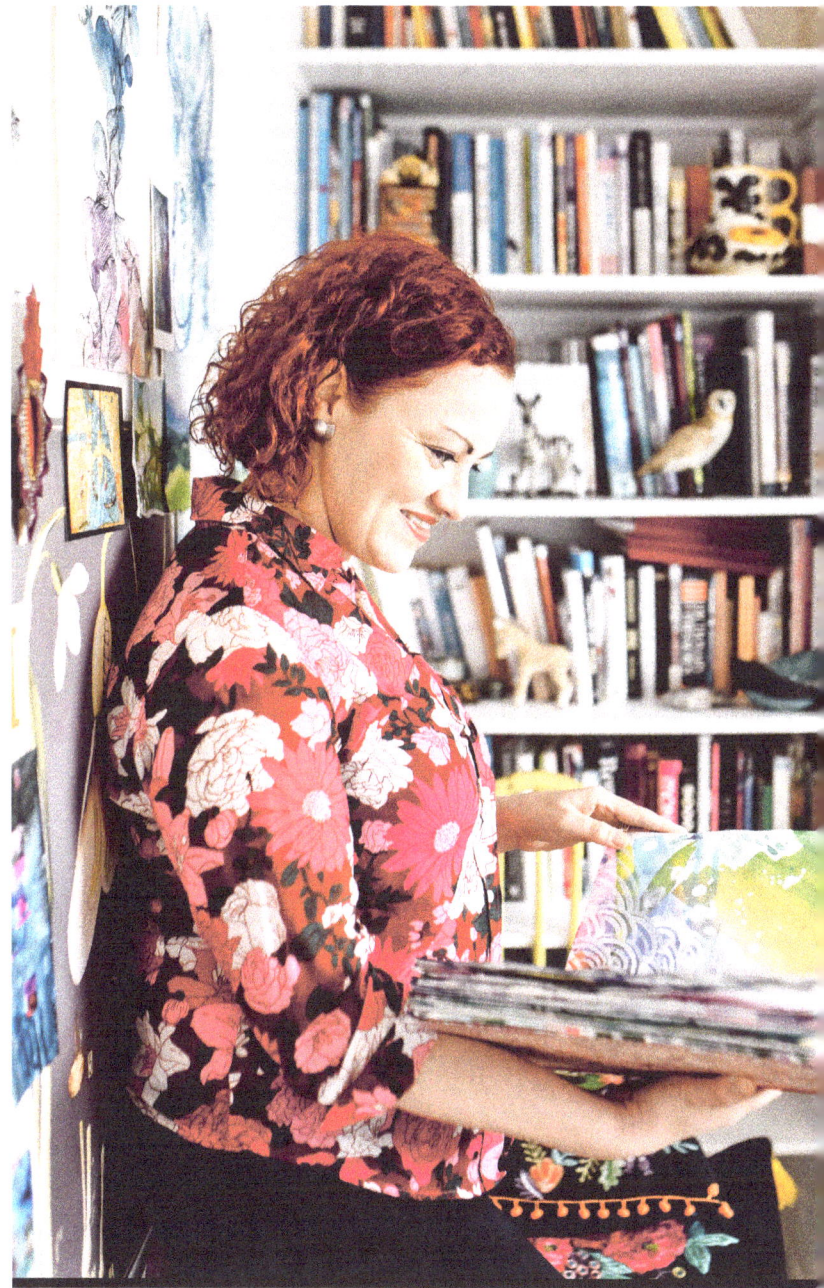

COLLECTING AND TREASURING

Collect things to include in your sketchbook, such as fragments of ideas, postcards, photographs, and the names of artists whose work you want to explore further.

I might paste in a fragment of a finished artwork I completed elsewhere but want to keep, or something I have found, a small photocopy, a visual reminder, or a prompt that I can return to. Treasuring these fragments and collecting them safely in the pages of my sketchbook allows me to flick through my current and old sketchbooks and follow a thread from long ago.

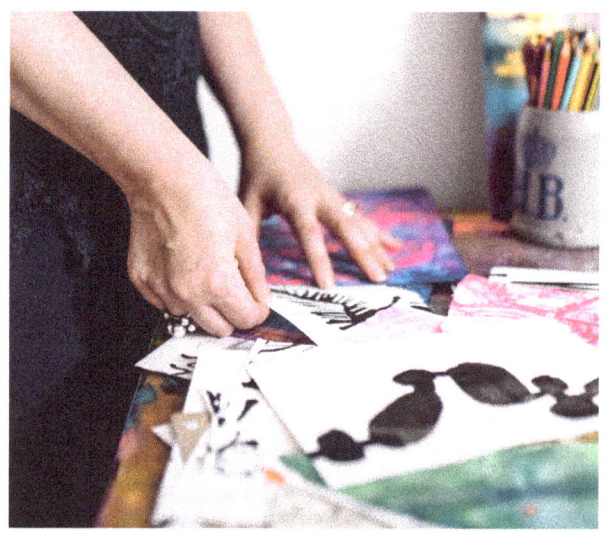

A sketchbook can be your place to gather the things you have collected in your hands, your head, and your heart. Paste items into your sketchbook that you may want to revisit later.

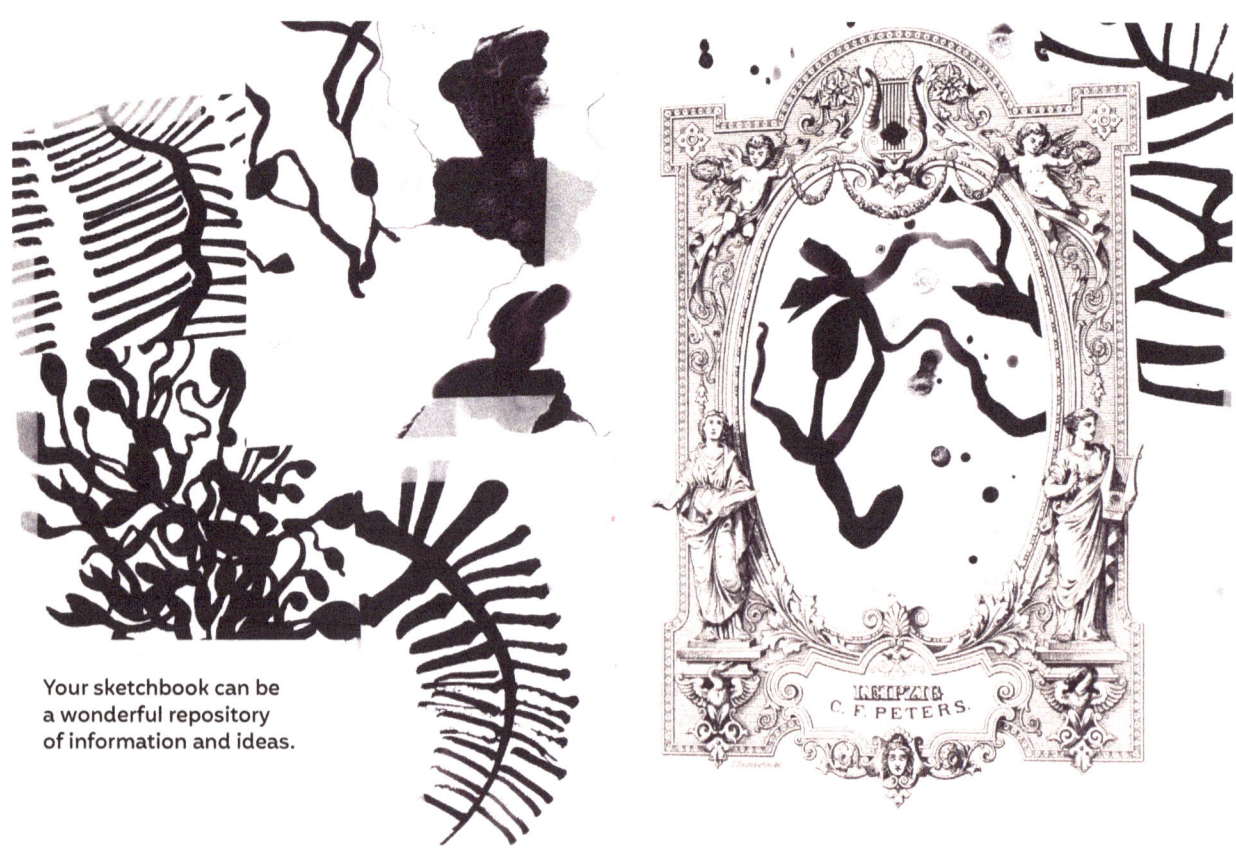

Your sketchbook can be a wonderful repository of information and ideas.

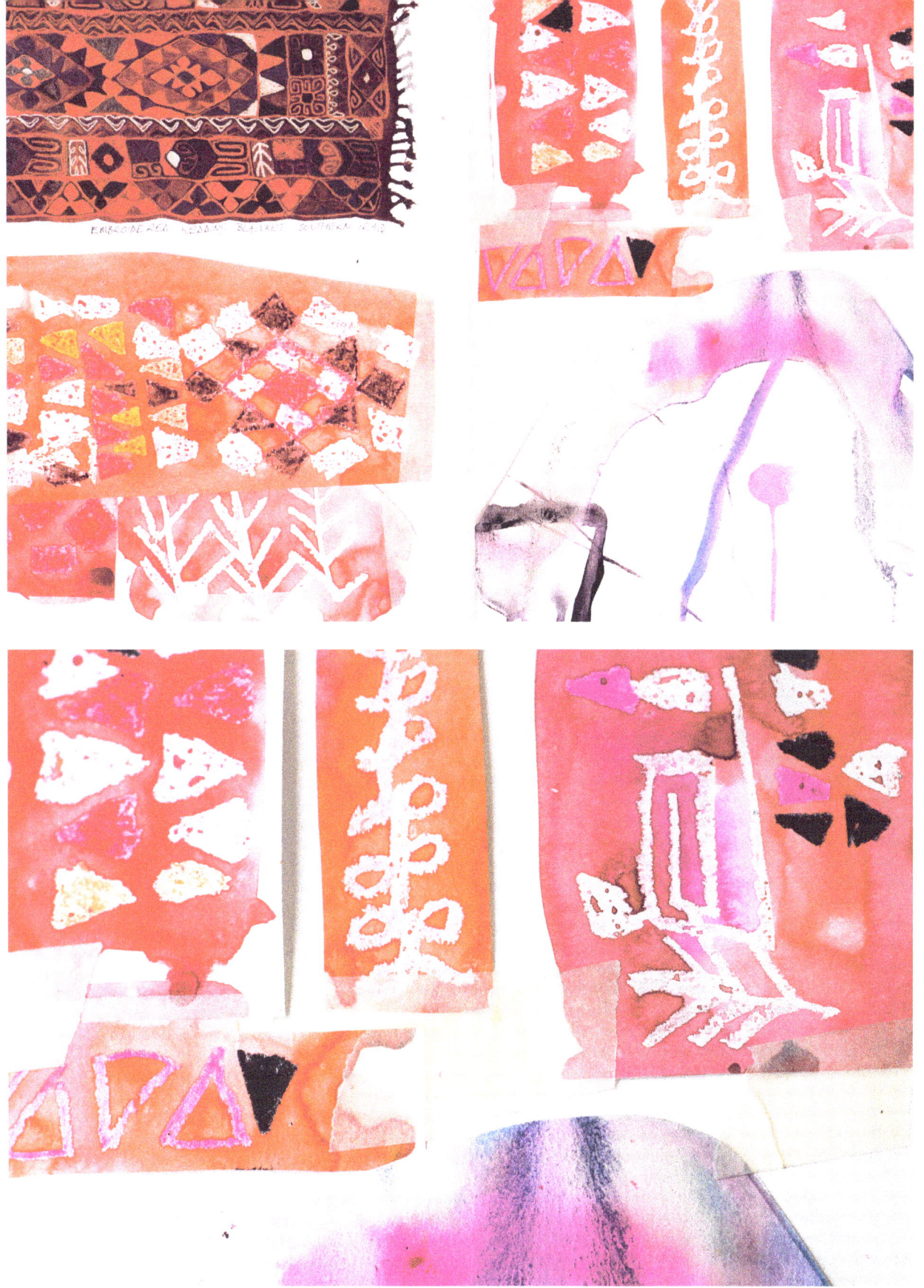

▲ Use your sketchbook to collect things that you find visually interesting, such as images from magazines, postcards, or small fragments of your art experiments that you want to keep for future reference.

WRITING

I often make connections and develop ideas through writing. If there is a subject I am interested in, I might go to the library, poke around online, or read books to learn more about it. I make notes as I read to help me think through how I could respond to it, what interests me personally about it, or what I could do in my sketchbook to develop my response. Sometimes stream-of-consciousness writing, in which I write down everything I can think of that interests me or that I know about a topic without stopping, can be a useful tool. This kind of brain-dump may contain the seed of an interesting idea.

You may want to make notes in your sketchbook. It is your sketchbook to experiment with, so do what makes sense for you. Try the following:

- Write some brief notes that describe your response to what you have created or reflect upon what you enjoyed about the process of creation.
- You might want to write technical notes about the colors you used, how you mixed a particular shade of paint, or anything else you want to remember about the tools or materials you used.
- If you are drawing on location, take notes about the elements of the scene that most appeal to you.
- Feel free to use your sketchbook as a visual notebook, capturing notes of artists, ideas, or thoughts to remind and stimulate you in the future—an idea filing cabinet of sorts for you to look back on and pull things out of.
- Describe the progression of an idea, the steps you took, or how you developed your thought process. Create a written record so you can replicate the process later.
- Capture thoughts about how to progress an idea, expand on it, or take it in a new or different direction.

▶ Writing in your sketchbook can help you connect with what you have created. It can be an opportunity to take stock and reflect on the process and outcome of what you have created or a way to record your observations and response. Or it can also be a way to remember the materials, colors, or combinations you used.

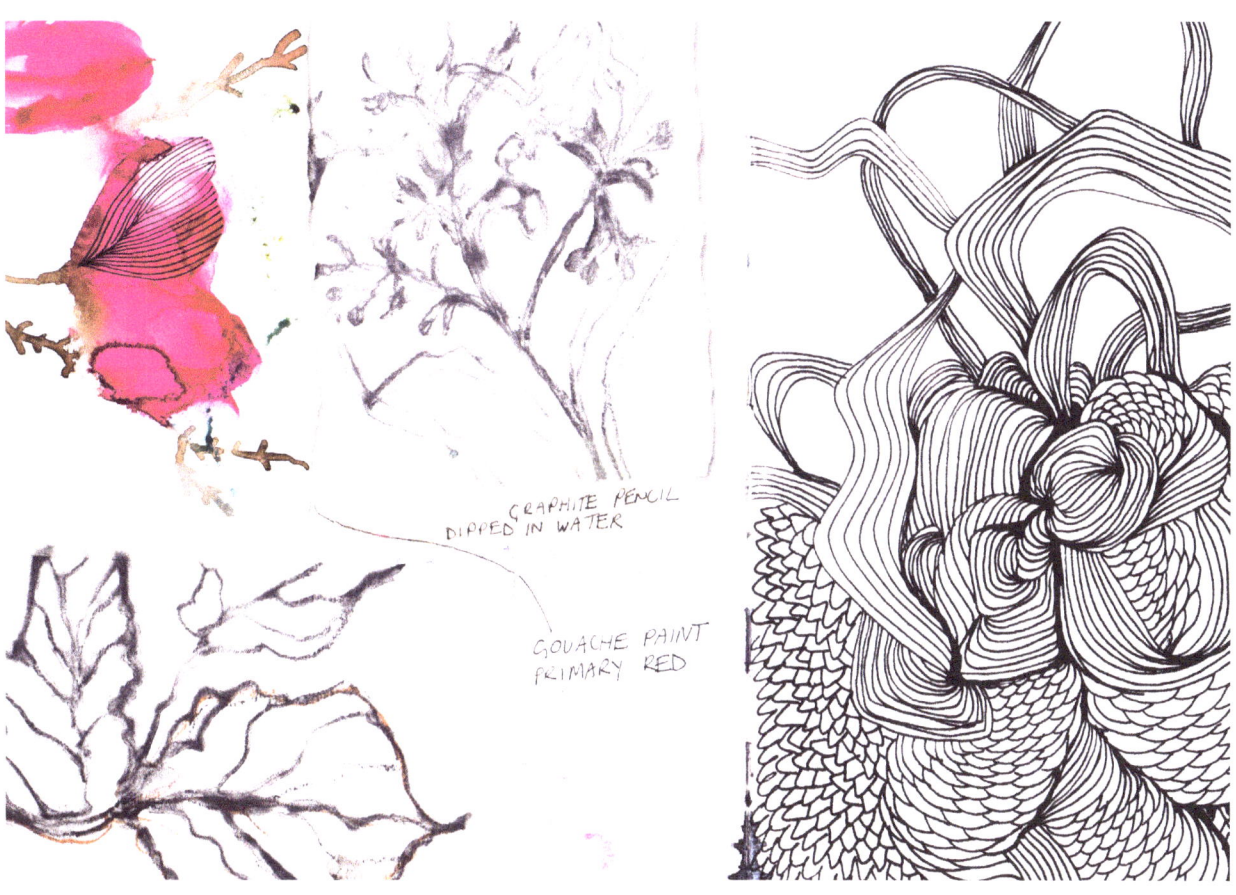

GRAPHITE PENCIL
DIPPED IN WATER

GOUACHE PAINT
PRIMARY RED

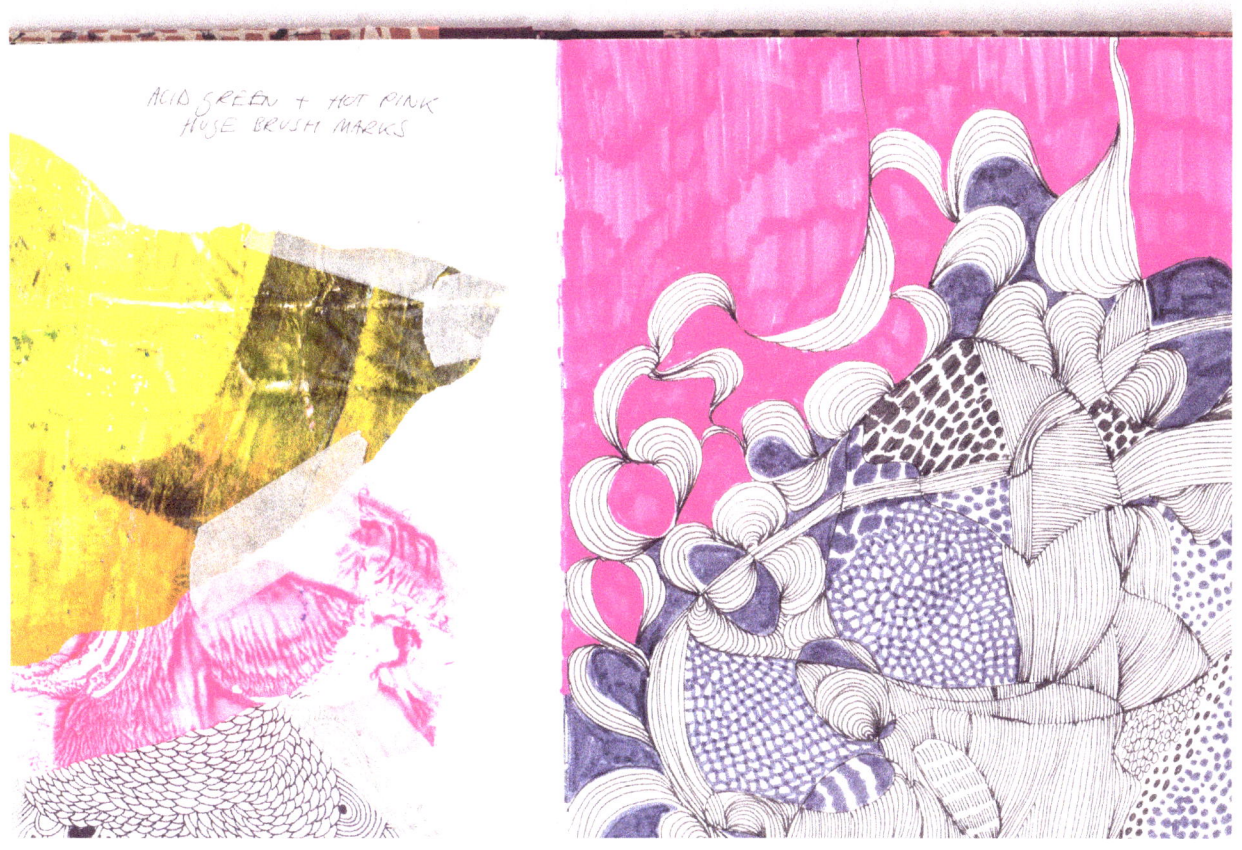

ACID GREEN + HOT PINK
HUGE BRUSH MARKS

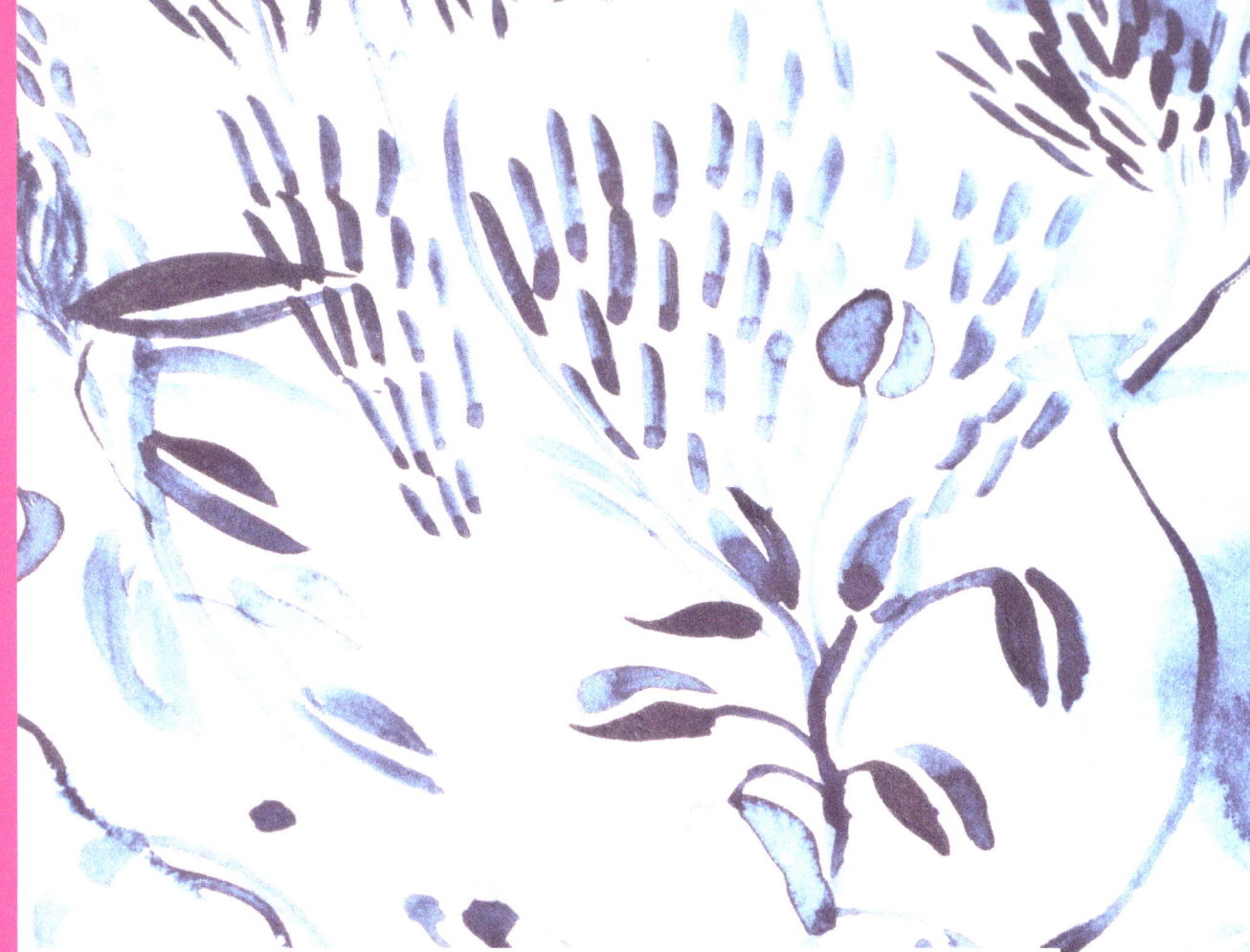

PRACTICE AND PROGRESS

You've tackled the techniques and learned how to dream up creative pages in your sketchbook that are a unique reflection of you. Now it's time to learn what may be the most important part of the process: how to maintain your expressive sketchbook routine and incorporate art into your life for the long term. Here are a few ideas for ways you can overcome common pitfalls and nurture your artistic practice thoughtfully and with a kind heart.

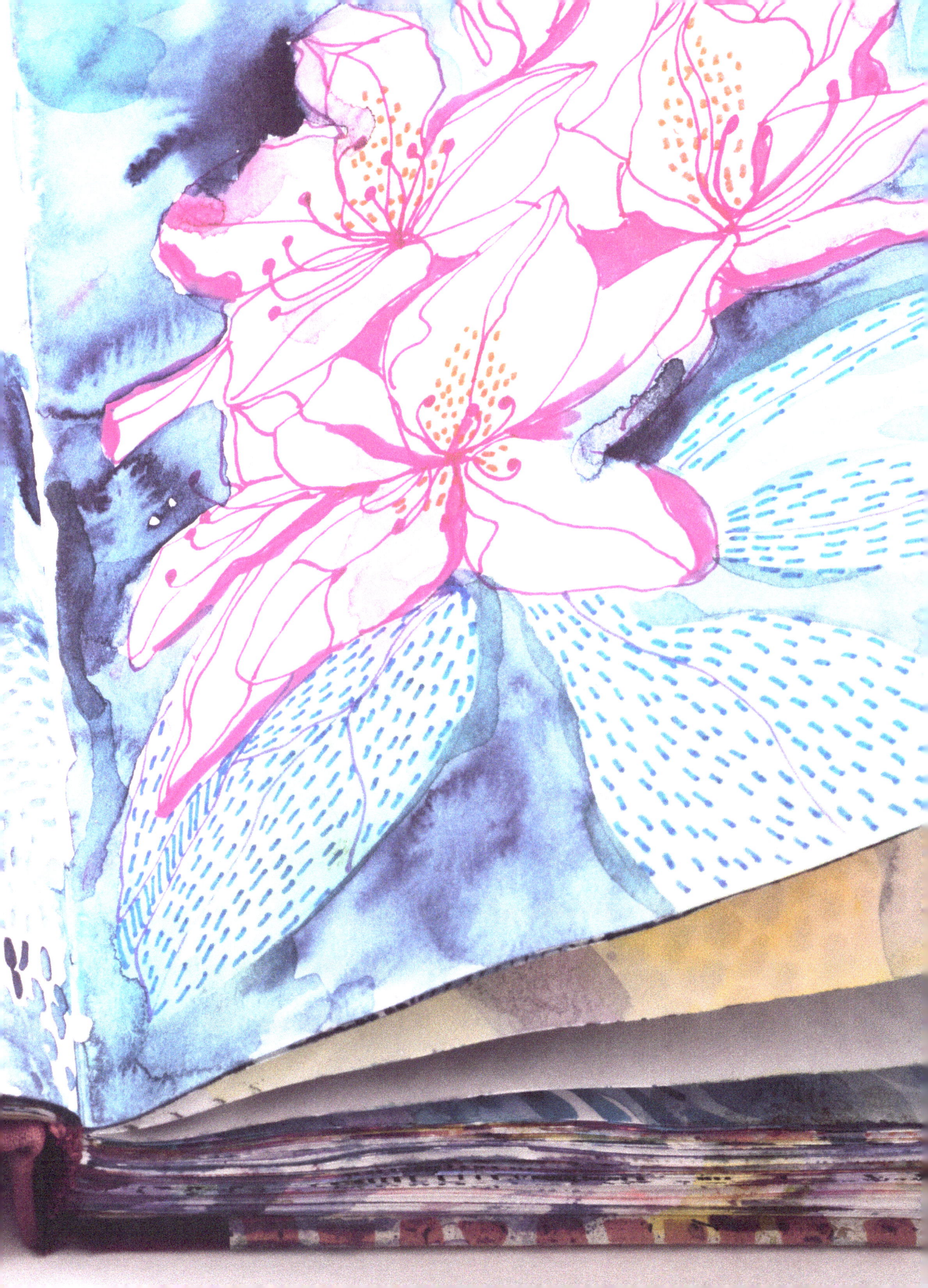

LACK OF INSPIRATION

What do you do when you have little inspiration? Don't wait around for it to find you. Instead, go and actively seek it out. On days when I'm feeling decidedly uninspired, I manufacture it. Taking a tiny step, doing something, approaching the blank page, and just starting are often enough to get the ball rolling.

When inspiration is elusive, assign yourself a small, achievable task or project that will somehow manufacture your missing inspiration. Work in your sketchbook, even if you don't feel like it, to find and nurture that inspiration. Ideas can come from action. Select an exercise to do, dive in, and see where it takes you. Small, incremental actions tend to build on each other.

▼ **Your art should contain the essence of you, as it reflects how you see the world and how you capture that vision on a page.**

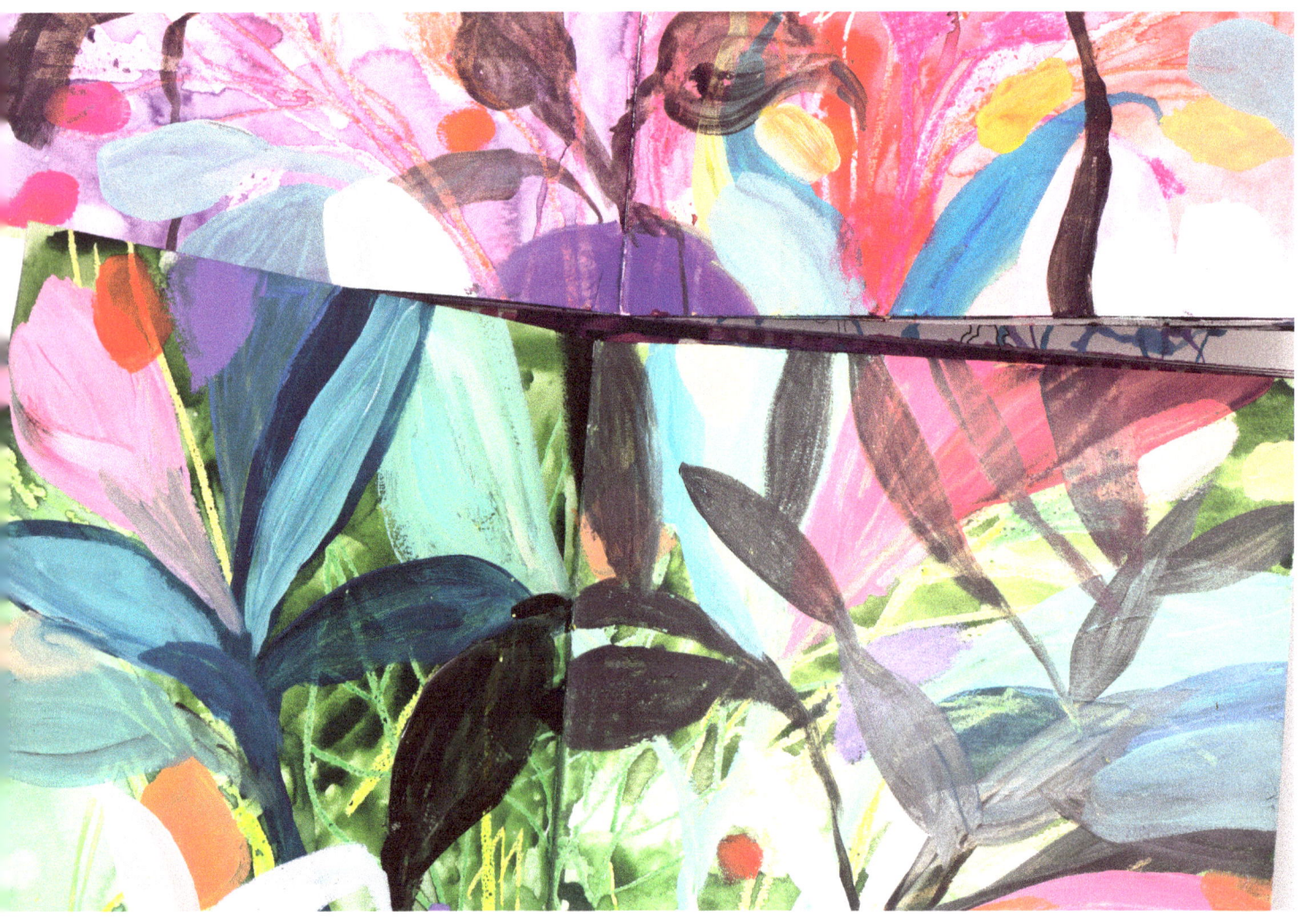

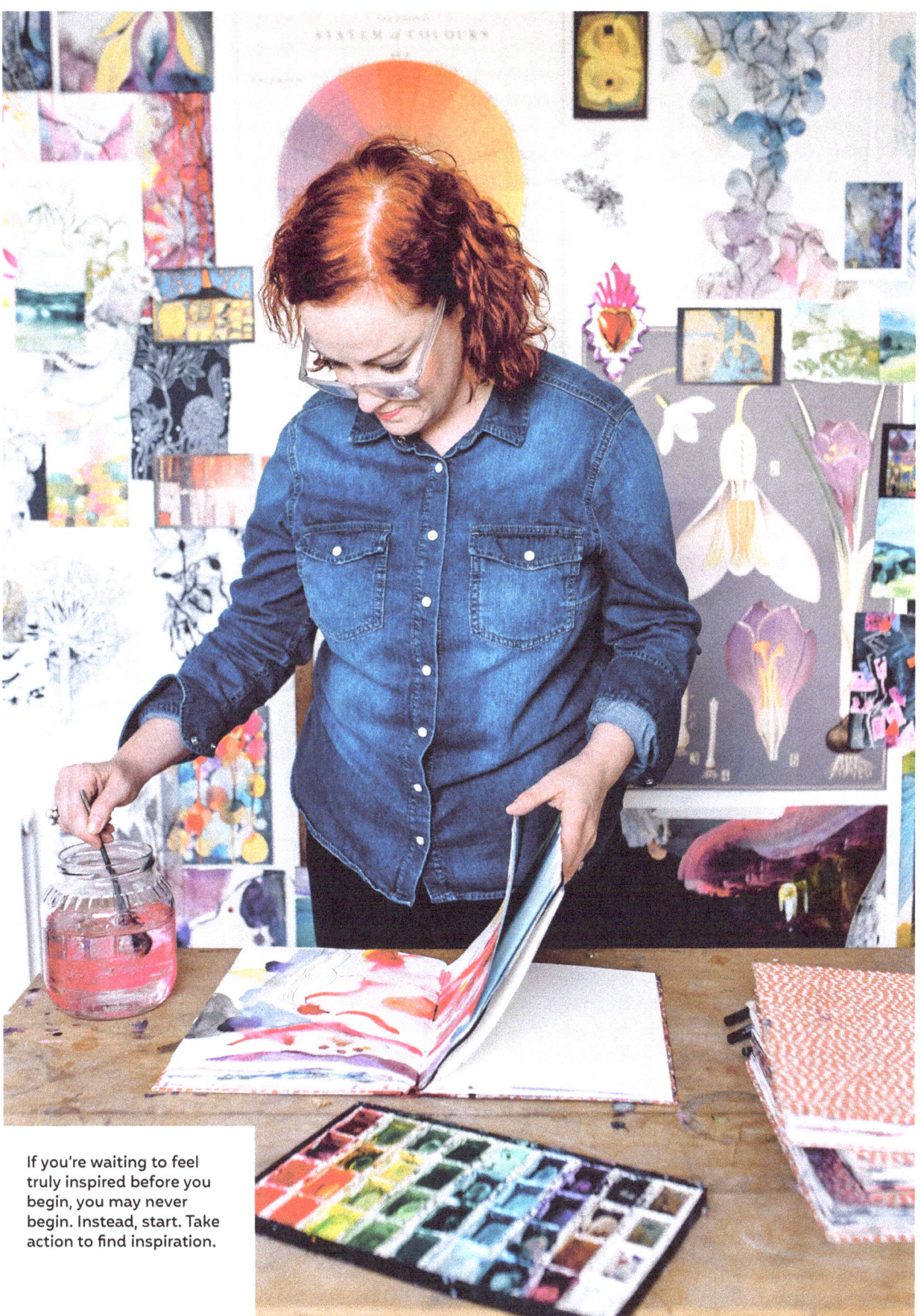

If you're waiting to feel truly inspired before you begin, you may never begin. Instead, start. Take action to find inspiration.

ASSESSING WORK

When you assess what you have created, turn away from negative judgment and instead explore your work with a sense of openness, curiosity, and detachment. If something isn't working, turn the page and start over or come back to it another day.

Never tear a page out of your sketchbook. If you absolutely must, repurpose it. If you don't like how a page has turned out, either paint over it or cover it with a collaged page. But before you do anything with it, take some time to think it over. I often flick past a page that I actively disliked when I first made it, only to find that a few weeks later I really rather like it. If you don't like a page, ask yourself the following questions before you do anything:

- What do I not like about it?
- What aspects do I like?
- What elements were successful?
- What elements were not as successful?
- What would I do differently next time?

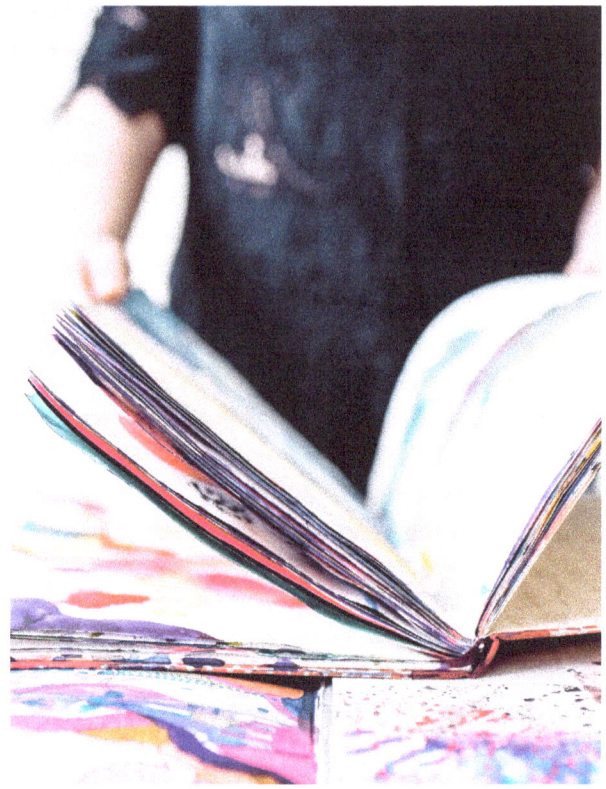

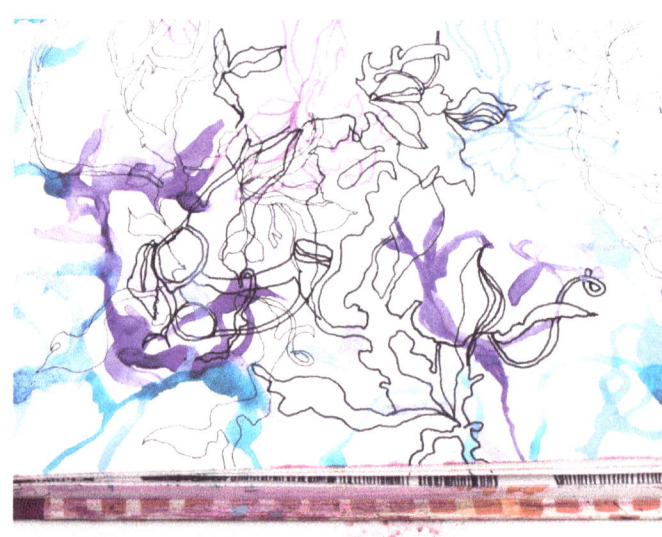

▲ If you have created something in your sketchbook that you aren't happy with, ask yourself questions about why you don't like it and listen to your answers.

Embracing Mistakes

There is always something of value in our mistakes. When we experiment, inevitably a page or pages of our sketchbook will look like a horrible mess.

In art, as in life, we can often learn more from these mistakes than from our triumphs. It is valuable to take the time to consider our mistakes objectively as they can teach us lessons. Remind yourself that creating pages in your sketchbook that you don't like is much better than creating nothing. The pain of not creating is greater than the pain of creating something you don't like. Taking risks is an in-tegral part of learning and creativity. Embrace the imperfect, enjoy the process, and guard against perfectionism.

Our mistakes can lead us to a breakthrough and encourage us to tackle our subject matter differently next time. When we allow ourselves to take risks in art, we find they can pay off beautifully sometimes. Other times, we learn what they can teach us. Our failures, mishaps, and mistakes contain lessons and growth.

When we are trying things out or learning new approaches, our sketchbook pages will not always turn out the way we would like them to. We can learn from our mistakes and mishaps.

Getting Perspective

If you dislike what you've created or don't know what to do next, walk away from it and return to it in a few minutes or hours, or the next day. Sometimes a little distance allows us to see our work more objectively. We're able to avoid being caught up in the finer details and instead view the work as a whole.

Achieve instant objectivity by holding up your artwork to a mirror, taking a photograph of it on your phone, or even looking at it upside down. Another way to get perspective is to move yourself physically away from what you are working on. Look at it from a more re-moved vantage point: try propping up your sketchbook on a desk and move away or just put it on the floor to achieve some distance. These simple techniques allow you to see what you are making with a little detachment.

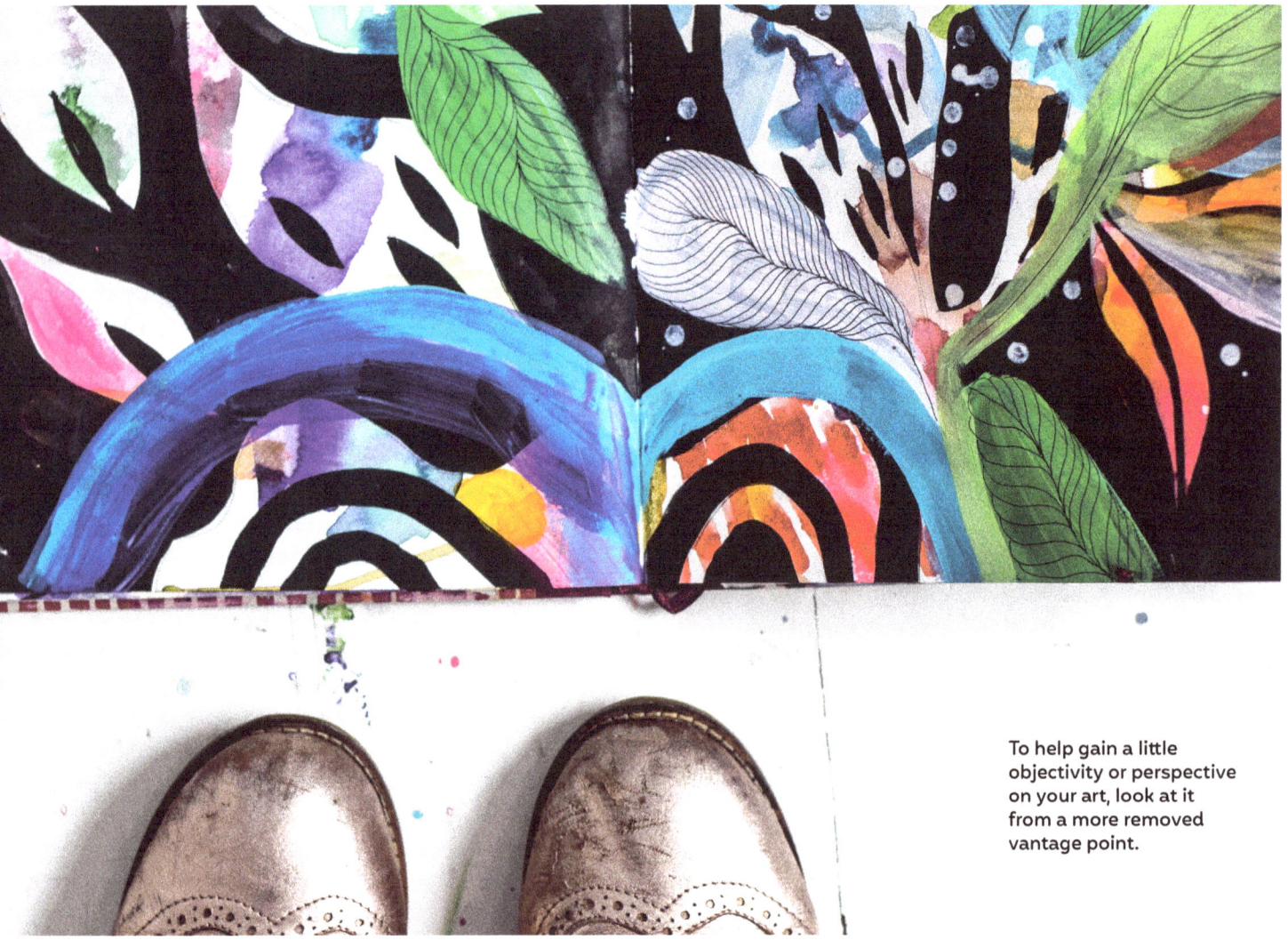

To help gain a little objectivity or perspective on your art, look at it from a more removed vantage point.

SELF-EVALUATION

Evaluation is an important part of the learning process. The great thing about a sketchbook is that you can look back through it and see your progression. Earlier in this book, I encouraged you to set some intentions around the use of your sketchbook. It can be useful to revisit these intentions, checking in from time to time to keep yourself accountable. Take inventory and ask yourself questions about your art making, such as the following:

- Am I learning?
- What have I learned?
- Am I doing what I set out to do?
- What aspects have I enjoyed?
- Am I allowing myself to experiment?
- Am I beginning to find a process that expresses my creativity?
- How do I feel about what I have created?
- How do I feel when I am making art?
- What would I like to do more of?

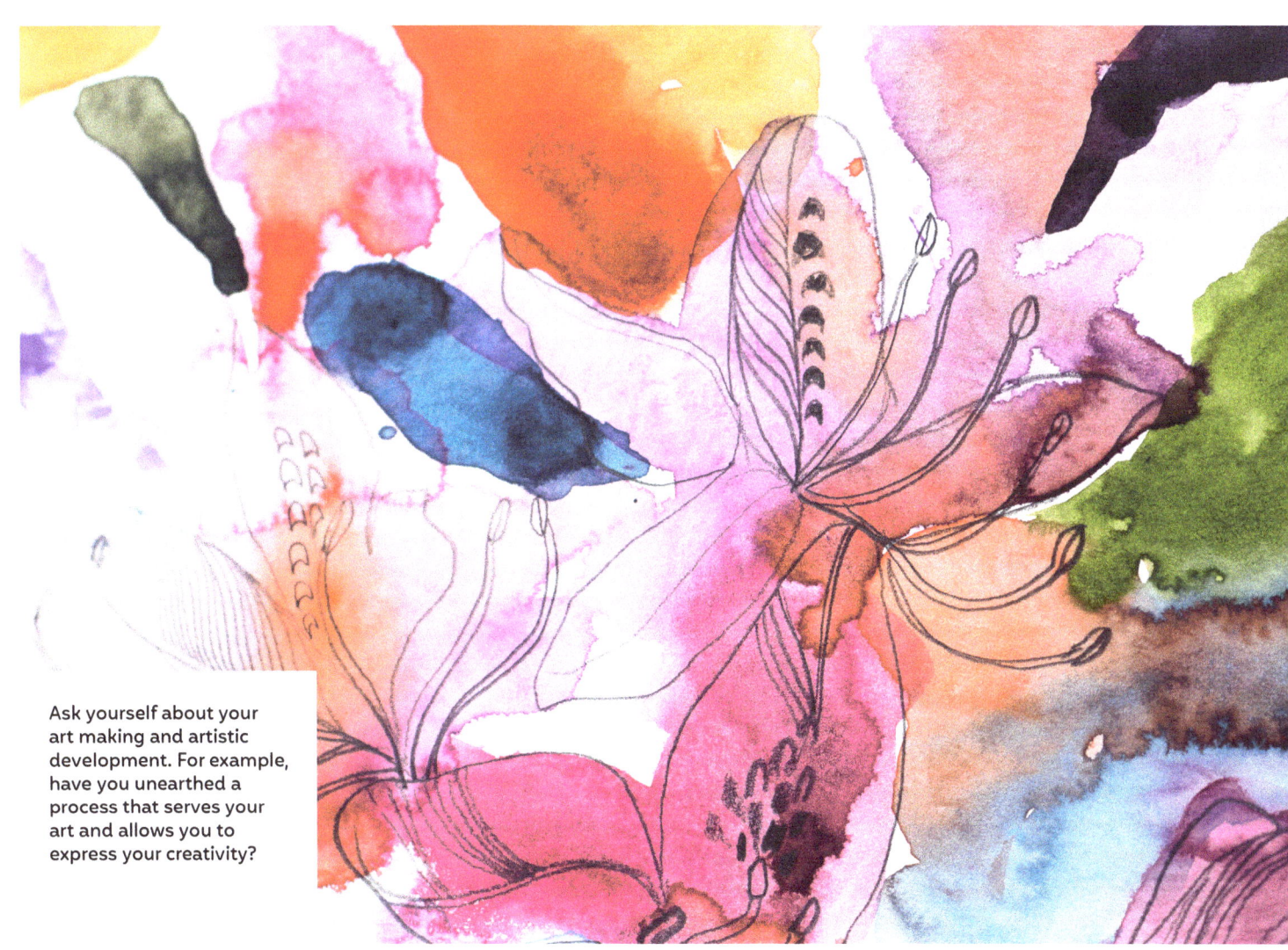

Ask yourself about your art making and artistic development. For example, have you unearthed a process that serves your art and allows you to express your creativity?

SELF-SABOTAGE

When we step out of our comfort zone and try something new to develop our artistic practice, we need to guard against the ways our minds may try to keep us safe and stuck within a negative, internal narrative.

Our minds can play certain tricks to prevent us from creating. We self-sabotage or allow our negative internal dialogue to get in the way of our intent to create. We may have anxiety and fear about not being good enough. We may be critical of our skills and abilities. We may allow procrastination and distraction to prevent us from creating art. We may not even try as a method of protecting ourselves from the pain of failing.

All these mental tricks may prevent us from making art as a way to avoid our inner critic, our judgment, and our failure. We may stop creating to prevent fear, but this also limits our joy. These safety mechanisms that our mind uses to protect us can stop us from playing, enjoying the process, improving, and expressing ourselves.

While we can't silence our inner art critic entirely, we can learn how to work alongside it. Let your negative inner dialogue chatter away in the background, but keep reminding yourself that you have so much to gain from making your own art.

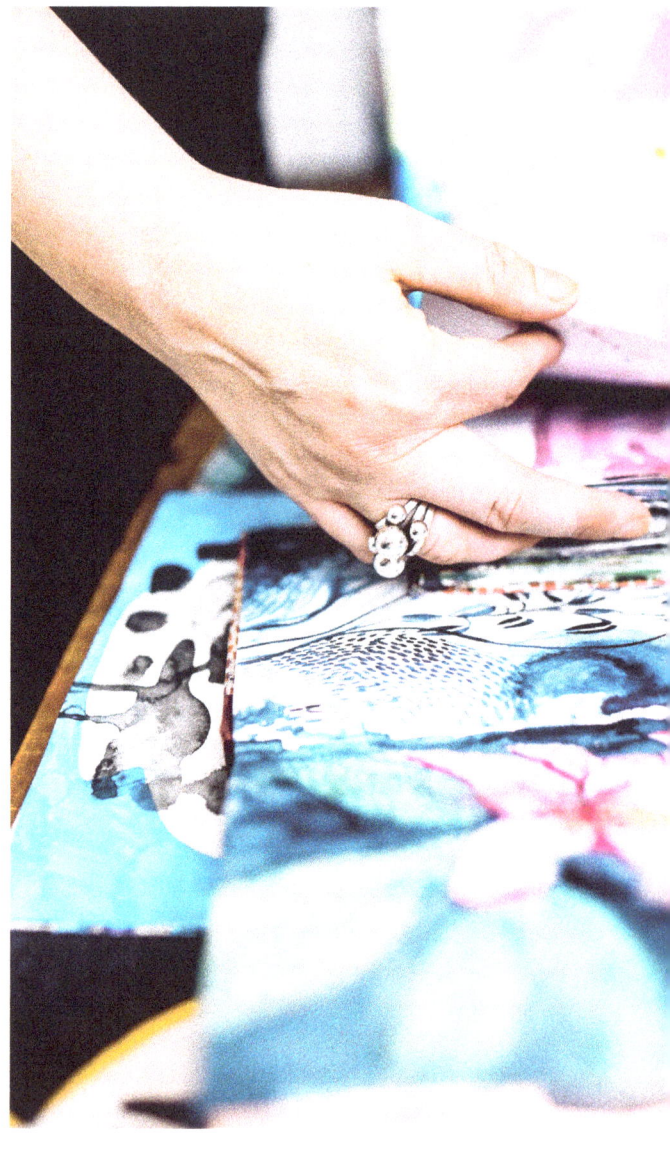

Learn to work alongside your internal art critic. Be clear on your intent, take action, make art, keep going, and keep growing.

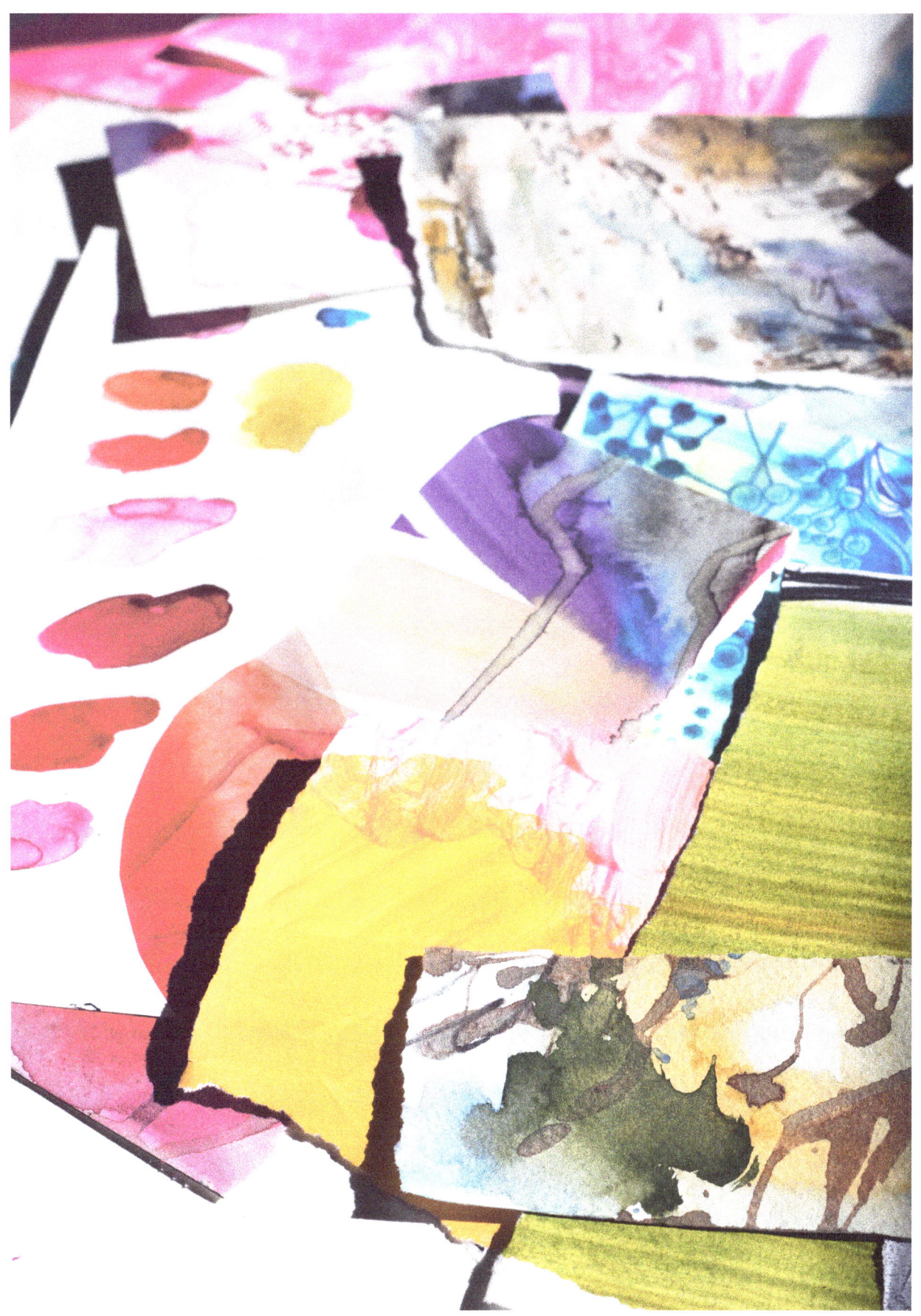

SELF-KINDNESS

Self-kindness is the key to developing an artistic journey that is meaningful. This doesn't mean that we love everything we create, but rather we don't judge our creative worth purely on the end result of what we have made. Conduct a more nuanced conversation with yourself about why you may not like something you have drawn or created. Insert a little objectivity, step back, and consider why you don't like it, how you could improve it, and what you have learned. Meet your vulnerability with kindness, as kindness helps your creativity flourish.

We live in a society that increasingly values consumption over creating, competition over kindness, and outcomes over effort. In your sketchbook practice, I encourage you to turn all these assumptions upside down. Relish the act of making something from nothing. Be more compassionate than competitive. Prioritize the act of creating art over your attachment to the end result.

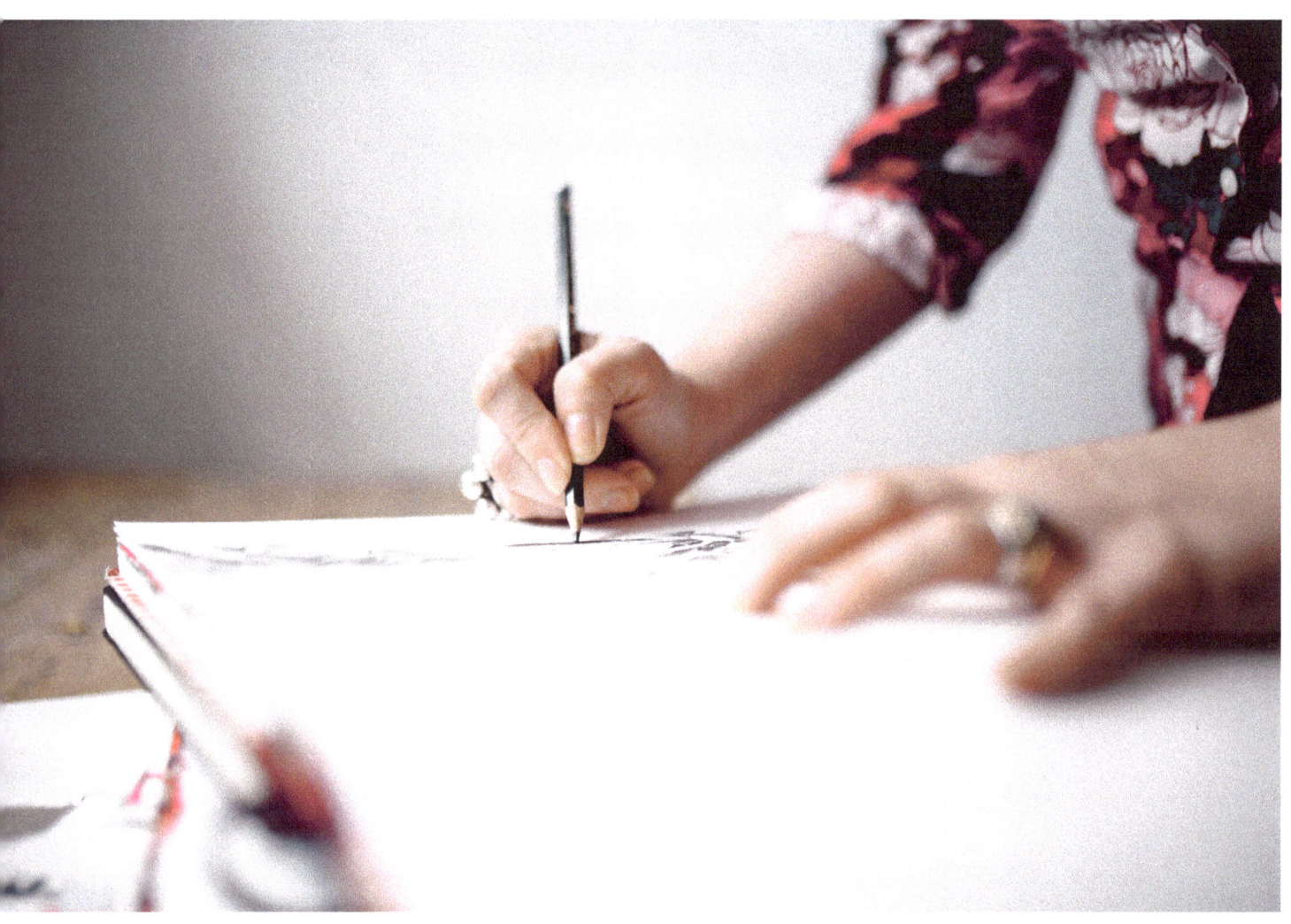

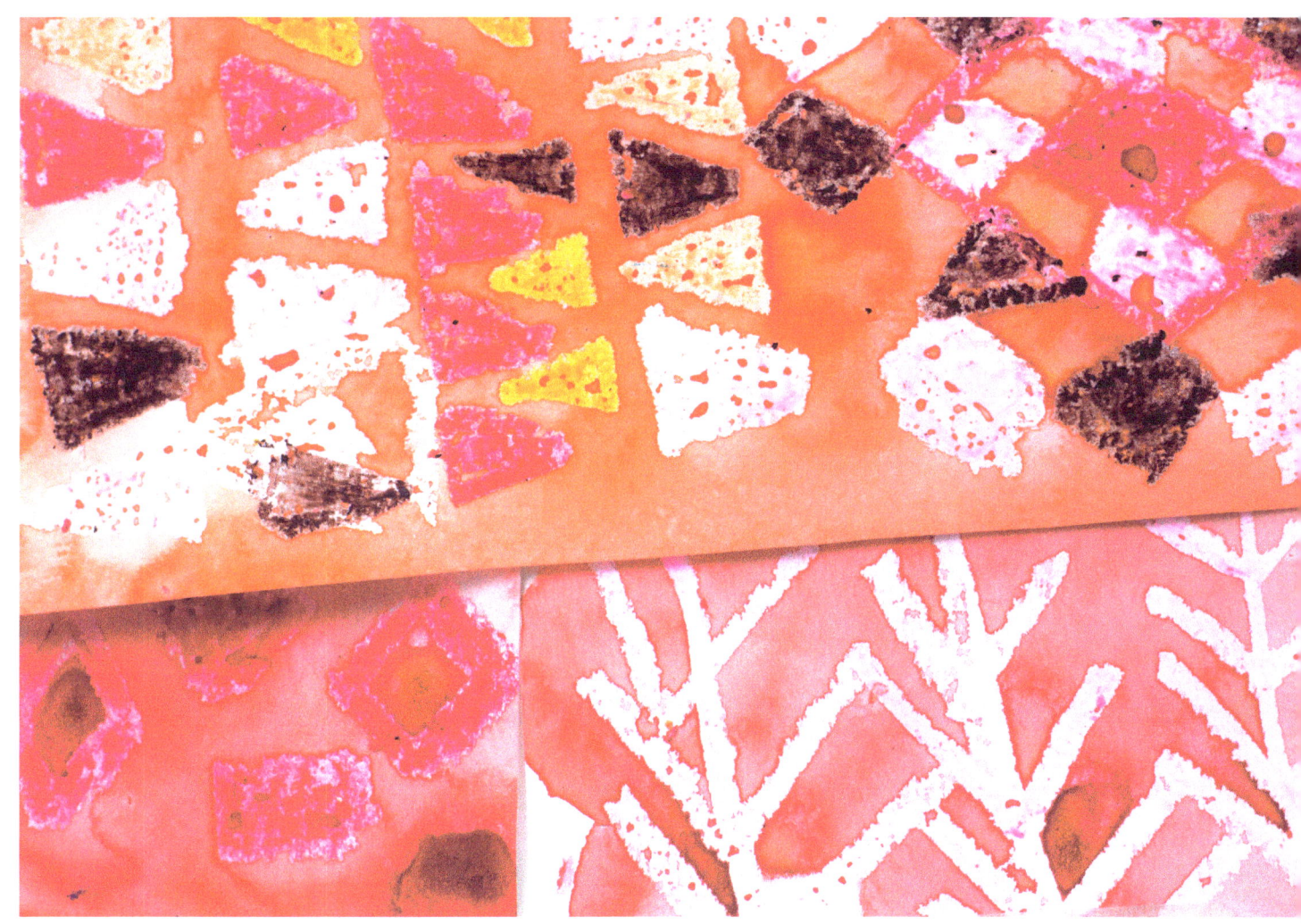

As children, we draw and color with an unself-conscious abandon. As we get older, we begin to censor our own creativity, comparing our worst results to others' best results. We can be unkind to ourselves, criticize our output, and dismiss our abilities.

Self-Confidence

The word *courage* comes from an old Latin word meaning "to come from the heart." When we create our own art with courage and confidence, we let what is in our heart pour onto the page. Confidence is listening to and trusting our inner wisdom and letting it be our guide. Become aware of your instincts and intuition, pay attention to them, and you will become your own mentor.

Think of your creative practice as a continuum of small choices. Creating art is a process of constantly making tiny choices and selections. We select our subject matter, our materials, where to place the next mark, when to start and stop, when to add, and when to subtract.

I've noticed that it is easier to follow my intuition and be more confident in my art making when I slow down and really pay attention. When I'm present and more focused on what is happening in the moment, I find that I release my attachment to judgment and better able to let the process flow.

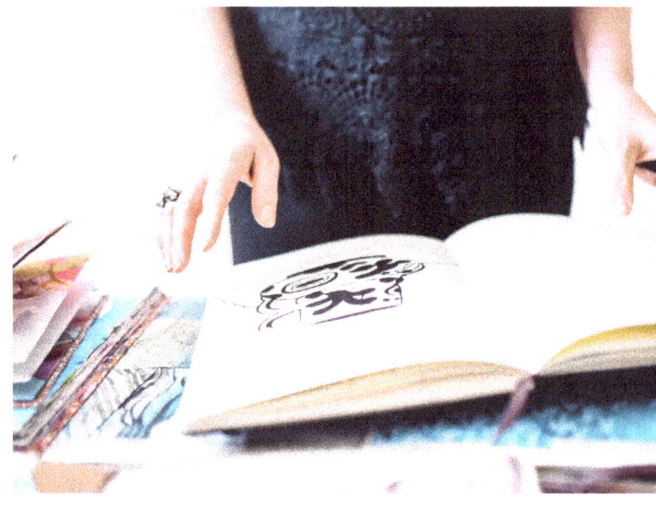

Understand and trust your choices. Also listen to your instinct to be bold and fearless in your art making. This level of consciousness means that you are making art that is truly personal to you and that more of you is showing up on the page. Setting your intentions and following your intuition can take you to wonderful places.

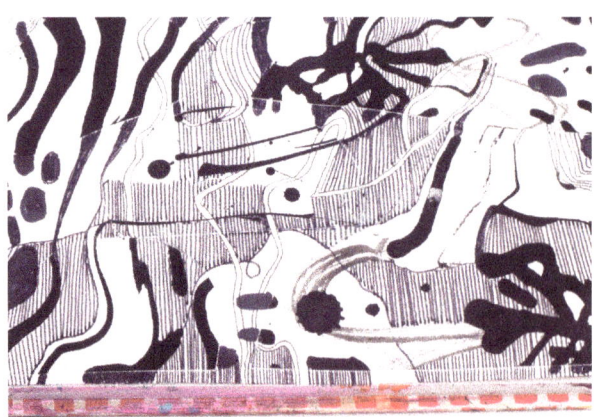

Confidence comes from tuning in and listening to your inner wisdom—it goes hand-in-hand with awareness. Being conscious of the choices you are making at every stage of your process helps you to understand more about who you are as an artist.

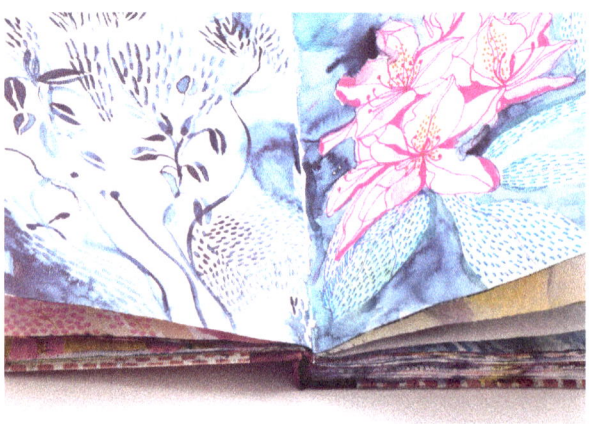

Self-confidence comes from listening to your inner voice while also connecting with your art as it develops on the page. Art making can sometimes feel like a delicate dance between your awareness and your art.

Developing a Practice

Creativity is a habit and a practice. Take pleasure in developing your own set of processes and approaches. Delight in your discovery as you begin to feel emboldened and brave in your artistic practice. Let your sketchbook be a place for your artistic voice to exist and flourish. Don't be afraid of the mishaps, mistakes, and wrong turns, as they contain wonderful lessons. Create art—*your* art.

ACKNOWLEDGMENTS

A huge debt of gratitude to all the lovely folks at Quarry Books for their vision, patience, and book-making brilliance, including Mary Ann Hall, Marissa Giambrone, Renae Haines, Joy Aquilino, and Lydia Anderson.

Also, a huge thanks to Georgina Piper for the wonderful photographs she took for me.

ABOUT HELEN WELLS

Helen Wells is an artist from the South Coast of England. Her artworks are intricate, organic, and depict illusionary surfaces or landscapes. With multiple layers, fragments, colors, and obsessive decorative details, her ethereal, patterned works bring to mind elements of the natural world or magical otherworlds.

Her artworks are in private collections all over the world and have been featured on numerous products from book covers to wine bottles. In 2014, as a cowinner of the Winsor & Newton Water Colour Revolution competition, her painting was displayed in London's Saatchi Gallery. She has appeared in magazines and exhibited her work at one of Gordon Ramsay's restaurants in London.

She became an artist later in life after working in an office job for many years. She credits her use of sketchbooks with finding her artistic style and the courage to develop her art outside of their pages. She is passionate about sketchbooks as a tool for self-discovery, play, and creativity and keen to share everything she has learned along the way.

www.helenwellsartist.com

www.ingramcontent.com/pod-product-compliance
Lightning Source LLC
Chambersburg PA
CBHW041923180526
45172CB00014B/1368